Spiritual and Religious

Spiritual and Religious

Explorations for Seekers

ROGER HAIGHT, S.J.

ORBIS BOOKS

Maryknoll, New York 10545

ORBIS BOOKS
Maryknoll, New York 10545

Fathers and Brothers MARYKNOLL
TOGETHER IN GOD'S MISSION OF MERCY

Founded in 1970, Orbis Books endeavors to publish works that enlighten the mind, nourish the spirit, and challenge the conscience. The publishing arm of the Maryknoll Fathers and Brothers, Orbis seeks to explore the global dimensions of the Christian faith and mission, to invite dialogue with diverse cultures and religious traditions, and to serve the cause of reconciliation and peace. The books published reflect the views of their authors and do not represent the official position of the Maryknoll Society. To learn more about Maryknoll and Orbis Books, please visit our website at www.maryknollsociety.org.

Published by Orbis Books, Box 302, Maryknoll, NY 10545-0302.

Manufactured in the United States of America

Library of Congress Cataloging-in-Publication Data

Haight, Roger.
[Essays. Selections]
Spiritual and religious : explorations for seekers / by Roger Haight, S.J.
pages cm
Includes bibliographical references and index.
ISBN 978-1-62698-161-4 (pbk.)
1. Theology, Doctrinal—Popular works. 2. Spirituality—Christianity.
3. Spirituality. I. Title.
BT77.H1755 2015
230—dc23
2015028779

In Gratitude to
The New York Workgroup

Elena
Teresa
Michele
Jeannine
Paul
John
Brad

Contents

Introduction

Most of these essays were written during the last six or seven years when I was preoccupied with spirituality. I have always felt that theology that did not have a bearing on spirituality lacked relevance and was somehow detached from its basic purpose. Spirituality was out front, and theology was oriented toward it. But these essays move in a different direction. Here spirituality appears first, and religion and theology follow, not chronologically but methodically. The same mutual relationship obtains. But these essays try to make clear that religion, church, and church structure have their source and ground in spirituality. Most of these essays (ten of the fourteen) address spirituality directly, and the other four have their mooring in the Christian life.

A number of reasons account for this shift of my direct attention from theology to spirituality as a discipline and a project. I recount the external reason in *Christian Spirituality for Seekers*:[1] I was asked by the president of Union Theological Seminary to be part of a team that addressed spiritual issues in the community. In doing this, I discovered anew the power of the Spiritual Exercises of Ignatius Loyola and the role that spirituality could potentially play in the larger project of a constructive theology. Spirituality provides the surest entrée into a number of theological issues that mark our situation. The best way to explain what that means moves from a brief enumeration of some of the problems these essays address to how the category of spirituality steers the discussion of them. These essays respond to several basic issues.

Most people are aware, through knowledge of specific data or on the basis of a general cultural impression, that Christianity in the West is in decline. Among the many reasons for this situation one looms large: people do not find the same kind of relevance for their lives in the doctrines or beliefs of Christianity or in its classical theological language as they once did. In a way, this statement is tautologous: it simply reaffirms the decline itself. Many of the questions that were posed in the intellectual culture of the Enlightenment and during

1. Roger Haight, *Christian Spirituality for Seekers: Reflections on the Spiritual Exercises of Ignatius Loyola* (Maryknoll, NY: Orbis Books, 2012), xi.

the subsequent rise of historical, secular, pluralist, and scientific consciousness are now the questions of a critical nonreligious culture. There is little patience for a careful theological response. The deeper third dimension of transcendence has been drained from secular life. Traditional language does not really connect with the events that transpire on the surface of things. The language that used to move us does not make sense to many members of recent generations.

From inside this situation I have retrieved the category of "seeker." The problem of meaning and relevance has left many people in a position that can be designated by this term. Seekers are those who both lack something for which they are looking, and at the same time possess it in some measure, enough to know vaguely what they are looking for. Asking a meaningful question presupposes some awareness of the subject matter. Seekers are both inside and outside Christianity and other religions. They have left their church, or joined a new denomination or another religion, or are where they were but in a newly precarious way. "Seekers" describes a wide spectrum of people. Yet, from certain perspectives, the category can be construed positively: it indicates a space that is uncomfortable but potentially generative.

Another problem is much more specific and can be designated as the relationship between religion and science. One side of this issue is methodological, and theologians engage it with scientists on the level of epistemology and metaphysics. The other side of the issue is more practical; it can be illustrated in a commonsensical comparison between the propositions of theology and those of science. For example, how do the ideas of God creating and evolution relate to each other? What does the personality of God mean in this vast randomly developing universe? But focusing the problem on specific issues conceals its massiveness. The classical Christian doctrines were formulated within the context of a comparatively simple conception of the universe. One needs only to scratch the surface of classical Christian doctrines with a few critical questions from the current scientific perspective on reality to show the enormous gap between traditional language and today's intellectual culture. This is not just a question of popularizing the critical theology that has already been developed. It has not been done. Most theologians have a lot of work ahead of them.

Finally, a major question for Christian theology revolves around finding a way to reconcile the classical doctrines about the absoluteness or definitiveness of Jesus Christ and Christianity with the new open and positive appreciation of other religions that increasingly prevails today. This problem has been on the table in various degrees of extensiveness over the past couple of centuries. But the debate is still intense and divisive. How are Christians to regard other religions and their mediators of salvation? Can this be done positively, not only in a way that is faithful to the Christian tradition, but also in a way that appeals to that very tradition?

I describe these four problem areas because they are addressed in the essays in this collection. But more importantly for this introduction, I see the turn to the category of spirituality as uniquely fitted to addressing them. The logic of this move can be schematized in three steps: First, I construct a definition of spirituality, one that secular culture can appreciate but that also includes a concern for transcendent reality. Second, I use spirituality as a bridge between the issues that are involved in everyday secular life and the worlds of the religions that more explicitly highlight the transcendent sphere. Third, I show how moving back and forth across this bridge brings to light the way in which theological constructions emerge out of secular spirituality, and in return shows how religious beliefs must use a language of transcendence that relates back to everyday life.

Let me briefly expand on this logic before turning to the essays in this book. The first point consists of framing a conception of spirituality that is comprehensive. In today's usage in Western culture, spirituality refers to the reflective depth and meaning-giving direction of a human life that defines a person's self. In the broadest terms possible it is the consistent way persons or groups lead their lives in the face of transcendence. Spirituality is an existential reality; it can be explicitly religious in character, or some guiding transcendent value may remain latent. The many forms of spirituality today show that a concern for some encompassing meaning-giving transcendent value is a preoccupation of Western culture.

Spirituality used to belong within the domain of religion. On the one hand, religion is still spiritual; religion is built on the corporate spirituality of a people. Without giving too much space to the study of religion, the term "religion" refers to the organized community, its institution and practices, in which the spirituality of a people is celebrated, nurtured, and protected. Religion is organized spirituality. On the other hand, today people claim to be spiritual but not religious. This does not make "spiritual" and "religious" opposing categories, but it does make spirituality the broader category. Spirituality is shared by all, some in an explicitly religious way and others in a nonreligious way, that is, without belonging to a religious organization. The point here is that spirituality has been construed as a basic anthropological constant, a common formal dimension of human existence; both religious and nonreligious people have a spirituality. This makes "spirituality" a bridge concept. It offers a "place" to look for transcendent dimensions in social life and to explain the relevance of religious language to general secular life.

The essays in this book move back and forth between spirituality and religion. For the most part they explicitly turn to the idea of spirituality as a way of getting into the meaning and relevance of religious language. Sometimes the underlying existential conception of spirituality remains implicit, and I do not formally appeal to it. Because this is not a monograph, because these essays were conceived independently of one another for different audiences, and yet are based on a common logic, they contain a considerable amount of repetition. The idea of spirituality is defined again and again in different essays. While this may be a distraction, I need to emphasize over and over again that I am not writing theology but spirituality. I also appeal more than once to the way the prior and grounding reality of spirituality gives rise though development to public reflective interpretation of transcendent realities, to more careful formulation of beliefs, and to the organization of a community by institutional offices and roles. All of this helps to reinforce the priority of spirituality to developed institutional forms that is the major premise of the method underlying these essays.

I also repeatedly go back to the idea of the narrative character of spirituality. From this perspective, Christian spirituality is following Jesus; it is essentially narrative because that is the way a person lives. This encourages an insight into the way spirituality is communicated most deeply through the influence of a way of life on another person. Because spirituality has a narrative structure, it affects others mainly through a communication or fusion of narratives rather than through a handing down of ideas, doctrines, formulas, and other information. The narrative character of spirituality also underlines how our actual relationship with God is forged by our action rather than our words. The evangelical principle that "you will know them by their fruits" (Matt 7:20) means that we fashion ourselves and our relationship with God most fundamentally by our actions. Words and actions need not be understood in contrast with each other, but the way these two dimensions of a spiritual life relate to each other remains basic and crucial.

These distinctions, as well as the audience to which the book is directed, namely, seekers and those who have questions about their Christian faith, help account for the activist character of the spirituality that is offered here. The point of these essays, singly and together, is not to offer a full account of Christian spirituality. I do not develop how assembly is at the heart of Christian life, how worship is an essential part of Christian spirituality, or how each person may encounter God in the silence of interiority. The point here is to show the interchange between Christian spirituality and life in the world, the connection between questions generated by secular culture and the transcendent response that Christianity offers the world. As with Dietrich Bonhoeffer in the *The Cost of Discipleship,* the point is not to revel in the vital religious life of the congregations but to challenge a bourgeois complacency with the world as it is and one's place in it.[2] It also offers to those committed to the human project a grounding for hope in the face of frustration.

These essays try to remain on the plane of spirituality as distinct from theology. I speak of a turn to Jesus and of disciples following Jesus without imagining that they thought he was Yahweh incarnate. I offer an interpretation of Jesus's ministry and the impact he had on his followers without entering into a fuller theological interpretation of Jesus as the Christ. I speak of an Easter experience without offering a theology of Jesus's resurrection. I speak of God being close to the whole world on the basis of God being creator, an idea that is close to the very idea of God in the Christian tradition. I do not explain how Vatican II can affirm that salvation is offered to all people on the basis of God's grace or offer an excursus on Karl Rahner's supernatural existential. I speak of God being experienced in various ways outside and inside the Jewish-Christian tradition without developing a theology of the trinity. I speak of how God is experienced in trinitarian language but not theologically of three persons within the Godhead. These limits to the range of the discussion should not be construed as reductionism. This book does not aim to say all there is to be said. It stays within the sphere of spirituality and describes it for a specific audience relative to special problems at this particular time.

With these distinctions as a background, let me briefly indicate the flow of the whole collection by noting the problem that each essay addresses.

The first two essays go directly to a discussion of spirituality. They explain an understanding of spirituality that positions it at the center of intentional human existence. This becomes the premise of the whole book; it allows spirituality to play a role that is analogous to the category of "experience" in much of modern theology. "Spirituality," however, is a more complex term than "experience," and this complexity gives it a wider and more incisive range of application. Spirituality is prior to and the basis of religion. It is also prior to theology because it provides the source and medium of theology. This is highlighted in

2. Dietrich Bonhoeffer, "Costly Grace," in *The Cost of Discipleship* (New York: Macmillan, 1963), 45-60.

the second essay, chapter 2, through the category of seeker. The seeker explicitly represents the dimension of spirituality that is always reaching for and thus receptive to transcendence through the media of worldly existence. Jesus Christ is introduced most fundamentally as a mediator of God's communication to humankind.

Chapters 3 and 4 discuss basic issues surrounding the place of Jesus in the Christian imagination. Christians consistently speak of or presuppose the uniqueness of Jesus. But this phrase can be understood in different ways in response to different questions. Chapter 3 is more an essay at clarifying the language Christians use about Jesus of Nazareth than a defense of a theological position. Chapter 4 turns to the death of Jesus by crucifixion, something that for many Christians contains the essence of Christian belief and thus provides the very foundation of Christian spirituality. Because of the spiritually sensitive location of "the cross," it requires careful discussion. The common language of the churches makes the cross central to the faith of many, and yet, for others, the same language is alienating. The spirituality of the cross has to remain a topic of an ongoing conversation.

Chapter 5 discusses the relationship between a spirituality of following Jesus and the church as a community of the followers of Jesus.[3] This analysis develops a structure that controls a good part of the argument of this book; it recurs explicitly in other chapters. Developmental sociology and the sociology of knowledge probably offer the best way into the relationship that obtains between spirituality and church. Just as institution grows out of the historical experiences of a community, so too does church emerge out of corporate spirituality. And just as human sets of cultural knowledge emerge out of subjective human experience, become objectified, and then set the parameters of our understanding, so too do the teachings and doctrines of the church emerge out of ecclesial spirituality.[4] Appreciation and internalization of this structure open up an approach to the church that situates Christian language in relation to secular discourse and allows one to understand how science, authority, liberation, and ecumenical dialogue in their turn can influence Christian spirituality in a constructive way.

3. I generally use the word "church" in a broad ecumenical way to refer to the whole Christian movement. Chapter 9 is an exception, because there I am addressing the Catholic Church. Usually "the church" and "the churches" are synonymous terms, except that the latter raises up the differentiations of denominations and individual churches, and the former broad inclusive term suggests the unity of the whole movement.

4. This construct offers a good example of where someone could interpret what is said in a reductive naturalist way. From a theological perspective this statement should be understood as presupposing the influence of Jesus and the Spirit of God (grace) at work in the corporate following of Christ.

Thus, for example, chapter 6 discusses why Christians do not have to fear the advances of science and the genuinely new appreciations of our universe, our world, and ourselves. These new conceptions constitute a new vision of reality that readily can be integrated into Christian faith when Christianity is not reduced to a set of beliefs formulated in the past but recognized as a living corporate spirituality. Analogously, in chapter 7, I bring personal spirituality and ecclesial authority into conjunction with each other. Surely the community must have a way to exercise its ecclesial authority relative to individual Christians or subgroups. But how often are people scandalized by an overreach in the exercise of authority in the church? We need a balanced modern view of authority that preserves and reinforces its religious and spiritual dimensions while at the same time is subject to critical reception in the light of Christian spirituality.

Chapter 8 discusses liberation and spirituality. For the past half-century the category of "liberation" has played a major role in Christian language and self-understanding. This chapter situates liberation in the context of Christian spirituality, giving it a place within the subjective foundations of Christian life. I then call on four medieval and late medieval witnesses to contribute some classical heft to the meaning of liberation. Only then can one begin to appreciate the deep eschatological implications of a spirituality dedicated to the social flourishing of freedom in history.

In chapter 9 I try in a brief space to compare liberation spirituality and ecospirituality as having their foundations in analogous structural experiences. It is meant to show some continuity between these two somewhat different spiritualities.

Chapter 10 is a period piece: it focuses on the Roman Catholic Church and specifically the American Catholic Church at this moment in history. It proposes that this church has a set of experiences and is developing an ecclesial spirituality that offers four gifts to the universal Catholic communion and also to the whole church. These are new appreciations of religious freedom, women in the church and in society, the role of the laity in the church, and a new set of attitudes toward other religions.

Chapters 11, 12, and 13 turn to Christian ecumenism and the relation of Christianity with other faith traditions. These three chapters work constructively from the premise of the priority of Christian spirituality to the organizational character of the churches and the definition of Christian beliefs; beliefs are reflective expressions of a deeper and more basic Christian spirituality. This structure provides a way to locate clearly where the groundwork for Christian unity lies and how comprehensive it is despite differences of lesser import. This structure allows a more realistic and constructive grasp of where "truth" in various spiritualities lies and how spiritual truth transcends diversity in its mediation and conceptualization. It provides the ability to distinguish levels of truth. This structure also shows how a nuanced view of religions, based on spiritualities that cannot be reduced to specific differences, allows one to appreciate how other religions can be true while being different and maybe opposed to one's own.

Finally, chapter 14 ends with a discussion of the doctrine of trinity as the central Christian doctrine. It too is based on the conception of spirituality that has been operative in the whole collection of essays, but it stresses the narrative character of spirituality and the church as a living movement. In keeping with these presuppositions, the discussion focuses on what theology calls "the economic trinity," and it proposes that trinity be understood in narrative terms. The centrality of the doctrine of trinity lies in its telling the essential Christian story. As a summary of the creeds, Father, Son, and Spirit offer a symbolic representation of how Christianity was fashioned out of Jewish-Christian spirituality.

Looking back over these essays and recalling the circumstances that occasioned them reminds me of the fact that a spiritual writer exists in complete dependence on a community and its tradition. The elementary drive to speak or write responds to a solicitation of people within a community. The completed work thus elicits a sense of gratitude for the implicit and explicit sharing of experiences and ideas that went into the extended conversation that actually produced these pages. I am grateful to the many people who were involved in the gradual formulation of the ideas contained in these chapters.

I especially want to express thanks to Pat Amer, who read this manuscript with care and a critical judgment that helped me to hone my thoughts with precision and clarity. I also thank Jim Keane, who edited this work with broad experience, the skill and sensibility of a writer, and insight into the subject matter and the prospective audience.

I dedicate the work to the New York Workgroup, which has met twice a year over the last ten years for critical theological discussion and friendly professional accompaniment.

CHAPTER ONE

Religion and Spirituality

The relationship between religion and spirituality is a wide-open field left barren by too many hikers all going in different directions. This initial chapter moves in a straightforward direction toward the primacy of the spiritual over the religious. The confession that "I am spiritual but not religious" usually means that people are reflective, perhaps deep and inquiring, not indifferent to ultimate questions, and maybe even believers. But they do not belong to or overtly practice a specific religion. For those who are religious, the growing number of people who call themselves "spiritual but not religious" does not represent a positive development. Churchgoers sense lazy indifferentism and distraction, and the statement elicits a quiet condescension. But they may be missing something deeper that is going on in the turn from religion and its theology to concern about spirituality. Does the tenacity of the spiritual point to a foundational primacy that it enjoys relative to religion and theology? Investigating what the priority of the spiritual may mean could be a way forward for religion at a time when mainline Protestantism and Catholicism in the developed world are in decline.

Two sets of reflections are enough to make this point. The first proposes an understanding of spirituality that rescues it from the sphere of special marginalized activity and shows in what sense every thinking person has some spirituality. Spirituality resides deep down in human behavior at a level shared with basic faith or trust. It bears a narrative structure that ultimately defines individual identity. Theology must be beholden to this spirituality, and religion has as its goal to reflect it and nurture it.

But all spiritualities are not the same, and every consideration of spirituality bears a trace of inner obligation and normativity. Although each one should become responsible for his or her spirituality, the issue involved may be too important to be decided by individuals in private. Spirituality needs public discussion. Therefore the second set of reflections turns to a method of seeking and finding a spirituality. It places Paul Tillich in dialogue with Ignatius Loyola about Christian spirituality. Paul Tillich provides a method of appropriating a spirituality by a correlation of narratives, and Ignatius Loyola offers an example of how this would work.

This seems like a long march, but the path is straight. It begins with a description of spirituality and its narrative structure.

Locating Spirituality

What is spirituality? Everything said about spirituality depends on the root meaning and the reference it bears. In this case, the meanings and the spheres of reference attached to the term "spirituality" are exceptionally diverse. The term has migrated from the sphere of religion to the marketplace of secular and popular consumption. Spirituality has resonances across the religions and disciplines that range from popular psychology and self-help to Meister Eckhart's metaphysics of nothingness. Is there a way of formulating a concept that is broad enough to include the many facets of this sphere of meaning and yet not lose touch with actual life?

The first part of this discussion offers a working definition of spirituality. It designates or stipulates in clear broad terms what the term refers to in this usage without comparing it with many other possibilities. As a working concept, its advantages will appear in the consistency of its application and the appropriateness to common experience. This description of spirituality shows that it has a narrative structure and describes how it relates to theology and religion.

A Working Concept of Spirituality

Since no commonly accepted idea of spirituality rules the day, it becomes necessary to establish a meaning for the term. A working definition, like a hypothesis, means that no arguments defend the conception over against other possibilities. Hopefully the interpretation offered here will make sense as the discussion moves forward. *Spirituality refers to the logic, or character, or consistent quality of a person's or a group's pattern of living insofar as it is measured before some ultimate reality.* Several elements of this terse definition need to be parsed.

This conception is intended to be open and inclusive: according to it, everyone has a spirituality even when one is not conscious of it. Spirituality refers to the style and pattern of a person's or a community's life. It may be consciously deliberated and trained; it may also be spontaneous and not carefully considered. But as long as people have character and identity, spirituality refers to the logic and consistent qualities embedded in their whole lives. This also means that we are not fully conscious or aware of the full depth of our own spirituality.

This construal locates it so far down within the depths of a person that it shares in the mystery that personal being is to itself. Spirituality in this sense also shares a certain unfinished and inconclusive character because, like personhood, it can range from being fragmented and disorganized to being integrated and disciplined. This working conception of spirituality also rescues this sphere from the margins of the bizarre or esoteric and places it within the sphere of ordinary life. The aphorism about being spiritual and not religious seems to imply a suspicion of purely formal and empty objective ritual. Using the term spirituality to designate something like personal identity in action connects it with the general ability of the human spirit to reflect, understand, decide, and act intentionally.

This notion of spirituality rests on the truism that we are what we do, that the overall character or pattern of our behaviors, with their direction and their guiding values, really constitutes the spirituality that in turn defines who we are. The French religious philosopher Maurice Blondel established this view in a classic work on human action.[1] "Action" for Blondel was an analogous term that characterized the dynamic nature of human existence itself as well as individual actions and routinized practices. He was a proto-existentialist who analyzed and interpreted the direction of human willing and action. One should not understand the formula "we are what we do" reductively, as though the self and its agency bear no reflective purchase over the way we respond to the world around us. Rather, decision and action translate the depth and agency of the inner self into character and identity. This continual process always lies open to possible growth, decline, or change of direction. Whether a development is indeed growth or decline ultimately finds its index in some internalized criterion that functions as ultimate value or reality. This identifies ultimacy formally and functionally rather than as this or that particular transcendent idea, value, or "object." At this point, ultimacy refers in an open way to that which centers a given life and measures its character. Paul Tillich would insist that the ultimate for which we live should really be an ultimate and not an idol.[2]

Given this basis of spirituality as the inner existential logic of the way a person's or group's life is actually lived in relation to ultimacy, spirituality as a discipline refers to the study of this dimension of

---

1. Maurice Blondel, *Action: Essay on a Critique of Life and a Science of Practice*, trans. Oliva Blanchette (Notre Dame, IN: University of Notre Dame Press, 1984; orig., 1893). "Action" refers to various kinds of concrete human actions. For the most part Blondel envisages the individual person as the referent, but action broadens to include society. Thus he also gives an account of social and group action as a continuous tradition.

2. Paul Tillich, *Dynamics of Faith* (New York: Harper & Row, 1957), 8-12.

human life. This study may be pursued within a framework of different religions, schools within religions, or more broadly as types of spirituality, as these can be measured by different human sciences like psychology, anthropology, and so on. But this proliferation of approaches still can be brought back to patterns of human living before ultimate reality. This working definition of spirituality, then, is not sleight of hand; it offers an inclusive way into a depth dimension of what is going on in what may otherwise appear as a fragmented human life.

The Narrative Structure of Spirituality

If spirituality congeals around the sum total of one's activity, it has a narrative structure. Noticing the implications of the idea that spirituality has a narrative character helps illumine some qualities of spirituality that will become operative in the discussion further on.

The category of narrative injects time into the equation of spirituality. Christian theologians have always been interested in history, but they have not sufficiently attended to the temporal and narrative character of experience itself. All human perception occurs in time: it has a before and an after. A prehistory leads up to attention, insight, personal consideration, and judgment; and significant experiences generate discernible effects and premises for new knowledge. All our memorable experiences and learnings have a story attached to them; they are rooted in a narrative.

Several decades ago, Stephen Crites, drawing on Augustine, showed how knowing itself has an internal structure that can be called narrative. Meaningful consciousness in the present is always accompanied by memory of the past and anticipation of the future. The three dimensions continually locate human consciousness in a history. "Consciousness grasps its objects in an inherently temporal way, and that temporality is retained in the unity of its experience as a whole."[3] Without memory, human consciousness would be locked in the meaningless present, which we have observed in our companionship with those who suffer various forms of dementia. And anticipation of the future is the open space that allows us to appropriate an experience within the horizon of the possibilities of our willing and acting.[4] Spirituality, then, must be understood in time and as history or narrative.

This temporal dimension highlights the complexity of the development of anyone's spirituality. Many different disciplines, such as

---

3. Stephen Crites, "The Narrative Quality of Experience," *Journal of the American Academy of Religion* 39 (1971): 298.

4. Ibid., 298-99, 303.

developmental psychology and socialization theory, for example, can help us understand the many factors at play in one's spirituality. The category of narrative suggests that each one's story, and the story of any group, may be understood as developing within a concourse and interaction with a myriad of other stories. All the events of one's life and all the memberships in groups that have their own stories show how infinitely complex are the ingredients that feed into each one's spirituality.

If one's spirituality resides in one's history so that one's whole story is the fullest expression of one's spirituality, how can one begin to read or decipher it? The interpretation of narratives provides a clue. Paul Ricoeur has noted that human time is a mixture of two elements: what passes away and what endures. Both the construction of a narrative and the understanding of a story seek to rescue identity within passing events. This opens up a way of understanding how we can retrieve our spirituality in our stories. "What we try to pinpoint is the temporal identity of what is enduring in the midst of what is passing away."[5] Across the twists and turns of our history we seek to collect the identity of the one who appears to be the constant and consistent actor. Our spirituality, then, does not quite lie on the surface of the here and now, nor is it completely apparent in any particular response. The deeper and real self can only be approached through the longer story.

The intelligible meaning of a story and thus a spirituality, however, is neither abstract, nor scientific, nor the result of hard empirical and instrumental reason that reduces data to mathematical formulas that work. Rather, this intelligible meaning occurs in the sphere of human subjectivity or life, which is always human being *for*. There is no intelligible human life that is not human being or life "for" something. This "for" has two important dimensions, ethical and metaphysical. The ethical dimension refers to the sphere of values that determine the moral quality of decisions and commitments. One's life is always lived by some set of values that implicitly guide it. The metaphysical "for" refers to destiny: the end game, the goal, the finality of one's life. What is one's life "for" in the end? To what will it add up? Or, more positively, what will it become? The depth dimension of a story, then, in the sense of having bearing on human existence at a deeper level than just "getting on," lies in its ability to offer comment on what life is for in an ethical and metaphysical sense. In one way or another human

5. Paul Ricoeur, "Toward a Narrative Theology: Its Necessity, Its Resources, Its Difficulties," in *Figuring the Sacred: Religion, Narrative, and Imagination* (Minneapolis: Fortress Press, 1995), 239.

stories involve some conception of ultimate reality and make a comment on it.

Priority of Spirituality to Religion and Theology

An existential and historical approach to spirituality in some respects establishes spirituality's priority to religion and theology. In the contrast between spirituality and religion, "religion" tends to mean overt participation in the public gatherings and worship of a given faith tradition. Is there a way of looking on religion publicly and socially that distinguishes it from spirituality without necessarily separating or dissociating it from spirituality? Although religion is notoriously difficult or impossible to define concretely and comprehensively, a purely formal conception of it will work for our purposes. Religion is *a set of beliefs, values, and practices that together identify what ultimate reality is and help establish the relationship that obtains between this ultimate reality and the practitioners.* This represents religion primarily in objective social terms that refer to the public institutions into which people are socialized and retain membership. Religions are constituted as social movements bearing a culture in which one finds responses to human questions of ultimacy.[6] On this level, religions are larger than us and draw us into themselves. But this does not exhaust the meaning of a religion, because its content is also internalized and resonates with the deepest religious experiences of the members. Thus we may talk about religions such as Hinduism, Christianity, and Islam as if they were objectified units. But we also know that religions are constituted by the very lives of the people who live them and would not exist apart from the people who bear them in their behavior. Religions are built by spiritual persons.

From this it follows that no line necessarily divides religion and spirituality. The possible separation between them, the ability to be spiritual and not religious, arose with modernity.[7] This new world culture arose in the West with a gradual acceptance of a plurality of churches in a single location, the separation of religion and state, the plurality of different faiths living together, and finally, as in Europe, the possibility and even a statistical probability of not being religious at all in a social sense. Thus while individual spiritualities can exist

6. Schubert M. Ogden, *Is There Only One True Religion or Are There Many?* (Dallas: Southern Methodist University Press, 1992), 5.

7. Charles Taylor tries to answer the question of why, after the early modern period in Western culture, in which everyone was expected to have faith, in our time it is socially acceptable that one have no religious faith at all. See his *A Secular Age* (Cambridge: Belknap Press at Harvard University Press, 2007), 3.

without religion, religions cannot exist without spirituality but are precisely the institutionalization of spirituality. Spirituality is prior to religion, and religion has as its purpose to reflect and support spirituality. When religion fails in this function, it loses its reason for being.

Spirituality is also prior to theology, because it supplies the source and subject matter for theology. Spirituality as it has been discussed thus far at least implicitly contains a reference to some ultimacy. When that reference becomes explicit, thematized, recognized, and identified by some mediation, reflection on it becomes what is called theology from the perspective of theism. There is more to be said about the issue of the nature of theology, because it has become complicated within Christianity. That complexity allows the position reflected here to be stipulated as follows: theology intends critically to appreciate, appropriate, and nourish the very spirituality that supports it. Spirituality is prior to theology as its source and the mediator of its subject matter. Theology divorced from spirituality bears a relationship to no perceptible reality at all.

Finding One's Spirituality

The second part of this discussion focuses on the process by which one finds one's own spirituality. For many people this process remains unproblematic: born into a religious or secular tradition, one gradually becomes socialized into one's religious or nonreligious faith and, during some period of time, critically reappropriates that faith so that it deeply influences one's spirituality. But if the aphorism that one can be spiritual but not religious increasingly describes our situation, it also complicates the common pattern of internalizing a given faith tradition. That hypothesis guides the following analysis. It describes a way of conceiving in Christian terms a search for a viable spirituality, a method by which a search could lead to an appropriation of a spirituality, and an illustration of this process.

Searching for a Spirituality

From one perspective, given the way spirituality has been described, our whole lives consist in fashioning our spirituality and constantly refining its borders. Spirituality consists in the way we live, and it constitutes our identity. But no one is willing to accept a static self-definition. The mystery of human existence and the openness of freedom in history forbid it. One can clearly distinguish at their extremes between lifestyles that, on the one hand, seem completely at sea and rudderless, and, on the other hand, those that are more settled because centered around distinct values and goals. Softening those extremes, one could say that each person passes through stages of self-criticism and appropriation to arrive at a mature spirituality. A description of the religious climate of the twenty-first century would note that the distance between questioning and actually finding answers relative to spirituality has widened considerably. Many can no longer make a conscious commitment to a definite object of faith. This raises the question of just how in our radically pluralistic religious and increasingly nonreligious secular life one can adopt any stable path or ascribe to any school of spirituality. Three observations address this question while still falling short of an easy positive answer.

The first notes the importance of the issue and cautions against the idea that one can responsibly make up one's own personal individual spirituality that is different from those of all others. Augustine's story is telling: his search for meaning proved futile until he finally turned to some public tradition for guidance. Sandra Schneiders describes the problem of a private spirituality: it is usually an "idiosyncratic, personally satisfying stance and practice which makes no doctrinal claims, imposes no moral authority outside one's own conscience, creates no necessary personal relationships or social responsibilities, and can be changed or abandoned whenever it seems not to work for the practitioner. Commitment . . . is easily circumvented by a spirituality which has no institutional or community affiliation."[8] Private spirituality is not necessarily irresponsible, but statistically it tends in that direction.

The second point provides a language to clarify what is being sought by a personal appropriation of a public spirituality. Stephen Crites describes two kinds of narratives that shape human lives: sacred narratives that help define and orient a people through time and mundane narratives of everyday existence. Sacred narratives may not be religious, but they are sacred because they shape us interiorly and become so internalized that people do not possess them but are possessed by them and dwell in them. For example, the secular event of becoming a citizen in a new country may be experienced as a sacred appropriating of a new story. These stories are large, and they create a world of meaning that in big terms provides a map for one's life. "For the sacred story does not transpire within a conscious world. It forms the very consciousness that projects a total world horizon, and therefore informs the intentions by which actions are projected into that world."[9] By contrast, mundane stories describe the world as it is actually encountered; they critically interact with sacred stories and bring them down to earth. In short, we live in a tension between

8. Sandra M. Schneiders, "Religion vs. Spirituality: A Contemporary Conundrum," *Spiritus* 3 (2003): 173.

9. Crites, "The Narrative Quality of Experience," 296.

two kinds of narratives, sacred and mundane. A conscious spirituality involves critical appropriation of the meaning-defining stories that actually orient people as groups and individuals in dealing with everyday events.

The third observation grows out of a new recognition of our religiously pluralistic situation as something that is good in principle and not a problem to be overcome. But it sets up a new situation. Kathryn Tanner has described how Pascal's wager on Christianity was simple compared with the far more complex situation where the religions of the world are represented in all major urban environments and where many subcultures reject them all. This new situation has implications for the search for a spirituality. Yet if God's grace is truly unconditional, it must be available to all, noncompetitively and without winners and losers.[10] But that still leaves us faced with innumerable sacred narratives and other secular spiritualities from which to choose. It does not lessen the need for a strategy that allows one to enter into a public spirituality noncompetitively but still completely. But how does one do that?

Correlating Personal and Sacred Narratives

Can one really commit to a particular public spirituality and appropriate a sacred story into one's own life? Today's sense of differences and individuality make public spiritualities seem irrelevant to personal need. How then can individuals with their own stories accept objective sacred narratives and make them explicitly their own and thereby complete the wager? This is not easy, and it may require diligent application. But it is possible, and Paul Tillich suggests a way in which it can be done.

Tillich stood within a line of hermeneutical thinkers beginning with Friedrich Schleiermacher and continuing through Martin Heidegger, Rudolf Bultmann, Hans-Georg Gadamer, and later Paul Ricoeur. This tradition has provided Western theologians with careful descriptions of interpreting the past. In this tradition, to know is to interpret: no knowledge without interpretation. Moreover interpretation always occurs from inside the story of the interpreter; we cannot escape our

---

10. Kathryn Tanner compares the phenomenology of Pascal's wager on religious commitment with the character of such a wager today ("Grace and Gambling," Presidential Address, American Theological Society [March 26, 2010], http://cas.uchicago.edu/workshops/theology/files/2009/10/Tanner-Kathryn-Grace-and-Gambling.pdf). If grace were considered truly unconditional, that unconditionality would mean that today's wager requires no works, no risk, and no limits or competition among winners. Thus, in the Christian view, the appearance that risk seems greater in our pluralistic situation is mistaken, and religious pluralism becomes a blessing.

individuality, and we can only understand the other by analogy with our own experience. Part of the brilliance of Tillich was his ability to internalize most of the fundamental insights of this particular hermeneutical tradition and fashion them into a method of interpretation which he called a method of correlation.[11]

Tillich's deceptively simple harnessing of interpretation to a formula of question and answer incorporates principles by which one can appreciate meanings proposed in objective terms from other situations and find their relevance to our day through existential correlation. "Correlation" means placing formulas from the past and the contextual experience within them in conjunction with present-day contextual experience. The deep questions of a given present generation look to the past for relevant answers. Applied to Christianity: "The method of correlation explains the contents of the Christian faith through existential questions and theological answers [from the tradition] in mutual interdependence."[12] This formula rests on the supposition of a common dimension to human existence and the existential principle of learning that answers to questions that are not asked can hardly be internalized with any depth. Since meaning can be appropriated only by analogy with a lived experience of the interpreter, spiritual truth especially requires an existential spiritual question in order to be understood sympathetically. "The answers implied in the event of revelation are meaningful only in so far as they are in correlation with questions concerning the whole of our existence, with existential questions."[13]

In Tillich's conception of the method, the question from the present situation of the inquirer gives the response a present-day form and relevance. But the content or objective meaning of the response comes from the public narrative. In the Christian sphere: "The Christian message provides the answers to the questions implied in human existence. These answers are contained in revelatory events on which Christianity is based and are taken by systematic theology *from* the sources, *through* the medium, *under* the norm [who is Jesus as the Christ]. Their content cannot be derived from the questions themselves, that is, from an analysis of human existence."[14] In other words,

11. The following theoretical account of interpreting the past in a meaningful way sets up the next section on the interpretation of narratives. The theory should be clarified by the extended example of Ignatius Loyola interpreting and appropriating stories from the past by correlation with his own possibilities.

12. Paul Tillich, *Systematic Theology* (Chicago: University of Chicago Press, 1951), 1:60.

13. Ibid., 61.

14. Ibid., 64.

a public spirituality retains its autonomy in its being received, but it can only be appropriated in a form that is analogous and responds to the individuality of the interpreter. Tillich's response to the question of how one appropriates a spirituality in the form of a sacred narrative is by a correlation of narratives. This process always retains a dialectical and tensive relation between the public and the personal, and the tension means that inquiry and interpretation never cease.

When Tillich's method of correlation is applied to narratives, it gives rise to the idea of a "fusion of narratives." This phrase of mine is a riff on the phrase "a fusion of horizons," drawn from Hans-Georg Gadamer's work in hermeneutics.[15] Gadamer's description of interpretation from a "standpoint" and "horizon" provides a visual metaphor for the way personal existential questions shape interpretation as Tillich explained. All public spiritualities were created and subsist in particular horizons, and they reflect them. When they are interpreted and brought to life in another context, one can speak of the correlation not only as a fusion of horizons but also as a fusion of two narratives, the narrative of the text and the narrative of the interpreter.[16] In this process the narrative world of the public spirituality is fused with the narrative of the inquirer. The meaning of the sacred narrative opens up possibilities for the freedom of the one seeking an explicit spirituality. The fusion works both ways as each narrative illumines the other within the consciousness of the one appropriating the public story.

How then does one appropriate a public spirituality as one's own? The process has been going on since history began. The self-transcendence of human consciousness allows appreciation of the other, and analogy with ourselves allows internalization. But can such a transposition retain the authenticity of the original and truly preserve the integrity of the individual in a later and different culture? The response to these questions requires considerable nuance: the authenticity of the transposition will not lie in the objective details of situation and culture, but in the logic of the human life that is represented and produced by the correlation itself. An authentic correlation and fusion of narratives can only happen existentially in those who accomplish it. It cannot be judged in purely objective terms.

The Example and Technique of Ignatius Loyola

To illustrate a correlation of narratives as a strategy for appropriating a Christian spirituality I offer a classic example in the person and the work of Ignatius Loyola. A Catholic Basque noble, contemporary of

15. Hans-Georg Gadamer, *Truth and Method* (New York: Seabury, 1975).
16. Ibid., 267-71.

Luther and Calvin, he was born in 1491 and died in 1556. The course of his life seemed to be one long quest, as he played the successive roles of Spanish courtier, royal fixer, convert to pilgrim and seeker, Parisian student, leader of a band of ordained ministers, founder and first administrator of the Jesuits in Rome, and, finally, author of their Constitutions. The turning point in Ignatius's life was a battle wound, a subsequent conversion experience during his convalescence, and the first outlines of his Spiritual Exercises written immediately thereafter. These initial drafts developed into a manual for a systematic prayerful consideration of the gospel narratives as a way of ordering one's life. The following analysis shows how a correlation of narratives describes rather exactly Ignatius's own conversion, his composition of his Exercises, and the experience of people who make them. In short, the following three points from the life of Ignatius describe by example how a correlation of narratives can generate or reinforce a spirituality.

First, regarding Ignatius's conversion: no one can doubt the power of narrative after considering this change in his life. Wounded at Pamplona and carried back to his family's manor house in Azpeitia in the summer of 1521, Ignatius had nothing to read but a life of Christ, made up of gospel stories with extensive commentary, and an anthology of brief lives of saints. The lives of two saints in particular inspired him. Later he himself, writing in the third person, described the experience thus: "In his reading he was deeply impressed by two saints, and his reaction was: 'St. Dominic did this, therefore, I have to do it. St. Francis did this, therefore, I have to do it.'"[17] He then copied out in a notebook all the words spoken by Jesus as recorded in the gospels. When he left home in the spring of 1522, he was setting off as a pilgrim bound for Jerusalem to follow Jesus, charged by the stories of Dominic and Francis.

The second point relates to the logic of the construction of Ignatius's Spiritual Exercises. The story of the initial sketches picks up where we left off. The first stop on his pilgrimage was at the shrine of the Black Madonna at Monserrat in the sawtoothed mountains west of Barcelona. There he spent a night in vigil before the statue of the Madonna during which he laid aside his arms and changed his clothes to those of a mendicant pilgrim. Before heading off, however, he tarried in the nearby town of Manresa and ended up spending almost a year there in a prayerful ascetic mode of life. During this period he developed the rudiments of his Spiritual Exercises. Most experts believe the keynote consideration of the Exercises was drafted at this time. It is deeply

17. Ignatius Loyola, "Autobiography," in *Ignatius of Loyola: The Spiritual Exercises and Selected Works*, ed. George E. Ganss, et al. (New York: Paulist Press, 1991), #7. Cited by paragraph number.

autobiographical, and it cleanly illustrates the correlation of narratives that governs the whole project of the Exercises.

The title of this consideration is "The Call of the King." In it Ignatius asks the one doing the Exercises to consider, in a context of quiet and prayer, a king and leader about to launch a great and noble campaign who seeks to enlist companions in the battle. Who could resist such a proposal of the highest good? He then compares Jesus to such a leader and commander-in-chief who addresses human beings in these words: "My will is to conquer the whole world and all my enemies, and thus to enter into the glory of my Father. Therefore, whoever wishes to come with me must labor with me, so that through following me in the pain he or she may follow me also in the glory."[18] In Ignatius's view, such a call elicits the highest possible level of commitment, so that anyone who did not answer such a summons would be "scorned and upbraided by everyone and accounted as an unworthy knight." But those who respond will strive to "distinguish themselves in total service to their eternal King and universal Lord [and] . . . make offerings of greater worth and moment."[19]

This consideration in the Exercises opens up a world of possible experience. First of all, this consideration mirrors his own transfer of complete loyalty from the earthly king of Spain to Jesus Christ. And this is what he invites the seeker to do. Ignatius, of course, had a high Christology; he does not hesitate to refer to Jesus as God and his divine Lord and Majesty. But in the Exercises Jesus is not represented primarily as someone to be adored. Ignatius represents Jesus as a human figure and as a leader to be followed. This is an imitation-of-Jesus spirituality in which one models one's life on Jesus in his ministry and simultaneously responds to the cause of the rule of God in the present world. The rule of God entails justice, concern for the oppressed and marginalized, a critique of purely self-serving power, and love even of enemies. Ignatius holds out a correlation of lives and a fusion of narratives as the basic structure by which the Exercises achieve their goal of assisting the reordering of one's spirituality.

The third point focuses on the experience of people making these Spiritual Exercises. The basic units of the Exercises are what he calls "contemplations" of individual scenes in Jesus's ministry as depicted in the gospel stories. The whole series of these contemplations follows the story of Jesus from his birth, through his public ministry, his passion and death, to his resurrection and appearances to his disciples. In

18. Ignatius Loyola, *The Spiritual Exercises of Saint Ignatius*, trans. and commentary by George E. Ganss (Chicago: Loyola University Press, 1992), #95. Cited by paragraph number.

19. Ibid., ## 94 and 97.

each case and all along the way a "correlation of narratives" describes exactly what is going on. Ignatius proposes an almost literal fusion of narratives in one's imagination. He asks that a person enter the gospel stories by imaginatively placing the self within the scenes of Jesus's life so that one sees what is going on, hears the voices, and mentally participates in the action. In these operations one positions oneself outside one's situation into another space in order to make these stories live. At the same time, the person making the Exercises brings the stories forward by correlation and appropriation of the possibilities they open up to one's own life. In this remembering of the Christian stories, the imagination forms the bridge between past, present, and future, between the stories of Jesus and a path for a given person's life now and into the future.

Let me sum up this illustration in a word. Ignatius Loyola was driven by the stories of the saints to imitate and emulate their lives. Four centuries later, William James knew exactly what was going on there when he described the social function of the saints as providing witness and example, that is, public stories of a level of virtue that we could not imagine possible without them.[20] We need stories to shape our own lives. Captivated by the stories of Dominic and Francis, Ignatius gave himself over to a new leader and set out to imitate him by following the lead of Jesus's campaign of basic values: resisting evil and doing good. And he constructed his Exercises in a way that mirrored his own experience and provided opportunities for others to merge their stories with the story of Jesus. The goal of the Exercises is an ordering or reordering of one's life. It does this by a correlation of one's own narrative with that of Jesus of Nazareth. The goal more generally and exactly is to align the goal of one's being and life with ultimate reality. Thus what has been exemplified here in the case of the Christian story and spirituality occurs in other spiritual traditions, religious and nonreligious, across the world. The pluralism of sacred stories is a blessing.

* * *

The question for religion in the twenty-first century might be asked in terms of Paul Tillich's aphorism that religion is the substance of culture:[21] will this remain true in the new critical world-culture that is emerging? The question appears to be vital in the light of the decline in religious participation among those who have internalized this world-

20. William James, *The Variety of Religious Experience: A Study of Human Nature* (London: Collins, 1960), 347.

21. Paul Tillich, *Systematic Theology* (Chicago: University of Chicago Press, 1963), 3:158.

culture. And this extends around the world to some extent wherever critical education is available.

The response to this question that is proposed here says that religion can represent the substance of a culture only if religion supports, nurtures, and expresses the spirituality of those who live in that culture. It cannot survive as the substance of culture if those who actively participate in social life have abandoned it. Religion can barely exist as a set of institutional behaviors that have no bearing on the daily dilemmas that mark the path of each person's story. Religion can only be the substance of culture if it provides a narrative that is relevant to the spiritualities that collectively make up that culture.

But this way of stating the case appears too negative. More positively, the story and stories that make up a religious tradition must be given precedence over the doctrines and moral codes that are so often equated with religion itself. Sets of beliefs and moral prescriptions are surely necessary and important; it is hard to imagine institutional religion without them. But they exist only to help support the integrity of spiritual life. Viewed from within, that spirituality exists as a way of life. It finds its most direct nourishment by a correlation and fusion of the sacred narratives of a tradition, with the possibilities they set before us, and the realities represented by the mundane stories of the present world. *Spirituality* is the substance of a new world-culture, and, in order to survive, explicit religious life must nurture that spirituality with new possibilities for the commitment of human freedom. Such is the importance of spirituality.

CHAPTER TWO

Spirituality as the Basis of Theology

We live in a period and a Western culture in which the practice of Christianity is declining. Religious sociologists propose a variety of reasons why people are drifting away from the churches. One or two single reasons cannot explain why so many people no longer actively participate in their parishes and congregations. People may retain their Christian faith apart from active community belonging, but without community support the character of that faith will undoubtedly grow thin and drift toward the idiosyncratic. No one can predict the results of this decline; it affects different cultures and countries in different ways and degrees. But the direction of this development appears analogous across the developed nations of Europe and North America. Whole groups of educated people in urban societies throughout the world are being affected by similar cultural forces.

Looking at this movement from inside the Christian faith, one has to conclude that the reasons why people are abandoning the churches do not lie within the faith itself but must rest with the way the churches present that faith. The various degrees of rejection of Christian faith should not be attributed to bad faith or evil inclination on the part of so many people but to the way in which the faith is practiced, communicated, and explained to people who make up our contemporary societies and cultures. This means that the church stands at a divide in its road forward that can be expressed by a question such as the following: should theology search for a way to communicate with a new audience residing in a significantly new Western cultural environment? Karl Rahner suggested as much many decades ago when he described the church as facing its most significant challenge since its adjustment to Roman and Greek culture and then to Constantine's Roman Empire.[1]

The role of the discipline of spirituality includes the task of appropriating Christian faith in ever-new cultural and contextual circumstances. The terms "secularization" and "religious pluralism" refer to

1. Karl Rahner, "Towards a Fundamental Theological Interpretation of Vatican II," *Theological Studies* 40 (1979): 716-27.

integral dimensions of our new situation and represent it symbolically. This chapter will not analyze the causes of these phenomena. Others are better able to decipher the mechanisms behind them. In what follows, secularization and religious pluralism are stipulated as commonly experienced developments. This chapter focuses instead on the following question: are there ways of reconstructing Christian faith in the face of these new social conditions? Here I use the term "construction" to mean "understanding." Reconstruction means interpreting the same thing in a new way. The word "construction" adds the notion that this is a human task, that although theology's content is revealed, it receives its form from human resources such as language, culture, and creative imagination. Since each theological construction is precisely a construction, an interpretive *understanding* of faith, it need not be confused with faith itself. There is no revealed theology.

The thesis of this chapter can be stated as follows: the decline of Christianity in the West in the face of a new positive appreciation of secularization and religious pluralism challenges Christian theology to reformulate its self-understanding. One formula and strategy for such a project would address "seekers" on the level of basic spirituality through considerations of the stories about Jesus in the Gospels. A spirituality of "following Jesus" would provide the grounds for reinterpreting the cosmic sacred story of Christianity on the basis of the spirituality contained in the story of Jesus.[2]

This proposal is laid out in six points designed to show how theology can begin to reconstruct its understanding of Christian faith in a way that responds to the inability of traditional Christian language to communicate to increasing numbers of people in the West. These six points define a distinct way in which individuals may appropriate their faith and a strategy by which theology programmatically can reconstruct itself. This is not the only possible program, but one that is plausible and potentially fruitful.

Seekers and Spirituality

The first question is whether one might find a suitable point of departure for reconstructing our Christian theology so that it might meet people in a culture of Christian decline. Such a point of departure lies within the phenomenon of the religious person who is also a seeker for a meaningful spirituality. What is it about the seeker and the idea of spirituality that makes the very search for a meaningful way of life a place to begin theological reconstruction?

---

2. This theme underlies the logic of my *Spirituality Seeking Theology* (Maryknoll, NY: Orbis Books, 2014).

The seeker is one who is looking for something, presumably something he or she wants but lacks.[3] Seekers are not squarely at home in any established religious faith and lack a single-minded faith commitment. They live on the edge of any creed and do not fully endorse any religion; they have no firm place within reality and certainly no master narrative that excludes others. But at the same time they are looking for meaning in their own lives and a wider framework that would supply a broader context for such a meaning. They want more coherence in their vision of things, more direction for their lives, and more comprehensive meaning. "Comprehensive" suggests width and depth, like a horizon within which discrete elements can be measured by being located within a larger perspective that provides the distance for comparative evaluation.[4] Certainly some things must be more important than others. The reference for the term "seeker," then, has to do with the large questions of the meaning and purpose of existence itself. Seekers live in this context, are not content with the answers to these basic questions as they have been proffered them, and are looking for symbols that can give more order to their lives.

The idea of a spirituality as it is used here corresponds with the description offered in chapter 1. Spirituality refers to the way persons or groups lead their lives in the face of ultimacy or transcendent reality however that is conceived. It applies to both individuals and communities. This broad definition aims at breaking down the frequent separation between spirituality and ordinary life and showing that the sum total of people's everyday actions defines who they are and connects them or separates them from transcendence. Spirituality has a narrative structure, is constituted by the behaviors and practices of persons, and may be understood as the logic or coherence of their lives in the face of ultimacy. Of course, what is taken as ultimate should really be so. But it is no longer the case that religion and spirituality imply each other. More and more people, in fact large segments of young people in the United States, describe themselves as spiritual but not religious, where "religious" means being a member of an organized religion or faith community. In this usage spirituality relates

---

3. I have described "seekers" in other works, particularly in *Christian Spirituality for Seekers*, xvii, 88-91. The notion of a seeker is open to many applications to people outside and inside a particular faith tradition. The particular relevance of the notion to this discussion lies in its association with many different kinds of disruption of and dissatisfaction with received traditions on the one hand, and, on the other hand, the contrasting positive searching for new forms of faith that resonate with an inner demand for coherent meaning in life.

4. One's horizon of consciousness "is the range of vision that includes everything that can be seen from a particular vantage point." See Gadamer, *Truth and Method*, 269.

to a dimension of life prior to and more basic than membership in a religious community and is compatible with being a seeker.

This first point does not imply that the point of departure for understanding Christian faith lies outside of faith itself. The sources of Christian faith are scripture, tradition, and the Christian community itself. But active appropriation of the meaning of Christian faith requires an appeal to experience. Seekers, whose good will and openness are implicit in their very seeking, represent the questions and concerns of the secular and religiously plural cultures that have to be met in theological reconstruction. Seekers, therefore, represent a dimension of our new secular and religiously pluralistic cultures that remains open to transcendent reality.

The Experience of Transcendence

Spirituality is a way of life corresponding to a transcendent value or ultimate reality. Is there an experience that points to such a reality? Not one but many experiences in human life support the idea of a transcendent principle of being whom Christians and others call God and to whom still other religions give other names. A survey of Christian believers asked whether they have ever experienced God in their lives would point to an array of personal encounters related to a whole range of types of experience that may be associated with the psychological, aesthetic, philosophical, moral, or scientific spheres of knowledge. The Christian tradition offers a large menu of analyses of how the human can be understood as instinctively open to transcendence, of how the very structure of the human spirit orients it toward recognition of some transcendent reality that embraces the finite world we know and the universe we extrapolate. The existence of God or any other transcendent principle of reality cannot be proved to exist, but the many different approaches to it highlight a human capacity and desire for transcendence that form the basis of seeking itself. Moreover, the questioning of seekers may indicate that they already participate in what they are searching for but lack ways of putting it into explicit language.

Finding a Conception of God

Many religions today offer places for the seeker to investigate the nature of transcendent reality. Several religions, notably the Abrahamic religions of Judaism, Christianity, and Islam, as well as other theistic religions, provide long traditions of meditation and reflection on the reality of God. The problem often encountered by the seeker today lies less in the scarcity of revelation and more in the many different and sometimes conflicting claims about the character of the transcendent order. In our adaptation to the situation of religious pluralism we now recognize that we can no longer think in terms of one true religion while all the others are false or seriously defective. More and more people who are reflective about their own monotheistic faith in God recognize that other religions contain truth about transcendent reality from which they can learn.

Shifting now to Christianity, Jesus of Nazareth points the direction for the Christian imagination when it speaks of God. Christian faith is faith in God as God is revealed in the teaching and ministry of Jesus. Christians of course relate to the whole Bible, in which both Testaments speak of God. It is impossible to understand Jesus apart from the religious tradition in which he lived. But within the collected writings of the New Testament, the Gospel stories of Jesus of Nazareth provide the main source of Christian faith and the centering symbol that points to God and makes God present to the Christian imagination.

The point being made here can sometimes be obscured by the massive weight of Christian tradition, that seemingly enormous amount of knowledge about God that Christians have accumulated over the centuries. Christian tradition refers to an immense storehouse of reflections and conclusions about almost everything that exists. Yet, despite the value of that tradition, the inner structure of Christian faith consists in clinging to God as Jesus has represented God in his teaching and ministry. All the wisdom about God collected by Christians through the years gravitates around and fills out the Christian's faith encounter with God as God has been made known in Jesus of Nazareth. The Christian tradition has added to, supplemented, and interpreted this faith encounter with God in Jesus but never supplanted it.

Jesus Represents God

The concept of God that a person encounters in Jesus of Nazareth has been the subject matter of theology for two millennia. An attempt at describing Jesus's representation of God for a seeker today would fall far short of the recorded history of the Christian experience of God. From the inspired authors of the New Testament, beginning with Paul of Tarsus and the evangelists, we have interpretations of Jesus and narrative accounts of his teachings. This person Jesus forms the central core of the New Testament. The New Testament always presupposes an encounter with God in Jesus even when the subject matter engages other issues such as morality and order in the communities. Of course, much if not all of the teaching of Jesus about God comes from the Jewish tradition and scriptures, because Jesus was a Jewish prophet, teacher, and healer.

Jesus proposed God as transcendent reality, the creator and ruler of the universe. Jesus's God was a God of power and might who created all that is and who cared for it as God's own cherished creation. As creator, God's word was self-fulfilling: God spoke and it was done. Jesus told of God's oversight and care of the world in providential terms that descended to individuals: "Even all the hairs of your head are counted" (Matt 10:30). God cares for each person even as God clothes in splendor the flowers in the fields.

As in the Hebrew scriptures, Jesus imagined God as the sovereign of the universe: God ruled as king, and a king cared for his people. God's rule formed the root metaphor for Jesus's operative conception of God, and all his teaching revolved around God's will being done and God's rule being accomplished in a new reforming way. Jesus's teaching of the rule of God applied to all sorts of situations and usually interrupted things because God's ways were not the ways of human beings. God's rule would turn society on its head and reverse many of the self-serving values that are engrained in any social system. God's rule requires social justice.

Jesus also stressed the personality of God. That God is personal was taken for granted within the Jewish tradition, and Christians and Muslims too think of God as personal. But what we know of the universe today, its sheer size and age, deeply challenges the idea that God is an individual person. The magnitude of the universe that science represents in numbers and formulas confuses our imagination: its size, complexity, age, and mixture of impersonal law and sheer randomness prevent us from imagining an even greater individual person behind it all. And yet Jesus's teaching challenges our imaginations to recognize that the power that surrounds and holds this universe in existence from within cannot be less than the very product of evolutionary process: personal being. Jesus called this power Father, but he also described God in a manner that has many feminine qualities, as, for example, God's tender care of those who need it. At the same time, the infinite magnitude of God explodes all space–time characteristics such as gender.

Another characteristic of the God that Jesus proposes to the world is love: God loves what God creates. The love of God for the world and its people appears throughout the teaching of Jesus, even when Jesus censures injustice and malpractice in the name of the rule of God. These prophetic words of rebuke frequently aim at preventing harm to those who are injured by certain attitudes and practices, or at undercutting some form of idolatry that usurps God's place. Jesus's spirituality of the rule of a God of love becomes socially actual in human responses of compassion for all who suffer, even enemies, as the parable of the

Good Samaritan shows. The love predicated of God by Jesus, then, suffuses the action of creation as the inner motive of God's power and might. The internal logic of reality itself rests within an all-embracing and self-communicating personal love. And this flows out into the world through the intentional personal and social actions of people's love for one another.

It seems ridiculous to sum up Jesus's representation of God in four qualities: God's transcendence, sovereign governance, personality, and love. The descriptions of human experiences of transcendence go on and on. One cannot imagine this as a reductionist synthesis as if the object of Christian faith could be so reduced. Yet if a person deeply internalized these teachings of Jesus, there is not much that he or she would lack from a Christian perspective.

Jesus Engenders a Spirituality

Consideration of Jesus of Nazareth raises the question of how he stimulates a spirituality in others. The model for understanding how this occurs is drawn from the way Jesus engendered a spirituality in his first followers. Their lives became entangled with his; they walked with him and followed his patterns of life, heard his teaching, and internalized his values. This same interaction of association and appropriation goes on today. The following description of this process finds its inspiration in Ignatius Loyola, who made a turn to Jesus about 500 years ago in his extended process of conversion over a two-year period, as described in chapter 1. How Jesus engenders a spirituality can be encapsulated in two steps: association and appropriation.[5]

The first step is association with Jesus. Jesus was a human being. In the eyes of Christian faith Jesus was more than a human being, but a human being nevertheless. As a human being he has a story that is accessible to all people. The humanity of Jesus means that all seekers, whatever their culture and background, can enter into the stories of Jesus that are found in the Gospels and that together make up the story of Jesus. At an initial level, one can approach Jesus as one would any other master of the spiritual life. If one wants to encounter Jesus more deeply, however, it is worthwhile to delay over the stories of Jesus and to enter into them imaginatively. In a given Gospel vignette one may associate oneself with one of the characters, or imagine oneself as a participant observer. In this way a person may be able imaginatively to receive the message and impact of the story from the inside. Of course, reading scriptural commentary may help this process, but on

5. This section reprises the description in chapter 1 of how a person can adopt a Christian spirituality.

this first level of vicarious and literary interpersonal contact one can learn from the Gospels themselves to feel what Jesus stands for, who he is, what kind of life he proposes in the face of God and God's rule.

The second step is appropriation of the story of Jesus. As explained in the last chapter, philosophers who have analyzed the logic of interpretation speak of a fusion of horizons. The idea of a horizon suggests metaphorically the open space before our vision in which we locate things and position them relatively to each other. All people have internal maps for understanding that are created by language, culture, and their own history. A fusion of horizon describes how understanding a vision of something from another culture requires entering into its meaning precisely as distinctly set in its own horizon. People today then draw it forward into their own horizon, merging it, so to speak, with the present. This fusion should both challenge people by the difference and sheer otherness of what is entertained, and yet be appropriated in the sense of being adjusted to the context of what people know in their own time to be true and have a bearing on their lives.[6]

What philosophers call a "fusion of horizons" to show how concepts of one culture can become relevant to another, we may call a "fusion of narratives" in the appropriation of Jesus into a spirituality for today's world. Persons enter the stories of Jesus and to the best of their ability appreciate them from the inside as past events. They allow the stories, and the whole story to which the many incidents give rise, to converge with their own lives in order to discover the possibilities they release for present existence and the future.[7] Because Jesus was a human being, he is imitable. People can imaginatively *try on* his teachings and values, reckon their potential within the parameters of the social, cultural, and personal possibilities of their own lives, and then *try them out*: put them into action. For example, today the love of the Samaritan for the victim along the road to Jericho may best be shown by making the road safe and establishing a social justice that eliminates banditry.

To appreciate better what is going on here it might be helpful to distinguish three kinds of story. An ordinary story describes everyday events and how our lives actually unfold. A deeper story, like the

---

6. Gadamer, *Truth and Method*, 271-74.

7. Ricoeur describes what one can learn from a story from the past not in terms of a one-to-one correspondence to the things located in the horizon of one's actual world. Rather one learns existential possibilities for living, ideals that can project for the self a new future. The world described in the stories of Jesus is not simply there objectively, but is there as intentionally construed and participated in. The reference that the text points to "is a *proposed world* which I could inhabit and wherein I could project one of my ownmost possibilities." See Paul Ricoeur, "The Hermeneutical Function of Distanciation," *Hermeneutics and the Human Sciences*, ed. J. B. Thompson (Cambridge: University Press, 1981), 142.

parables Jesus told or the stories about Jesus himself, sets out ideas and values in action that have a bearing on how a person leads his or her own life. A sacred story, a metanarrative, organizes the world so that one does not quite control it because it defines the meaning and destiny of life itself.[8] The Jesus story, which is made up of the Gospel stories about him, hovers between the second and third type of story. For this reason, when one enters into it and by a fusion of narratives allows it to communicate direction to one's life, one has begun to internalize a spirituality.

A Jesus Spirituality as a Basis for a New Theology

How does a Jesus spirituality come to bear on theology? A direct answer to this blunt question would affirm that it happens the way it did the first time and has continued ever since. Spirituality provides the basis and the criterion of an effective theology.

This response assumes a historical developmental perspective on what happened with the disciples of Jesus after his death and resurrection. They had developed a spirituality of the "way" taught by Jesus through a process of association and appropriation (Acts 9:2). But they had a major problem of explaining both to themselves and to the public what went on in Jesus's death, because it corresponded with no messianic script. Who exactly was Jesus, and how did it all fit together? Deciphering all this took time and great effort, a properly theological effort of understanding how God was at work in these events. The theology of the New Testament was thus literally generated out of the disciples' Jesus spirituality, by consultation with the tradition of the Hebrew scriptures, especially Isaiah, and the inspiring energy of God as Spirit. Spirituality provided the matrix of theology. The term "spirituality," more fully than "experience," points to where existential human conviction passes over into the kind of certainty that generates decision making and public communication in writing. Primary religious language, the language that articulates religious experience in relatively spontaneous terms, often expresses spirituality in a narrative form reflecting "what happened to us" and the life of the movement. Second order or reflective language, the language of theology, turns precisely to the language of spirituality in a critical, reflective, analytical manner. This describes not only the genesis of the New Testament but also the continuous history of theology.

If spirituality in action provides the experiential source of theology, then it also provides one of the criteria for measuring its adequacy. If a theological formula or proposal for understanding Christian faith

8. Crites, "The Narrative Quality of Experience," 296.

cannot be squared with the basic life of faith, it cannot stand. This logic does not apply to every spiritual practice, because they are many and diverse: some deep and others merely occasional and local in their relevance. Other criteria may be invoked to criticize particular spiritual practices. The point here refers to the basis of spirituality itself, that is, commitment to God as revealed in Jesus that remains identical even when it elicits different historical forms in different cultures and contexts. A theology that is inconsistent with the fundamental logic of faith and spirituality mediated by Jesus of Nazareth has drifted from its grounding and lost its vital first principle. A spirituality of following Jesus is both the source and the criterion of an effective theology.

In summary, a spirituality centered on Jesus of Nazareth provides the existential relation to God that supplies a starting point, the experiential source, and the criterion for the reconstruction of theology that can respond to the decline of Christianity in the West. This formula does not bypass the history of theology and doctrine up to this point. Rather it provides a strategy for reappropriating it in a way that meets our current problem.

* * *

The simple logic that holds this proposal together bears a threefold significance for our situation today. The first point has to do with the problem that faces us. We live in a world of intercommunication and interdependence. This world presents a culturally secular face, a neutral world shared in common, in which many religions flourish on the premise of religious freedom. Part of the decline of Christianity in the West can be associated with the loss of an exclusivist and supremacist self-identity which can no longer be maintained in our world, not pragmatically and not theologically. Many of the doctrines and much of the language based on those premises need to be reinterpreted or reconstructed. The question is how to do it.

In response to this, secondly, one can imagine the Christian vision being constructed by two stories. The first story is the story of Jesus: it has four versions in the collected vignettes about Jesus's ministry in the four Gospels. This is the small story of Jesus, and basic story, the inner core of Christianity. It is surrounded by a big story, a sacred story, a metanarrative, that interprets the small story and situates it in cosmic terms of being. This story begins anthropomorphically with God and creation, includes a fall and the sending of a redeemer; it goes forward with the story of the church leading to the end of time. This metastory relates to the small story of Jesus not by necessary logic or deduction but by reflective existential and speculative interpretation. The community reflected on its spiritual life intensely during the period of the writing of the New Testament and afterward, and it developed over centuries the big story that embraced and encompassed the little story within itself. The metanarrative, told in Christian doctrine, then became the introduction to Christianity and provided the lens with which people then understood Jesus, frequently without going back to the stories about him. And when they did, they frequently read the developed doctrines about him into his consciousness as he performed his ministry in Palestine. But virtually all of the elements of this metanarrative have come under attack: creation, fall, redemption, church, and end time. Even the possibility of metanarratives in our Western culture remains questionable. Whether or not these assaults on the Christian story succeed, the Christian metanarrative has to be reinterpreted.

Third, according to the formula proposed here, we should not go first to the metanarrative to interpret Jesus but should return to the story of Jesus and reinterpret the metanarrative on the basis of a spirituality of following Jesus and where it leads in our contemporary world. This replicates the process by which the metanarrative was created in the first place. Such a proposal addresses both secularity and religious pluralism. It offers both a formula for each individual Christian to reappropriate his or her faith and an outline for a strategy for reconstructing the discipline of Christian theology in the West. For all seekers, both those outside and those inside the circle of Christian faith, Jesus appears in history as a human being; he is approachable by all, friendly, attractive to the religious imagination, with a message of ultimate justice and hope. This is not the end of the human quest, but for Christians this is where it begins. Jesus will in fact be found to teach many of the things taught by other religions. As for individual seekers, Jesus will open up for them a personal loving God who both loves human beings and, out of love, questions them. For insiders, associating more closely with Jesus, "again for the first time" as Marcus Borg has said, can revitalize one's faith. This association with Jesus cuts through the metanarrative with a more immediate personal relationship with God. That relationship will be found to be both comforting in our new world and challenging, because Jesus proposes a spirituality of active social concern. At the end of the day, it appears that in fact this describes what most critical or thinking Christians actually do.

CHAPTER THREE

The Uniqueness of Jesus

The word "uniqueness" is an analogous term and loaded with a variety of meanings in relation to Jesus. Each one of them is contested, because they all touch on fundamental issues in understanding the inner character and being of Jesus Christ. Since Jesus is at the center of Christian faith, much is at stake in these issues. The strategy of this chapter is to describe three distinct spheres of reference in which the language of Jesus's uniqueness comes into play. In each case the question of Christian spirituality will be used to measure the options. In every case spirituality cannot decide one position that excludes the others, but it does point reflection in a certain direction.

The three areas of discussion concern, first, Jesus's uniqueness as a historical figure. In this sense every human being is unique because we each have our particular identity as an individual. What is Jesus's uniqueness on this level? Is it a uniqueness that clearly distinguishes him in a substantive way from his Jewish tradition? In many respects the meaning of "uniqueness" on this level approaches that of "identity," and the question of Jesus's historical identity overlaps with the object of the quest for the historical Jesus. The second area concerns Jesus's uniqueness as savior or path to God. This level of meaning usually entails the question of how Jesus compares with other savior figures or religious mediations as revelations of or ways to the transcendent reality of God. Does Jesus's uniqueness entail an absolute character that makes him incomparable to other religious mediators? The third area concerns Jesus's divinity. When Jesus's uniqueness refers to an absoluteness that stems from his divinity, this divine identity often places him in a completely other class than all other religious mediators. These three broad topics will provide a good overview of the topic of Jesus's uniqueness and provide a framework for conversation.

Uniqueness as the Particularity of Jesus

The first dimension of the uniqueness of Jesus relates to his historical individuality. How is one to describe what he said and did? How is this related to what other religious figures have preached? And how should we compare it to the message about God that is contained in the Jewish scriptures and religion in which he was raised? To a large extent this is a historical question that should be able to be resolved through the discipline of history.

To answer these questions we turn to New Testament scholars who use historical-critical methods to uncover as best they can how Jesus presented himself in his ministry and to determine the content of what he said and did. Historical Jesus research has been contested in its methods and in its results, from the beginning and from multiple points of view. Frequently the different positions on the merits of trying to describe Jesus as he appeared to his historical contemporaries lie embedded in fundamental frameworks or paradigms for appreciating Jesus as the Christ. These frameworks contain emphases that have to be protected and positions whose compromise would cause uncomfortable adjustments in the understanding of Jesus Christ and the role he plays in religious life. For example, some people may look on Jesus in such a way that his divinity was overtly displayed in miracles such as a direct command that stopped a storm (Mark 4:35-41). A historian's reconstruction of that story as fictional or embellished in order to make a theological point may disrupt a literalist construal of the scene.

A historical approach, however, may also protect faith in Jesus Christ from objections and problems that ultimately stem from incredible beliefs but are not essential to it. For example, an overly docetic language about Jesus implicitly depicts him as God disguised as a human being. This kind of talk was rejected early in the tradition. But some theological language, even though it is traditional, has become in various degrees dysfunctional or confusing because it respects neither the historical fact nor the doctrine that Jesus was a real human being. Moreover, in order to cut through to the central logic of Christology it seems important to have a conception of how Christology emerged in the first place. Like everything else in history, Christian faith and its accompanying Christology had a beginning in time, and a full understanding of it would include an appreciation of its genesis. An ability to understand the historical development of Christology, however, requires some kind of reconstruction of the figure of Jesus of Nazareth and some idea of the narrative of how he became lodged in the imagination of his disciples as the Christ.

A second reason makes the historical uniqueness of Jesus important to Christology, namely, the role of the imagination in all reference to Jesus Christ. Jesus of Nazareth lies behind all the predicates that Christian faith applies to Jesus Christ; he is the historical referent even when Christian faith speaks of and refers to Jesus as risen. On the supposition that all our knowledge has specific content that is mediated through our sensible contact with the world, there will always be some imaginative construal of the content referred to as Jesus Christ.[1] To the extent possible, therefore, that image should be chastened by some consideration of the way the historical figure Jesus appeared.

These complications lie behind the desire to say something about Jesus of Nazareth and his individuality and uniqueness. The project requires consultation of the work of New Testament scholars who try to get behind the embellishments of the Gospel stories about Jesus to the way the historical figure appeared to the people who witnessed his ministry. This does not quite mean seeing him as they did but reconstructing a type of figure that can be pieced together on the basis of evidence that more or less probably reflects the situation in which he appeared.

Two things help to determine an image of Jesus: the public role he assumed and the content of his message. What follows does not develop these categories at length, nor does it expand relatively common knowledge in this respect. The point is rather to illustrate a way of thinking in order to move toward understanding the uniqueness of Jesus on the historical level as a particular person.[2]

Jesus's Public Roles

A good place to begin is with the roles that Jesus assumed. What kind of a religious figure did Jesus appear to be? Most of the historical analysis of Jesus's ministry shows that he appeared as a prophet, a healer, and a teacher. Many scholars maintain that he was primarily one or the other, but all of them admit that Jesus in some respect fits into these three roles which overlap in his person.[3]

---

1. The epistemological framework from which this position is drawn is that of Aristotle mediated through Thomas Aquinas. See Thomas Aquinas, *Summa theologiae*, I, qq. 78-79.

2. I am sympathetic to the authors who address the question of method in approaching the historical person Jesus of Nazareth in the collection of essays edited by Beverly Roberts Gaventa and Richard B. Hays, *Seeking the Identity of Jesus: A Pilgrimage* (Grand Rapids: Eerdmans, 2008). I found the essays of William C. Placher, Dale C. Allison, Jr., and Francis Watson particularly insightful. I also agree for the most part with Terrence W. Tilley in his *The Disciples' Jesus: Christology as Reconciling Practice* (Maryknoll, NY: Orbis Books, 2008), who deals with the same issue. These authors show a limited sympathy for the project of the Jesus Seminar and that of John Meier and at the same time have much more to say about Jesus's identity than can be gained by history alone.

3. This material is drawn from an earlier work, *Jesus Symbol of God* (Maryknoll, NY: Orbis Books, 1999), 55-118. I was not as conscious then as I am now of the constructive potential of the category of "narrative." I attend to it more consciously today. I thus appreciate the motif that runs through the Gaventa and Hays collection to the effect

As a prophet Jesus announced the word of God; he spoke in the name of God, he offered God's blessing, and he warned of God's judgment. For some, Jesus met a general expectation of a final prophet in his day. However, one finds some rather significant variations among scholars on what exactly Jesus's prophetic message was: to whom was it addressed in particular, and what exactly was its content? But most are agreed that its center of gravity revolved around what Jesus called the kingdom or reign or rule of God. What exactly the "kingdom of God" refers to is not so easily defined in precise terms even though it can be seen below the surface of much if not all of his teaching and action. This is so because it refers to a rule of God that Jesus frequently indicates in his parables is different from the set of human values that is in place. The rule of God might be paraphrased formally as referring to the way the world would be if it were actualized according to God's will and values. Jesus announced that this kingdom of God was coming about through the power of God. It is not entirely clear whether Jesus meant that a new situation would come about relatively sooner or later, how it would be effected concretely, what things would look like after its arrival. But the sum of his teachings as represented in the Gospels presents God as concerned about history and attentive to people's lives.

Jesus was also a healer. New Testament scholarship is useful here in drawing present-day imagination away from a concept of miracle whose essence lies in breaking laws of nature by a power that practically demonstrates divine power in a quasi-empirical way. Jesus's world was as filled with real powers and principalities, angels and demons, as our own is with electronic signals. Jesus's wonderful healings were exercises of power, but it is not so easy to recreate in our imaginations the way the lines of agency ran in the minds of his audience. He seemed to be an exorcist and a worker of signs of God's power relative to religious faith. He was more of a faith healer than one who consciously defied the laws of nature. There were other such figures at the time of Jesus. As a healer Jesus attracted crowds, and he healed people who had faith in God, and the power of God's Spirit was recognized as being at work through him.

---

that Jesus is best revealed in the whole story portrayed in the Gospels and that "to come to grips with the identity of Jesus, we must know him as he is presented to us through the medium of narrative" (Gaventa and Hays, *Seeking the Identity of Jesus*, 20). Dale C. Allison, Jr. concurs: titles do not get the whole story, nor does a constellation of them (teacher, healer, wisdom figure, "Son of God" or *Kyrios*). The story is the thing (Allison, "The Embodiment of God's Will: Jesus in Matthew," in *Seeking the Identity of Jesus*, ed. Gaventa and Hays, 118-19).

Finally, Jesus was a teacher, an itinerant teacher of the wisdom of God, who attracted people where he taught and had a group of followers who accompanied him in his ministry. There were other such teachers in Jesus's time, but the distinctiveness of Jesus's teaching as far as we know from the Gospels lay in his various sayings and especially his parables.

This first approach to Jesus's uniqueness shows that he combined in his person several public personae or roles. People would have recognized him as a prophet, as a healer, one who cast out demons, and a teacher of religious wisdom.

Jesus's Message

A second route to Jesus's historical uniqueness derives from the first and consists in considering the content of his message. It was said that the prophetic message of the kingdom of God was at the center of all that he taught. But what are some of the specifics? And how did this relate to what was already being taught in Judaism?

The way to determine what Jesus communicated about God and about human beings in relation to God requires some analysis. One way of going about this might work from the premise that he taught in a variety of ways by his words and by his symbolic actions. He taught in parables, which were sometimes enigmatic, and almost always showed God's ways to be different from the ways we think. He taught in short sayings, in beatitudes or blessings, and in short formulas for prayer like the "Our Father." He also taught by his healings, his welcoming people, his concern for people's welfare. After considering his various teachings, one might then compare them with what was taught about God in Judaism and note whether there is distinctiveness or uniqueness by contrast. This describes what follows, beginning with a generalized summary of Jesus's teaching about God.

God is transcendent in Jesus's teaching. God is creator of heaven and earth, sovereign Lord, as he is most frequently represented in Jesus's centering metaphor of the rule of God. But God is also personal; Jesus related to God interpersonally; Jesus conversed with God. He prayed.

Jesus referred to God in what today would be called anthropomorphic terms. Although God was for Jesus creator of the universe, judging from his language Jesus related to God like a person. On the one hand, Jewish tradition recognized the transcendence and absolutely incomprehensible holiness of God, and at the same time Jesus's language about God portrays God in straightforward images as the father of a prodigal son or the direct source of power that could cure an illness or exorcize a demon. Jesus's anthropomorphic language, therefore, was not simplistic but a symbolic means of talking about a transcendent God.

God can be described as loving in Jesus's teaching; he taught consistently and in many different ways that God's being was a personal benevolence, an active overflowing love for the world. In parable, by healing, in his exorcisms, in his symbolic table fellowship with sinners, in his pointed aphorisms, and by his outgoing receptiveness Jesus communicated the love of God and God's concern for the world. This infinite loving embrace and its universal scope reaches out to each individual in Jesus's ministry. The awesome character of God becomes transformed into personal solicitude for particulars, for details, in the lives of individuals. "Why, even the hairs of your head are all numbered" (Luke 12:7).

God is therefore savior. This means God liberates or will liberate human beings from anything that imprisons them. This salvation was also extended in the spiritual sphere of sin and guilt: Jesus promised and extended God's forgiveness to sinners. On the level of social relationships he symbolically dramatized God's forgiveness by his own reaching out to the marginalized. Jesus the prophet also symbolized God's justice and righteous anger at situations and incidents of injustice that diminished human lives. Jesus stood for God's justice in history and promised it in God's future.

The God of Jesus supplies the grounds for moral disgust at what some human beings do to others, including oneself, and at the unjust situations people are all willing to tolerate. Jesus's prophetic outlook urges reaction against injustice and hope for a reign of God that is continually asserting itself into our world. But the absolute future is where one has to look for any kind of final reconciliation between God's justice and mercy. Jesus did not solve the mystery of why the innocent often suffer and the unjust often flourish. But he holds out the possibility of God's eternal sphere where full justice may be achieved. "Thy kingdom come. Thy will be done, on earth as it is in heaven" (Matt 6:10).

These broad lines represent the drift of Jesus's teachings. As schematically outlined they in no way approach the actuality of their historical delivery, which spontaneously would be filled in by the imagination of the hearer. The question of uniqueness involves a consideration of whether these teachings were novel relative to his Jewish forebears. Or is the distinctiveness of Jesus's teachings hardly remarkable and only due to the particular flavor he gave them in his representation? After analysis, many exegetes find that Jesus's teaching about God was not significantly different from what was taught before him as represented by the Jewish scriptures. Every big idea of Jesus about God can be found in one or other part of the Old Testament.[4] If this is the case, the uniqueness of Jesus's teaching consisted in the way he condensed this teaching in his own ministry and person, in the historical milieu that conditioned his delivery, the intensity of his commitment to this message, and how he was willing to die for it. But it was not so unique that it stood out over against the substance of the religious tradition of Israel. Another way of saying this is that there is no major difference between Judaism and Christianity within the teaching of Jesus. It is not necessary to exclude teachings of Judaism from a consideration of the essential character of Christianity as if the teachings of Jesus should be different from the teachings of Judaism. In sum, thus far, on the level of the historical uniqueness of Jesus, what appears is an individual uniqueness of personal identity that is in continuity with Judaism.

It should be apparent that the question of Jesus's uniqueness, especially as it has been delimited here, narrows down the broader question of Jesus's identity. The expansiveness of the many and far-ranging approaches to Jesus's identity in other historical treatments illustrates this. For example, the historical meaning and relevance of Jesus the individual historical figure cannot be confined within the limits of his own historical appearance, because of the way he actually continued to accrue meaning after his death, and this continues in our own time. This provides another dimension to the narrative character of the uniqueness of Jesus: its meaning changes with the history of interpretation.

There has been some insistence that the most adequate way of discovering the identity and in this sense the uniqueness of Jesus should pass through the narratives told of him as distinct from his teaching or the titles abstracted from this story. But there has not been enough "narrative criticism," that is, an explicit mining of the genre of narrative relative to Jesus, to generate the dynamic meanings it releases. Future work in Jesus research might include such critique and an interpretative method that correlates the narratives of Jesus's ministry

4. Gerhard Lohfink writes: "The proclamation of the reign of God coming now is the definitive historical realization of what has always been before Israel's eyes and what it sought to live in the Torah: for Israel there can be only this *one* God and he must become Lord of one's whole life, of every hour of the day of all spheres of life" (Gerhard Lohfink, *Jesus of Nazareth: Who Was He? What Did He Do?* [Collegeville, MN: Liturgical Press, 2012], 174). Relative to the Sermon on the Mount, often considered Jesus's distinctive teaching, Lohfink comments: "There is not a single statement there that does not have an Old Testament background" (187). But Jesus did not simply reproduce and repeat OT teaching, nor insert completely new content into it, but sifted it into his own voice for his own time and brought it forward with a new light (187-88).

with the stories of people today. Inspiration to do this can be found in the Spiritual Exercises of Ignatius Loyola.

This first dimension of Jesus's uniqueness has a direct bearing on Christian spirituality when it is conceived as a following of Jesus. Uniqueness in this first sense defines Jesus's personal identity as a human being. As an individual, Jesus is like all others unique. This uniqueness places him squarely within the stream of all human beings. This means that Jesus is able to be comprehended as other persons are; Jesus is approachable as a fellow human being; and, most importantly, Jesus is imitable. Jesus can be a model for the human. One can find in Jesus's ministry and teaching something that is genuinely human and able to be appropriated. Too often this is lost in a language that so emphasizes Jesus's divinity that it separates him from the human condition.

Uniqueness and the Status of Jesus among the Religions

We now pass to a second sense of the uniqueness of Jesus. This deeper religious sense of the word "uniqueness" emerges in the context of Jesus's relationship with other religious revealers of God or savior figures or more generally focal points of religious response to transcendent reality. Here the sense of "uniqueness" approaches or becomes synonymous with "absolute." Is Jesus the absolute mediator, way to God, or savior in comparison with whom all others are deficient or preliminary? Or is Jesus one savior among many? This is usually where the largest problem lies today. On the one hand, historical consciousness has mediated a growing appreciation and acceptance of other religions at various levels, an attitude that cannot imagine that they could have no value. In fact people in developed and pluralistic cultures are tempted to believe that God, precisely as they know God through Jesus, not only tolerates these other religions but, insofar as they do not directly contradict the message of Jesus, that they are valid and positive paths to union with God. Thus they lead to or bear within themselves ultimate salvation. But, on the other hand, this temptation seems to contradict the understanding many Christians have been brought up with, that Jesus is the one and only savior sent by God. As the New Testament says at one point, there is salvation in "no other name" (Acts 4:12).

This tension between received doctrine and our current sensibilities has received more attention in theology over the last two decades than any other problem; it is still one of the major theological issues being debated today. In some respects it provides a test case on the degree to which a person has recognized historicity and allowed its free flow and open-endedness to reorient one's imagination. It also represents an area where the general sensibility of churchgoers and the church's theologians may not be on the same page. In the broad arena of Christian theology, this issue remains a truly open question with opinion ranging across the board. The discussion that follows briefly points to two typologies of responses to this issue and then suggests a route for resolving the tension, not in order to close the issue, but to invite discussion of other ways of negotiating it.

Three Distinct Views of Jesus's Absolute Uniqueness

The following three theological views of the status of Jesus relative to other religions are written from the perspective of his role in human salvation. Theologians never hold such views in the simplified way in which they are typified. They are not usually so blunt and unqualified in their thinking. For this reason this description of three types of position could be misleading. The point here is simply to illustrate a wide spectrum of views that can be called right, left, and middle. Aristotle says that virtue consists in the mean between two extremes. But all three have their internal coherence. Some instantiations on either side may be close to the middle. The descriptions that follow do not supply any details on the supposition that, speaking generally, these positions are intuitively clear in their differences from one another.

The first broad view is called "exclusive" because it holds that there is no salvation for human beings outside of an explicit conscious faith in Jesus Christ. Traditionalist or conservative Christians frequently hold this view. Its main impasse is found in its implication that a good loving God could allow so many people to fail in reaching the goal for which they were created. The position itself seems to create an obstacle for believing in the God of Jesus. Is Jesus unique here? Yes, and absolutely so.

The second view is referred to as "religious pluralism." It holds that there is one final destiny for all human beings or all creation, and that there are many paths to this goal. These paths are not all "equal" in any obvious sense because they are all different and historically unique. But neither is one superior to another in principle. The phrase "in principle" is deliberately vague; it strives to suggest an unattainable neutral view as an a priori context, that is, prior to concrete comparative analysis. It suggests further that all religious mediations embody positive religious views and all have limitations. They should, moreover, enter into dialogue with one another to learn more about transcendent reality that no single way could possibly represent fully. While this seems reasonable in itself, it also cuts across the faith commitment of many of the religions themselves. Is Jesus unique here? In a historical sense, yes, but in the religious sense of being absolute, he is not. That is the point of pluralism.

The third or middle position, often called inclusivist, tries to hold on to advantages of each side and in doing so guard the Christian tradition. It grants that Jesus as a human figure is particular and individual, one among many. But Jesus is also the incarnation of the Word of God, the divine Son, or second person of the trinity, and there is no salvation outside this Word of God. Other religions can channel God's presence and grace to their members because this same Word of God that was incarnate in Jesus is implicitly or secretly or anonymously or latently at work in other religions. Thus there may be salvation outside of a knowledge of Jesus, but there is no salvation outside of the Word of God that was incarnate in him. This is the official position of the Catholic Church, and it may be the common view among the members of most of the mainline Protestant churches.

Four Distinct Views of the Relations between Religions

The handy and commonly referred to typology just described does not exhaust the field of typologies. In fact, one could design a typology of typologies, because each one may be set up around a distinct axis of interest. Paul Knitter has offered a more nuanced survey of the field around a focus of the status of Christianity relative to other religions and their ability to enter into dialogue with one another.[5] Each of his four types or models is illustrated by the positions of theologians who may be quite different among themselves. This typology thus combines the abstractness of types and the distinctiveness of specific theologians who more or less exemplify them. The following simple enumeration of these types illustrates how wide-ranging the positions have become.

The first of Knitter's models resembles the conservative exclusivist type mentioned earlier, but it is renamed in a more positive way as "the replacement model." This view is dominated by the conviction that there can only be one true religion and that in the end, dialogue notwithstanding, Jesus mediates that revelation.

The second model, moving from the right gradually toward the left, resembles the middle, inclusivist type, but is called the fulfillment model. This means that other religions find their own internal dynamisms fulfilled in the event of Jesus Christ. Dialogue is highly recommended in this view because of the conviction that the God operative

5. Paul F. Knitter, *Introducing Theologies of Religion* (Maryknoll, NY: Orbis Books, 2002).

in Jesus is secretly at work in other religions as well. Sometimes a trinitarian perspective and the role of God as Spirit are exploited to understand how Christians can affirm real revelation going on in other religions without undermining their own christocentrism.

Knitter's third bundle of views is called the mutuality model. Roughly it calls for many different and autonomous religions being true and yet is open enough to be called to enter into dialogue with other religions. Several bridges enable the mutual crossing over and communication between members of different religious bodies: a common human nature, an openness within this nature to transcendence, a recognition that incomprehensible mystery surrounds the transcendent order, and common concerns about human well-being, especially on a broad social and political level. This model does not quite correspond with any of the three in the first typology.

Knitter's fourth model is also quite distinct; he calls it the acceptance model. It is so thoroughly marked by a sense of differences among religious cultures, languages, and systems that it remains skeptical about any real communication between them. Finding little or no common ground among religions, it counsels a polite dialogue that does not expect any deep mutual learning or appropriation. The maxim that real differences make for real dialogue ironically employs a radical historical consciousness to relieve a firm Christian faith of any pressure it might feel from other seemingly viable religious faith traditions.

Each one of these understandings appears fairly clear in itself and in its distinction from the others. But all one has to do is ask some probing questions and the responses will begin to complicate matters. Still, while staying within the framework of these caricatures, every Christian theologian could state his or her position that is more or less coherent and yet find that inevitably it will be contested. What follows is one such effort.

A Solution to the Dilemma

The middle position on Jesus's uniqueness in the first typology (inclusive Christology) and the "Christ as fulfillment" of the second seem to be perfect: they preserve the absoluteness of Jesus and allow for a certain pluralism of religions. The problem, however, lies in the fact that they do so precisely on Christian premises that ensure the superiority and absoluteness of Christianity and the inferiority and dependence of other religions. All outside of Christianity are really saved by Jesus Christ who is the incarnation of the saving Word or Son of God. This is not something that other religions willingly accept. They do not imagine themselves dependent on a Christian economy of salvation but as independent and autonomous. Is there a solution to this problem that can bridge the parties and create a more level field for interreligious dialogue?

There are solutions to this problem, but none is proposed in a way that makes it acceptable to all: all resolutions remain contentious. But this in its turn should release some pressure and allow for critical discussion among churches, theologians, and ordinary Christians. On that premise, a way of approaching the issue from a Christian standpoint might be pursued on the basis of two principles. These are meant to foster mutual understanding among the religions while protecting the autonomy of all. The reasoning here does not speak for other religions, but these principles are offered in a way that might invite a positive response. The first point recommends a positive attitude toward pluralism, and the second looks for a statement about the closeness of ultimate reality to us that all religions might affirm.

The reason why this problem of Jesus's uniqueness has arisen lies in the fact that Western developed nations have become accustomed to pluralism, where pluralism means diversity within a common field or framework. For example, democratic societies are used to one government and nation holding together different parties and a host of different political and religious views. When it works, this pluralism is not something negative when compared with its opposite, uniformity through totalitarian government and social control. The Catholic Church, with its Vatican II decree on religious liberty, has begun to approach such a positive view of free religious expression. The next step for it to take would be to recognize that religious pluralism is the natural condition of the human race, not something to be conceded temporarily in the hopes of overcoming it. The step after that would be to realize that this is a good thing. From it flows the conviction that religions need not be in competition with one another, but together can reflect the one human spirit's quest for the sources of truth and goodness, and of human existence and its destiny. At some fundamental level, what is required here is something like a sense of mystery and transcendence that can be translated into a faith that is both really affirmative and really humble. The question is whether Christian faith can be appropriated both in a way that one's life depends on it and noncompetitively.

The first point requires a change in attitude from the absolutism that has traditionally revolved around Jesus the Christ. Such openness requires an all-embracing perspective on the formal level that will provide a unity to the whole religious sphere within which the differences among the religions may coexist and communicate with one another. This is not difficult to find within Christianity. Theologians like Friedrich Schleiermacher and Karl Rahner, when they discuss the philosophy of religion, find dimensions in the human subject as such that reflect a vague consciousness of reaching out toward and being impacted by a truly transcendent power and reality. And this philosophy of religion has its counterpart in the Christian doctrine of creation. Because the creator creates out of nothing and is always creating, making it the very ground of being, the creator is immediately present to each creature.

But the second point is noncompetitive humility. This begins by recognizing that the only way the creating ground of being can be named lies in this-worldly symbols and language.[6] For what Christians name as God, through mediators of the Old Testament and ultimately Jesus, other religions will have other names derived from other mediators. This field of a direct immediate presence of ultimate reality or truth to the human condition, a presence that requires a name or a mediation to be distinctly recognized, is a candidate for becoming a meeting place for discussion across religious boundaries. In other words, each religion recognizes the distinction between the conceptions of ultimate reality and the transcendent reality itself to which they point.

On the basis of these two principles, it appears that, if Jesus is a true mediator of God for our salvation, other religious mediators cannot contradict that fundamental truth. But there is more to be said. Jesus is not an exclusive revealer of God, because what Christians name God is immediately present to all human beings, as other religions testify. God is experienced in other mediators in ways that imply that other names of God are also true. God is absolute, but no religious mediation can be. Thus Jesus is not a comprehensive mediator of God, because a single finite and limited mediation cannot exhaustively reveal the fullness of God's reality. One set of names cannot wholly communicate the full mystery of ultimate reality. On the deeper level of the pluralism of religions, Jesus as a mediator of God is not unique in these senses even though he retains his historical uniqueness.

This view of Jesus's nonuniqueness as a mediator of ultimate reality has a bearing on Christian spirituality. It brings Christian faith-in-action in line with other secular convictions. It correlates with Christian belief that God is present to all people in a loving relationship that has to manifest itself in and through the actual cultural media in which they exist. It confirms the conviction that all people have a right

6. The requirement of a this-worldly medium for any positive conception of transcendence is well argued by John E. Smith, *Experience and God* (New York: Oxford University Press, 1968), 68-98.

to be free from all social coercion in their deepest relationships with ultimate reality. The reason for this right is the conviction that these relationships are real. It is difficult to see how any reserve about the possible validity of other religions in principle would not also foster various kinds of feelings of superiority that so easily lead to discrimination. Positively, however, this view of Jesus's nonuniqueness as a religious mediator, that is, his being one among others, strengthens faith in the God of Jesus as being in contact with all humanity.

Uniqueness and the Divinity of Jesus

This resolution to the question of Jesus's uniqueness will not be accepted by many Christians because they will infer from it a compromise of the divinity of Jesus. The divinity of Jesus is a hidden player in this discussion. In the eyes of many, it is really the divinity of Jesus that accounts for Jesus's uniqueness, so that for them the term "uniqueness" is really synonymous with Jesus's divinity. Is there a way to think about Jesus's divinity and at the same time abandon Jesus's religious absoluteness? For many this is impossible. They reason that, if one promotes the religious comparability of Jesus and other religious saviors or mediators of God's presence to humanity, one has by definition abandoned Jesus's divinity by lowering him to the level of other religions. But another way of construing such comparability, still from a Christian perspective, remains possible. Instead of thinking that one is lowering Jesus to some common level, one may think that comparability raises other religious mediators up to Jesus's level in principle. There is no demotion here, but only promotion of the quality and character of other religions on the basis of the direct presence of God the creator of heaven and earth to all creatures and human beings. The presence of God is complemented by the mediation that makes it operative in human consciousness. This way of thinking is encouraged by the two principles just mentioned: God's presence to all religions and the need of a name to identify that presence. But much more would have to be said theologically to justify such a revised Christian perspective on the many religions.

Although it is hardly possible to make such a case in a paragraph or two, one can at least imagine a direction in which such an account might travel. It would begin by describing how Jesus came to be named divine. This conviction had its origins in the experience that God had acted in Jesus of Nazareth for the salvation of those who encountered him, his disciples. Gradually it came to be seen that what was true for the disciples was true for all people. Thus fairly early in the Jesus movement, after the Easter experience of Jesus's being alive within the sphere of God, preaching in his name reached out beyond the circle of Jews to Gentiles. But if God acted in Jesus for human salvation, the reasoning went, then Jesus must have acted with and by the power of God, because only God can save.[7] But how does one express such an idea? There were various ways in which God was said to be active in the world in the Old Testament. God influenced the world by God's word; God's speaking was the command of God's will. God structured and ordered the world by God's wisdom. God's glory shone forth in various aspects of the world. The spirit of God, God's invisible power, was a life force in the world. All of these expressions gave the first Christians a language to say that God was at work in Jesus. This experience and language provided the basis to begin speaking of Jesus's divinity. This language developed by reflection and debate, so that Christians finally came to affirm the divinity of Jesus broadly and unambiguously in the fourth century. The reasoning consistently followed the basic logic that God was at work in Jesus because we encountered God's salvation in him; God being at work in Jesus as Word or as Spirit "explains" or at least names his divinity.

But this raises another question: can the Christian see an analogous process going on in Torah relative to Judaism, or in the Qur'an in Islam, or in Gautama in Buddhism, or in the scriptures of many forms of Hinduism? Perhaps more pressingly, what would be necessary conditions for a Christian theologian to move toward such a judgment if he or she were moving from a more traditional position? Two premises seem to be crucial. The first is that one must entertain the possibility of thinking within the framework of a theocentric worldview as distinct from the epistemological christomorphism of one's actual faith.[8] Practically speaking, this entails openness to a view that considers a philosophy of religion, or within the Christian sphere a reflection on creation theology, that is in some sense prior to christological reflection. Second, one has to be convinced that such a framework can be pursued and religious pluralism can be affirmed without subtracting from Jesus Christ's divinity. What is sacrificed in this understanding is not the incarnation but its happening only once or its being restricted to the single event of Jesus Christ. Can one find a sense in which this way of thinking does not subtract from but enhances the plausibility of Christian language about Jesus's divinity? This question opens up a perspective in which what Jesus reveals of God and God's love of and presence to all people in turn encourages one to think that God is

7. I take it that this logic pervades patristic debates over the nature and character of the mediator, Jesus Christ. The reasoning still has persuasive power today.

8. "Christomorphism," having the form of Jesus Christ, defines Christian faith structurally as being faith in God as mediated (given form) by Jesus of Nazareth.

operative in other religions in a way analogous to how God is operative in Jesus and Christianity.

These two conditions are less logical premises and more indicators of a fundamental conviction that God should be conceived as savior in a way that is equally available to all. When this conviction is in place, one can begin to construe the traditional concepts and language of faith in a new way. Christians can coherently integrate their commitment to God as mediated by Jesus, their conception of what God has done in Jesus Christ, and, at the same time, their conviction that God acts analogously within the dynamics of other religions.

Spirituality has a final word in this third dimension of the uniqueness of Jesus, his divinity. Spirituality refers to the way a person's or a group's concrete behavior in the world unites or separates them from God. In Christianity, this requires a reading of the ways of God, first of all, in the patterns of life displayed in Jesus of Nazareth. And, secondly, one relates to God in the interactions with people and the world of one's actual situation. In both cases this involves dialectical perception or understanding: people encounter God and relate to God in their interchanges with the material and finite world. This world does not display divinity or make it available overtly. Rather divinity has to be conceived as absolutely transcendent and simultaneously radically immanent to all finite reality. This conviction says that divine presence is not rare but the very condition of all existence. This principle allows the Christian to be spiritual in the small world of the church, and also to recognize true God operating with the abandon of love in other religions and in the secular world itself. This vision, which provides the basis of a spirituality of encountering God in daily life, also allows one to see divinity, divine presence and revelation, in other religions.

There is much more that has to be said on this last dimension of the uniqueness of Jesus that is also quite contentious. It requires responses to many questions relative to the tradition and formulations of exactly what needs to be protected in it. It requires special attention to the meaning that is conveyed by the term "divinity" when it is applied to Jesus. But these cannot be developed here. The goal here has been simply to open up lines of thinking and conversing about these basic issues.

* * *

Relative to the questions revolving around the "uniqueness" of Jesus, this discussion has at least established that this little word is laden with different meanings and that all of them are contentious. First, on the level of his historical identity, Jesus of Nazareth was a unique individual the way all of us are, and this gives Christianity a historical uniqueness. Christianity has its own identity that goes back to Jesus. But on the second level of religious uniqueness it is spiritually coherent and fulfilling to accept Jesus as God's true revelation while at the same time recognizing that God works independently of Jesus in other religions for people's salvation. Therefore Jesus is not necessarily unique in the sense of being absolute while other religious figures are inferior or dependent on Jesus. If this is not the majority position among Christians at present, more and more Christians are embracing something like it. Third, this view need not undermine the divinity of Jesus, which is often the hidden meaning of the idea of uniqueness. To think so presupposes a competitive and perhaps even an adversarial relationship among religions. For Christians, a broad humanistic philosophy of religions and the doctrine of creation open a perspective in which the strict divinity of Jesus may be paralleled with the divinity, or the transcendent ultimacy, of other religious mediators.

CHAPTER FOUR

The Spirituality of the Cross

The cross has always been a problem, for insiders and outsiders. The apostle Paul wrote to the Corinthians: "Jews demand signs and Greeks seek wisdom, but we preach Christ crucified, a stumbling block to Jews and folly to Gentiles" (1 Cor 1:22-23). Then he added, "but to those who are called, both Jews and Greeks, Christ [is] the power of God and the wisdom of God" (1 Cor 1:24). The goal of this chapter is to find power and wisdom in the crucifixion of Jesus. But this is no easy task. Much of the traditional language about the cross no longer seems plausible. Even the language of worship and formal liturgy raises serious questions.

Part of the problem comes from taking literally the surface meaning of much of Christian speech: Jesus had to suffer; it was fitting for Jesus to suffer; God sent Jesus his only Son to suffer and die; since we are saved by this suffering, it must have been something good; Jesus is a sacrifice that the Father God found pleasing; Jesus suffered for us by taking on in himself the suffering that was a just punishment for our sin; Jesus was a scapegoat, loaded with our sin and then destroyed in our place. In all of this, suffering appears as a way of perfection, so that asceticism represents the noble Christian life; as a follower of Christ it is good to suffer; self-sacrifice is a Christian ideal, and a penitential life is virtuous. These ideas find backing in much of Christian theology. They recur in the language of Christian sermons and spirituality.

But these phrases are beginning to stick in our throats; they do not sound right; they are becoming an embarrassment. We cannot comprehend how Jesus could literally be God's son; and we cannot imagine God sending Jesus to the kind of death he endured or being pleased with it. It would be worrisome if this language subtly took suffering, which is evil when it is imposed upon someone, and turned it into a good. That would not only make suffering tolerable and useful but give it as well a positive value.

What do we do when Christian language loses its plausibility, especially in this central case, for everyone seems to presume that the cross is at the center of Christian faith? Does this collapse of the credibility of this language at the heart of our faith endanger Christian faith itself? It will if we cannot find a way of understanding the meaning of the cross in a new, positive way. This is what this chapter sets out to do.

The approach to the issue that follows has four parts. The first calls attention to different ways of interpreting the death of Jesus. This initial reflection yields two ways of appropriating the meaning of the cross: one is historical and the other is spiritual. The second part of the discussion deals with the historical reasons or causes of Jesus's death, and the third sifts through some spiritual understandings of the cross. Finally, the fourth part offers an interpretation of the cross for spirituality in our time. The idea throughout is to find in the cross God's power and wisdom.

How Does One Address the Question of the Cross?

We need a preliminary discussion of a proper way to enter into a discussion of the cross. Explaining how one goes about formulating a question about the cross and deciding how one will go about responding to it in some measure influences what the answer will be. What is the proper question about the cross and how does one gain leverage to decide the role of the cross in Christian faith? The method employed here can be called a narrative historical-spiritual approach, and it requires a brief description.

To begin negatively, one cannot simply take the New Testament and read the answer to a probing question in various verses or passages among the many writings. At other times and among some churches today, citing the Bible provides answers to delicate questions and problems. But educated Christians have become aware of how the scriptures came to be written, how deeply they are tied to a culture distant and different from our own, and how rarely they address directly the questions we entertain in our time. One usually cannot take the overt meaning of scripture for granted, as if it were written in a present-day idiom. Readers have to adjust to the cultural terms of a past time and attend to the historical circumstances in which a text came to be written. It remains true that the New Testament was inspired. But that inspiration itself occurred in the complex historical way in which the texts were composed, edited, and assembled by a community, and it occurs in the readers of the Bible. Thus a brief outline of how the New Testament was composed provides a key for explaining the road toward understanding the cross that is traveled here.

The simple fact that the New Testament went through stages in the process of its development tells us much about how we should interpret individual parts of it. It is not necessary to describe these stages in technical language in order to show the relevance of the developmental process. One could, for example, consider that development as moving through five stages. The first would be the historical events of Jesus's public ministry that led to his execution. A second stage may be identified with the Easter experience. This refers to the time and manner in which the disciples became aware, because it was revealed to them, that God had raised Jesus from death. This changed everything for them; it turned a state of desolation and confusion into a condition of joy, enthusiasm, and mission. This led to a third stage of the gradual formation and development of Jesus movements. Although Luke in Acts speaks about the movement that began in Jerusalem, some appearance stories are set in Galilee. One has to imagine that other Jesus movements began in Galilee, where Jesus performed most of his ministry. These movements preached Jesus as the prophet messiah who had been ratified by God's raising him from death.

A fourth stage of this development that overlapped with the Jesus movements consisted of reflection on the Jesus event. This involved telling the stories about Jesus and discussing them in the communities that made up the movement. It included writing these stories down and sharing considerations of them expressed in hymns, letters, and other writings. Collecting the stories about Jesus, writing and editing Gospels, and compiling other writings into a package could be considered a fifth stage of this development. The composition of the Gospels was a complex process that is still not clearly understood in a way that all accept. The larger process of gathering the contents of the New Testament was not controlled, and it continued into the second and even the third century. It took a good deal of time beyond the first century for the followers of Jesus finally to decide which writings among many should be included in what became the church's foundational document.

Once one considers this history of the development of the writings of the New Testament, looks at the different characteristics of the many genres that make it up, and then scans the distinct contents of each book, one can see quite plainly that the New Testament contains many different interpretations and appropriations of the events that made up Jesus's ministry. Different authors representing different communities facing different issues interpret the words and deeds of Jesus somewhat differently relative to their own situation. These differences establish something that is absolutely basic: there is a distinction between what actually happened during Jesus's ministry and the way it is portrayed, explained, and interpreted in the writings that were written later. The result is that the New Testament rarely contains a single specific response to any question addressed to it. The

New Testament witness involves a variety of perspectives and several answers to most questions. The many New Testament conceptions of basic issues in Christian faith may be significantly different from each other. The New Testament is pluralistic.

The pluralism of the New Testament beginning with the Gospels has a great deal of relevance for the answer to the question of why Jesus was crucified and the meaning of the cross. It means that no single answer trumps the others. But, more importantly, one also finds two distinct approaches and kinds of answer to the question of the meaning of the cross: the one is historical and the other is spiritual. The historical question asks about what led up to Jesus being crucified. What did Jesus do to provoke it? Who was responsible for it? What were the motives for this chain of events? What exactly happened? These historical questions are quite different from the questions that interpret the cross in a spiritual way. They ask: what is the meaning of Jesus's crucifixion? What does it reveal about Jesus and about God? How or where are we to locate the cross of Jesus in our religious imagination and reactions? What bearing does it have on my life?

The next part of this chapter turns to the historical question, and the third explores the spiritual question and answer. Then, in the light of an imaginative construction of what happened in Jesus's ministry, I offer a spiritual interpretation of the cross that has bearing on life in the developed world of the twenty-first century.

Historically, Who and What Caused Jesus's Crucifixion?

The first question is historical: what caused Jesus's crucifixion? Who was responsible for Jesus's execution and on exactly what grounds? Was it the Romans or was it Jewish leaders? Because the texts of the New Testament, especially the Gospels, were written well after these events, and because they are so laden with theological interpretation, we do not have very exact historical knowledge of the events leading up to Jesus's execution. But each of the following three aspects of the historical question deserves some commentary: what can be said with some assurance about Jesus's death? Second, where can interpretations go wrong? Third, what can be said constructively on the historical level?

As to the first issue, we can say with some positive assurance that Jesus was killed because of his ministry. Jesus obviously alienated certain groups among his people, whether in Galilee or Jerusalem, but especially in Jerusalem. Some commentators believe that Jesus's so-called cleansing of the temple must have angered the leaders of the temple cult. Given the temple's place in Jewish life, this could have been the reason for Jewish religious leaders to want him removed. Many Gospel stories point to conflicts between Jesus's teaching and various groups within Jewish religious culture. Some scholars emphasize the nervousness of the Roman occupying government at any sign of religious uprising, especially at a time of religious commemoration when many pilgrims were gathered in Jerusalem. The more Jesus had a following not loyal to Caesar, the more they had reason to want him out of the picture. But in the end we do not have enough historical knowledge to be able to reconstruct these events in any detail or to measure the relative balance between these two protagonists. But it seems clear that elements from both sides were involved.

Second, it is important to notice how trying to answer this question can go wrong. Sometimes people take a theological interpretation of Jesus's death and turn it into a historical reason for his death. For example, some hold that the reason why Jesus died is that, from the beginning, he was meant to be a bloody sacrifice atoning for human sin. This turns Jesus's historical ministry into a divine drama: the script was written in heaven, and Jesus was acting it out. Or Jesus was the Son of God, the first Christian, and the Jews knowingly rejected him and killed him. This ideological reason is used to justify anti-Semitism and is utterly ignorant and confused. A moment's analysis reveals what is happening here: later theological interpretation becomes solidified and gradually gets turned into historical data or facts. This does not fit the free, contingent, and random character of historical events. Jesus's crucifixion was not a historical necessity; it happened because of what Jesus preached. His ministry confronted the interests of some who took offense and freely reacted against him. With the exception perhaps of Judas's betrayal, we do not even know whether or not those who led Jesus to his death were acting in good faith but with severely limited awareness. In the end, it is hard to see how the answers to these kinds of questions about the details of how Jesus died are ultimately relevant.

Third, then, what can be said positively about Jesus's death historically that is relevant for later and deeper spiritual interpretation? It seems to be all-important to understand that Jesus was executed because of what he preached and how he acted in a manner consistent with his message of the rule of God. One can find a certain continuity between the way he lived, referring to his public ministry, and the way he died. This correlation can be perceived at different levels of interpretation. The values that Jesus espoused, which were God's values as articulated in his parables, healings, and symbolic actions, countered entrenched values and interests among his listeners, drew them into conflict, and occasioned their action against him. These values contradict selfish human values, and they frequently lead to conflict. The consistency between Jesus's ministry and the reaction it caused among some helps to explain what was going on in Jesus's execution.

Notice too the consistency that connects Jesus's representation of the values of the rule of God and his sense of mission, of being sent to communicate God's values to Israel. Jesus remained faithful to that commitment to the end. Everything we know of Jesus points in this direction. Jesus's end was a death that was inflicted on him and not something he sought. Any language that even suggests that Jesus was seeking to die is interpretation that distorts the evidence. But at the same time, one has to imagine that Jesus appropriated his death into a larger commitment to mediating God's values and remaining faithful to them even in the face of death. Only in this sense can we talk of Jesus voluntarily accepting his death as a by-product of his fidelity to God's cause. One can find no saving value in Jesus's death as a passive being killed, but only in his positive and free witness to the values of the reign of God.

Understanding the Crucifixion Spiritually

We can now address the question of how we might understand the cross of Jesus spiritually. Spirituality refers to how people live their lives in the face of transcendence. A spiritual interpretation thus finds within the empirical historical events a meaning that bears on persons' way of living in relation to what they believe is transcendent and ultimate. The idea of spiritual interpretation refers to how we connect Jesus's suffering and death with God, God's intentions for human existence, and God's liberation of freedom that comes to human beings through Jesus. How is God involved in the cross of Jesus? What is the place of the cross in the way we understand God and our liberation through Jesus? The question of the necessity of the cross looms large in some theological approaches to Jesus's death by a gruesome execution. Was God behind the cross of Jesus?

The first part of this chapter explained why there are many different interpretations of Jesus's death, not only in present-day theology but also in the New Testament. Some of them make more sense than others to the cultures of our time. The interpretation offered here is not the only one that is possible but is one that strives for plausibility. Such a positive construal will make more sense against the background of various interpretations from Christian tradition.

No one single theology of the cross has ever exclusively dominated Christian faith. The view that perhaps has come closest to universal acceptance in Western Christianity is the theory of Anselm of

Canterbury from the eleventh and twelfth centuries. His view is based on the conviction that original sin and the history of sin it unleashed so disturbed the relationship between humanity and God that eternal justice required satisfaction. A human being had to repair the breach, but because the offense against God was infinite, only God could accomplish it. Hence Jesus Christ, God made man: his offering himself as a sacrifice was both an act of a human to pay a human debt, and a divine act that rendered satisfaction proportionate to an infinite injury. Jesus's death satisfied cosmic justice. This "satisfaction theory" has had a hold on the imagination of the Western church right up to the present time.[1] But the New Testament contains a plurality of views of how Jesus is savior. They are not reducible to one. While many gravitate around the cross and hence explain it as a vehicle of human redemption, others do not make Jesus's suffering central.

As a framework for thinking about the cross it is also good to recall that the many views of how Jesus saved that are present in the New Testament also developed over a period of time. The Easter experience that Jesus is risen occurred some time after Jesus's execution. This experience helped to overcome the deep embarrassment and confusion of Jesus's disciples at the event of his cross and death. They did not expect a suffering messiah; the idea of messiah did not signify one who would suffer but one who, more like David, would lead Israel to renewed stature, prominence, and faithful well-being. A suffering messiah did not make immediate sense. But at the same time, if Jesus was indeed God's messiah ushering in a new age, as they experienced in the new awareness that Jesus is risen, then they had to factor the cross into the theological understanding of how Jesus saved. Interpretations of how Jesus saved had to include the fact that he was executed as a criminal.

The way the early Jesus movement and then the earliest communities of Christians interpreted Jesus as savior and the cross as part of that role was by searching the Jewish scriptures, the Old Testament, for types or models to help them understand what happened in Jesus's case. In other words, they looked for clues in God's dealing with Israel that would give them examples or prophetic foreshadowings of what had occurred in the death of Jesus. This process transpired

1. Anselm presented his theory in *Why God Became Man*. See *A Scholastic Miscellany: Anselm to Ockham*, ed. and trans. Eugene R. Fairweather (New York: Macmillan, 1970), 100-183. It is important to recognize its theoretical status: it "explains" the historical events of Jesus's execution by constructing a divine or heavenly story of God, the ground of justice, needing "satisfaction" and therefore sending his divine Son on this earthly mission. This theory communicates its theological insight by means of an anthropomorphic mythological story that should not be read as a literal scenario.

over a period of decades. It generated a large variety of metaphors and analogies for understanding how God was at work in Jesus's suffering and death for our salvation. The evangelist Luke refers to this process of reflection in his Gospel and his Acts of the Apostles. In the story of the encounter of the risen Christ with the disciples on the way to Emmaus, Luke has Jesus say to them: "'O foolish men, and slow of heart to believe all that the prophets have spoken! Was it not necessary that the Christ should suffer these things and enter into his glory?' And beginning with Moses and all the prophets, he interpreted to them in all the scriptures the things concerning himself" (Luke 4:25-27). These words, appropriated from his sources or composed by Luke fifty years after Jesus's death and resurrection, reflect the process of how the community began to interpret the meaning of the cross using the Old Testament. Luke has Jesus say that the cross was "necessary." In its context that means that it can be seen to have a rationale when interpreted in the light of such passages as those in Isaiah describing a suffering servant of God.

The Acts of the Apostles displays the same process actually going on. For example, the speeches that Luke places in Peter's mouth some time after the Jesus movement was underway (Acts 2:14-35; 3:11-26; 4:8-12) are theological interpretations, based on Old Testament texts, expressing how God was at work in Jesus's ministry and death.

The images and models for integrating Jesus's crucifixion into an understanding of how he brings God's salvation are many and varied. Jesus is understood as the suffering servant described in Second Isaiah; Jesus was a sin offering or a sacrifice whose suffering was offered for our sins; Jesus's death functioned as a redeeming ransom for our sins. Ideas such as these derive from complicated, culturally determined conceptions in Jewish tradition prior to Jesus; they provided a language by which the early Christian movement could make some sense out of Jesus's death by a Roman execution on a cross. Once one grasps or understands what is going on in this process of interpretation, it follows that one cannot take these ideas as objective descriptions of what happened. Misunderstanding these metaphors as objective descriptions of an actual transaction between God and Jesus, or between God and the human race through Jesus, turns them into something negative: God is depicted as cruel, as one who is pleased with human sacrifice, or at least as a manipulator of human events. Rather these interpretations represent the human spirit using figurative and symbolic language in search of understanding; they make profound sense when they are seen as the effort of those employing them to understand how God could have been at work in the cross of Jesus. That question had to be addressed by the New Testament writers in first-century Jewish terms, and it has to be taken up anew in each age and culture, because the answer must make some sense precisely within the interpreter's culture.

Making Sense of the Cross Today

This final part turns to a view of how Jesus's death by crucifixion might be construed as meaningful for spirituality today. The inspiration for this interpretation comes from the way the disciples of Jesus reflected on the Old Testament to find a language that described or expressed their experience of salvation from God. But in this case the New Testament rather than the Old Testament provides the source. The interpretation is presented gradually through a description of how Jesus might be experienced as liberator. This is not an objective argument that can be judged as right or wrong, but only a more or less successful characterization of how spiritual experience today might be judged faithful to New Testament and traditional language. Thus the interpretation poses the question whether or not this can represent people's experience of faith today.

Jesus Reveals the God of Absolute Mystery

A base line for beginning consists of taking stock of the awesome mystery of God. Karl Rahner, the great twentieth-century Catholic theologian, spoke most authentically when he described God as absolute and incomprehensible mystery. All sorts of nuances can be drawn out of this deep abiding impression, from a reflection on the absence of God to a description of a feeling of God's overwhelming presence. In all of this, however, even in our deepest encounter with God, God remains an elusive unfathomable mystery, a God of power and might that is gentle and personal forgiving love, distant and near, and yet always infinitely ungraspable. We do not really know the thoughts or ways of God, except through the analogies and symbols that God infinitely transcends.

But despite our ignorance Christians find God at work in Jesus of Nazareth. This statement provides the short but accurate definition of what a Christian is: one who finds God and God's salvation in Jesus. The question of salvation has bearing, first of all, on human existence. It refers to being made whole and bearing an identity within being itself. As a question it lies imbedded in the mystery that encompasses human life itself: is it meaningful? Does it have ultimate value and purpose, or is it, like everything else, common and expendable? Does human life have a destiny beyond its appearing and vanishing? Is there a way of grounding the value of each new beginning of human life, each new person? Is our own life worth any more than our actual achievements now, as fleeting as they are? These are secular questions, the human questions that the rhythm of time imposes on each one.

These questions about existence are meaningful because they point to the many bonds that actually construct human freedom on a personal and social level. Not least among them are moral failure and death. They all entail a bondage of freedom to self-interest from which human beings cannot escape. If they have an answer it will possess a sacred dimension because it must transcend what we actually see and do. In the end, then, Jesus takes his place in the Christian imagination because he responds to these secular questions of constriction and liberation. He provides a response to the religious question with a power we do not possess. Christians encounter in Jesus God working on our behalf. In Jesus the Christian finds liberation offered by the mysterious and transcendent God that he called Father.

Putting these two reflections together, that is, God's mystery and Jesus's representation of God, provides a way of understanding what is going on in the Christian act of faith. A way of describing the logic of faith goes like this: although we do not know what God is like, because God remains pure mystery, still we allow Jesus to define for us what God is like. "Who" or "what" is God, the Christian is asked? The Christian responds: I do not really know, but in faith I allow Jesus to tell me, to reveal, what God is like. The direction of this response does not follow a line in which we know what God is and we find the God whom we already know in Jesus. Rather the logic runs like this: God is absolute mystery, but in Jesus we experience an opening of the imagination to what God is like. Jesus reveals God to us. Christian faith is allowing Jesus to be the parable of God communicating God's self and God's will or rule to us as a human race.

Jesus Recapitulates Human Existence before God

But, moving forward in this reflection, if Jesus reveals God to us, then Jesus also reveals the meaning of human existence before or in the face of God. If Jesus was one through whom the power of God shone forth, then at the same time he stands as a revealer of the way in which human existence should in its turn relate to God. Jesus is not only representative of God to human beings, he is also our representative; he models authentic human existence subsisting in an intimate relationship with God. Jesus is the revealer of spirituality in the Christian view of things. This view plays itself out in the spirituality of an "imitation of Christ" or a following of Jesus. From the beginning, taking Jesus as an inspiration for how to live has been a constitutive element of Christian faith.

If Jesus is drawn into Christian faith as the revealer or representative of God and of human existence, so that he reveals God and reveals what it means to be human before God, then one can say with the patristic theologian Irenaeus that Jesus recapitulates the dialogue between God and human beings. To "recapitulate" roughly means to sum up or to summarize a whole in its principal points. Recapitulation succinctly expresses the logic of a whole argument or drama. Saint Paul inspired this concept of Irenaeus with his idea that Jesus was the second Adam. In Romans and in Corinthians Paul says that Jesus saves by doing successfully what Adam failed to do. "As one man's trespass led to condemnation for all, so one man's act of righteousness leads to acquittal and life for all. For as by one man's disobedience many were made sinners, so by one man's obedience many will be made righteous" (Rom 5:18-19). In other words, Jesus successfully completed the course of human life and thus becomes the new head and model for the human race.[2] If the salvation that Jesus won for us essentially consists in revealing a God who is absolute mystery, then this Pauline view of salvation means that Jesus is an authentic revelation and summing up of who God is and what it means to be human before God.

Jesus Reveals Resurrection in the Face of Human Suffering

There is one more factor needed to situate the role of the cross in this spiritual interpretation of how Jesus saves, and, once again, it can be made by an appeal to Irenaeus. Interestingly, Irenaeus thought that Jesus was relatively old when he was crucified. The reason for this is that Irenaeus had a developmental conception of human life: it begins in an infancy of ignorance and dependence and gradually, through learning and formation, grows to adulthood, achievement, and finally old age and death. If Jesus recapitulated the whole drama of human existence, he had to have lived life into the stage of relatively old age. Only what was fully represented would be fully revealed and saved. Most scholars of the New Testament think that Jesus was relatively young when he was crucified, certainly by our standards today. An informed opinion is that Jesus died at the age of 36.[3] So by our stan-

2. Irenaeus, *Against Heresies*, in *The Ante-Nicene Fathers: The Writings of the Fathers down to A.D. 325*, vol. 1, ed. A. Roberts and J. Donaldson (Grand Rapids: Eerdmans, 1953), 3.16.6, p. 443. For a commentary on Irenaeus's Christology, see Haight, *Jesus Symbol of God*, 215-19.

3. Raymond Brown, *The Death of the Messiah: From Gethsemane to the Grave. A Commentary on the Passion Narratives in the Four Gospels*, 2 vols., Anchor Bible Reference Library (New York: Doubleday, 1994), 1376.

dards, Irenaeus was wrong on that fact. But the same logic as used by Irenaeus can be applied to a different aspect of Jesus's representation and recapitulation. Jesus did not die in old age of natural causes; he died a cruel death as an innocent victim of injustice. But suffering is the fate of all human beings to one degree or another, and innocent and dehumanizing suffering actually is the lot of most human beings. Therefore, whether or not he chose it, the course of Jesus's ministry in the end reflects in an extreme form something fundamental in human existence as a whole, namely, innocent human suffering. And, as Paul suggests in his letter to the Philippians, it is because Jesus was faithfully obedient to God's cause even through a death on the cross that he was exalted in resurrection (Phil 2:8-9). It was in that faithful action that Jesus reveals what an authentic commitment of human freedom looks like. Jesus revealed it by dramatizing a faithful spirituality. And his resurrection by God confirmed both the character of God and God's validation of Jesus's commitment to God's rule.

Human existence as we know it shows some dark sides. All human life includes negativity: it is prone to sickness, a victim of outbursts of violence that we both perpetrate and suffer, and programmed for final diminishment and death. These passivities and negativities are essential constituents of human existence in actual fact; we know of no other actual life. The cross says that through Jesus we can read God being a part of and embracing that reality. God's power and might as creator also encompass the negativities of existence; they are not outside God's presence or concern. Moreover, finally, the saving power of God for human flourishing will have the last word in this drama of human existence. The resurrection, which cannot be dissociated from Jesus's cross, is not only the actual destiny of Jesus, but also the promise of God to all human existence. The cross represents the reality of human existence that cries out for liberation, and resurrection is its answer.

To sum up: a spiritual understanding of the cross of Jesus has to be a part of a larger conception of salvation by God and Jesus's role in it. Salvation has been manifested to Christians by God through Jesus, and the cross has to be located within that economy of salvation. The conception of salvation offered here is inspired by Paul's view of Jesus as the second Adam and the new creation. It borrows too from the letter to the Hebrews the idea that, as the second Adam, Jesus is the pioneer who goes before us and shows us the way by giving us a schematic map of the dialogue between God and human existence. The Christian looks "to Jesus the pioneer and perfecter of our faith, who for the joy that was set before him endured the cross . . . and is seated at the right hand of the throne of God" (Heb 12:2). To be human involves negativity, sometimes in the form of a suffering that defies any suggestion of coherent meaning. Jesus saves by representing God's concern as Jesus enters into that negativity and takes it on. His suffering is not detached from his ministry but precisely the consequence of it. Thus Jesus reveals God and human response to God in two ways. Human beings are not meant to wait for human suffering to end but, as Jesus did, to engage it, resist it, and struggle to overcome it. God as Spirit is the empowering agent in that effort. But in the end, despite accomplishments in this endeavor, when suffering and death overcome us, God's embrace includes that death and raises it into life. That life in God bends back and gives meaning to the spirituality that leads there. God's love and justice represent the character of this all-embracing absolute mystery. But it can only be appreciated in the negativity of the cross that all human beings must undergo. The cross, then, is the actual necessary condition of all human existence, and in that measure surrounds the figure of Jesus Christ as the new Adam, the representative, recapitulation, and pioneer of human existence. In the end, confidence in resurrection makes the cross meaningful by negating its ultimacy. In the end, only God and the resurrected life that God promises are ultimate.

CHAPTER FIVE

Spirituality and Church

The church in the United States is downsizing. This phenomenon affects all the mainstream churches and is beginning to be felt among evangelicals. We are experiencing a major shift in how people understand their spirituality, their faith, and their relationship with the institutional church. A large percentage of Christians understand that religions are voluntary associations. There is little social pressure to be religious. More and more have come to an awareness that they do not have to belong to a church to remain believers who are spiritual. Coming to this consciousness can affect people deeply, especially those who were brought up thinking that their salvation depended on church membership and practice.

This chapter does not probe all of the ramifications of this new situation; that would be a major challenge and would extend well beyond spirituality into psychology and sociology. This chapter has the more limited goal of clarifying the relationship between spirituality and church membership. This will not settle any of the many tensions and strains entailed in belonging to the church today. But it will provide a way of looking at the relationship between spirituality and religion positively, a way that clarifies that relationship, and in so doing provides a framework within which other problems may be discussed consistently and intelligently.

This chapter has a simple four-part structure. First, it describes the conception of spirituality that forms the basis of the discussion. This may be repetitious at this point in the book, but it will not hurt because so much is determined by the way spirituality is construed. Second, an understanding of spirituality in a broad way as human behavior in relation to transcendent value enables one to understand why spirituality enjoys a certain priority in relation to being a member of the church. This can be shown historically by describing in a developmental way how the church evolved out of spirituality. With this priority of spirituality to church membership in place, it will be easy to show how each of these two dimensions of being a Christian relate to each other. The third part will show that far from being any antithesis between spirituality and church membership, the survival of Christian spirituality depends on there being a church. And fourth, looking at spirituality through the church will allow one to see what ecclesial spirituality might look like, at least in an ideal form. At its best, the reciprocal relationship between spirituality and church membership can enhance personal spirituality and be absolutely fulfilling.

The Concept of Spirituality

The term "spirituality" has been released from the writings of solitary mystics and the cloistered precincts of monasteries and convents. One can now pick up books on spirituality in the kiosks of airports and train terminals. They deal with anything from formulas for self-improvement, to psychological self-examination, to Eastern practices of meditation and mindfulness. Spirituality covers a range from schools of prayer and relating to God to techniques of assisting people in their religious lives. This eclectic expansion of the sphere of spirituality has the merit of relating it to everyday secular life. But it requires that anyone using the term be clear about a particular usage and meaning.

"Spirituality" here refers to the encompassing logic of how people live their lives with implicit or explicit reference to ultimate reality. More than anything else, the cumulative actions of people define who they are as persons. This usage capitalizes on the democratization and secularization of the term: everyone has a spirituality. Spirituality is not the stale stuff of a fading religion; it is the positive élan that drives each person's life. The notion goes far deeper than "lifestyle" and thus should not be equated merely with what transpires on the surface of time and place, the ad hoc of doing this or that. It includes but cannot be reduced to practices that intentionally direct attention to transcendence. The word "spirituality," by recalling the human spirit, calls up the depth of the intentional direction of human lives, singly or in groups, toward some implicit or explicit goal. While spirituality includes the entire range of people's human activities, its formal or defining mark lies in its reference to ultimate reality. In Christianity, ultimate reality is God. Spirituality for Christians thus refers to the quality of one's whole life as it stands before God. Spirituality opens up to inspection the entire range of "the Christian life" as this is directed toward and is measured by God as God is revealed in Jesus Christ.

Spirituality so understood always carries two dimensions. The one may be called existential and consists in the actual decisions and concrete actions that make up the daily course of life. It is the way persons direct their lives: the direction they chart, the decisions they make, the pattern that develops and identifies them as who they are. Frequently spirituality means a set of definite practices, of meditation, prayer, disciplined behavior leading to good habits. The usage here does not exclude such practices but reaches out for a larger framework of reference. People define themselves by their actions; they are what they do, not reductively but positively. Spirituality points to the way conscious and free persons create themselves in this and that decision and more clearly in the series of actions that make a life. Over time people become more and more responsible for who they have made themselves to be as distinguished from a passive "what they have become." In other words, one's spirituality is in some measure within one's control.

The other dimension of the term spirituality refers to the understanding, rationale, or reflective analysis that governs or is contained in existential living. This second dimension may be embedded within a person's behavior and not explicitly examined; or it may be an intentional theorizing about the character and quality of Christian life. Spirituality in this second sense, when it is formally objectivized, constitutes the discipline analyzed in books and studied in traditions. But the real point of this distinction between existential and formal spirituality is not to separate these inseparable dimensions of spiritual life but to insist that the two should always be held together in any understanding of the term spirituality. The theoretical reflection always refers back to life on the ground; seemingly mindless routine behaviors arise out of latent motivations, implicit goals, or reasoned teleologies.

With this very concrete and practical sense of spirituality in place, one that always implies a theoretical or formal coherence, we now shift attention to how Christian spirituality and church are related to each other.

Christianity Began as a Spirituality of Following Jesus

One way to explain how spirituality relates to church and being a member of the church consists in showing historically how the church grew out of a spirituality of following Jesus. Nothing can replace a narrative in the explanation of a historical institution. The history of origins does not remove the need for other forms of analysis, but it remains foundational. A major area of research today has to do with the origins of the church. Once one has a basic grasp of how the church came to be, many things begin to fall into place. History cannot displace theology, but theology that contradicts history makes no sense at all.

On that premise, it is fairly obvious that the church began as a spirituality of following Jesus of Nazareth. All the Gospels, but particularly Mark, Matthew, and Luke, tell the story in slightly different ways of how Jesus appeared in Palestine as a religious teacher, prophet, and healer, drew crowds with his ministry, and gathered followers. It is quite important at this point, when one is trying to think historically, to recognize that Jesus and his followers were not Christians but Jews. It was only considerably later, years after Jesus's death and resurrection, that his followers were referred to as Christians by outsiders. The point here is obvious but important, namely, that what would become decades later a Christian church got started by what has been categorized as spirituality, a commitment to follow Jesus and lead a life that reflects his teaching about God and God's rule.

Jesus is portrayed in the Gospels as operating out of a sense of calling and being sent by God. It would be natural for the disciples of Jesus during his public ministry to experience a sense of sharing in this mission. This idea gets formalized in the Gospels when Jesus is portrayed as sending the disciples on a mission essentially modeled on his own. "And he called to him the twelve, and began to send them out two by two, and gave them authority over the unclean spirits" (Mark 6:7; also Mark 3:14-15). Jon Sobrino makes a historical case that these sendings of the disciples on mission provide the deepest foundations for an emergent church.[1] But even apart from such actual sendings, whether they actually happened that way or not, one has to imagine that the disciples of Jesus shared a sense of his "mission," his urgent sense of calling and his response to the imperative of bearing witness to the values of God's rule to Israel. In other words, a sense of mission lies at the essential core of the appearance of Jesus, his ministry, and the religious appreciation of him. Therefore, from the beginning, "mission" represents a stimulus toward the formation of what will later be called church. This missionary impulse will also influence the fundamental character of the church.

This general historical picture of Jesus's ministry and his attraction of followers has some considerable theoretical relevance. One is already able to say that a profound relation to God as mediated by Jesus of Nazareth existed prior to any church, certainly by a priority of time. But this priority of time correlates neatly with a priority of importance and significance. In fact, church, as something that developed later in history, absolutely depends on the spirituality of following Jesus. The spirituality of following Jesus explains why a church later arose. One

1. Jon Sobrino, "Evangelization as Mission of the Church," in *The True Church and the Poor* (Maryknoll, NY: Orbis Books, 1984), 253-301, esp. 257-65.

cannot say that a spirituality of following Jesus depended on the prior foundation of the church. That would be a perfect historical example of putting the cart before the horse. Jesus and following Jesus generated the church which came later. It will become clear in what follows that the reason why the church arose was to ensure that the spirituality of following Jesus would be preserved.

How Jesus Spirituality Became a Church

The next step in explaining the relationship of spirituality to the church consists of tracing (here broadly and abstractly) the process by which the followers of Jesus gradually evolved into a church that was distinct from Judaism. This took many decades and was a process that lasted at least into the second century and in some respects into the fourth century. It was not a development that was organized or unfolded consistently; it occurred earlier in some places than in others. But the truly important thing in all of this lies less in the stages of development and more in the fact of development itself. Our language frequently gives the idea that the church was set up in Jesus's time. It was a common occurrence that, in the process of constructing the Gospel stories, situations and events contemporary to the composers were retrojected into the Gospel scenes that portrayed Jesus's ministry. Scholars who study the scriptures critically are, practically speaking, unanimous in their view that Jesus did not found a church. Rather a church gradually and incrementally developed over decades based on a spirituality of following Jesus. What follows tries to capture the logic of this development in a series of analytical characterizations of what happened.[2]

A first principle for understanding the development of the church can be found in the idea that the Easter experience of Jesus's disciples, namely, that he had been raised from death, functioned as a commissioning for them. Recognition that Jesus was risen was received by the disciples as a "mission" to communicate this conviction; they were

2. Some presentations of the story of Christian origins and the difficulties of presenting anything like a detailed history of this development are Edward Schillebeeckx, *The Church with a Human Face: A New and Expanded Theology of Ministry* (New York: Crossroad, 1988), 13-123; Roger Haight, *Christian Community in History:* Vol. 1, *Historical Ecclesiology* (New York: Continuum, 2004), 69-139; Daniel J. Harrington, *The Church according to the New Testament: What the Wisdom and Witness of Early Christianity Teach Us Today* (Chicago: Sheed & Ward, 2001); Rodney Stark, *The Rise of Christianity* (San Francisco: HarperCollins, 1997); Gerd Theissen, *The Religion of the Earliest Churches: Creating a Symbolic World* (Minneapolis: Fortress Press, 1999); Hal Taussig, "The End of Christian Origins? Where to Turn at the Intersection of Subjectivity and Historical Craft," *Review of Biblical Literature* 11 (2011): 1-45.

charged to pass on its religious significance to others. Jesus spirituality became a church because of this sense of "mission," the idea of being sent. Anyone attentive to the stories of Jesus appearing to his disciples after his death will notice that the theme of mission or "being sent" appears in many of them. In John's Gospel, Jesus appeared to the disciples who were in a closed room and said, "Peace be with you. As the Father has sent me, even so I send you" (John 20:21). And at the end of Matthew's Gospel, Jesus appeared to the disciples and gave them the so-called missionary mandate to spread the good news to the whole world. This association of the coming to awareness that Jesus had been raised from death by God, the conviction that this message should be shared among all people, and the followers of Jesus being impelled to carry this forward represents a deep structure of Christian faith. This foundational experience was needed for the Jesus movement to take off. The experience of Jesus resurrected and alive was not something simply to be shared among intimate associates who had come to that awareness, but something that should be spread among all people: it had universal relevance.[3]

The next question is how this primal mission movement became a church. The answer to that question on the level of history is theoretically simple: it happened gradually through historical development. It was accomplished with a great deal of local controversy, and, theologically, not without the power and inspiration of the Spirit of God. One version of how this happened is the second volume of Luke's two-volume work, the Acts of the Apostles. Unfortunately, many of his stories, especially those regarding the first twenty years, have disputed historical value. We do not have very much information about how the Jesus movement spread up to around mid-century, when we have the firsthand accounts of Paul's authentic letters.

One story in Acts tells of events around the years 48–49 that are verified by Paul as historical and very significant.[4] At that time the leadership of the church formally decided that this still-Jewish Jesus movement, or messianic Judaism, should be opened to Gentiles without circumcision. In other words, one did not have to become a Jew in a formal sense to become a follower of Jesus. This major decision

---

3. Continuing the ministry of Jesus does not fully describe the sense of mission of the earliest followers. One also finds a sense of eschatological urgency that, however it developed, is reflected in Luke's account of the ascension in Acts (1:11). The Jesus who ascended on the clouds will, like the Son of Man (Dan. 7:13-14), come again, and we must be ready.

4. Philip Francis Esler thinks that Luke has adjusted this story to his own ends. Nevertheless, the decision, whatever its motivations, helped open the Jesus movement to Gentiles. See Esler, *Community and Gospel in Luke-Acts: The Social and Political Motivations of Lucan Theology* (Cambridge: Cambridge University Press, 1987), 105-9.

in effect opened up the Jewish Jesus movement to all in the Roman Empire in a more direct way. The decision turned out to be a turning point in the process by which the movement of Jesus spirituality moved toward becoming distinguished, but still not separated, from Judaism.

When exactly did a community of the disciples of Jesus become a church distinct from Judaism, one that would have an identity of its own as a Christian church? It is impossible to answer that question without some elaboration. Many factors would have to accumulate before the Jesus movement would cease to be simply a distinct tradition within Judaism. In fact different Jesus communities evolved somewhat differently in different cities and cultures: some were more Jewish in character, others more Greek or Roman in character. One can discern different forms of organization in different proto-churches. This separation may have been accomplished earlier in one city and later in another. It took decades for the Christian communities to begin to assemble a body of writings that they shared as distinctively their own.

This schematic narrative of how the church developed enables one to describe in a historically developmental way what the church that developed actually was. The church was the Jewish Jesus movement that gradually took on its own distinctive identity; it became separate but always religiously dependent on Judaism. That distinct identity began to be publicly defined by various institutional forms that still define the Christian church: faith in Jesus as God's representative, baptism, the meal of discipleship that recalls the meals of Jesus with his disciples, and participation in assemblies where Jewish and then gradually Christian scriptures are read and people comment on them.

One could give a fuller description of the early church in the late first century. In various contexts it may be important to consider the different organizational patterns that the churches adopted. But what is more important for this consideration lies in the deeper constitutive structure of the church in answer to the question of what the church is. The story of the first-century development shows that the church can be defined as having a core that consists in the spirituality of following Jesus, and around that core various social structures are formed to preserve it, to ensure its leadership, and to normalize or socialize its overt spiritual activities. In short, the developmental story shows that the church consisted essentially in a Jesus spirituality, a spirituality of following Jesus, that acquired an institutional structure. This structure is both dependent on and the servant of the spirituality and not the other way around.

This story of the gradual formation of the church has been forgotten;

in some respects it has been blotted out by the frequently repeated phrase that Jesus founded a church. This story, which communicates something essential about the nature of the church, has been short-circuited from the active memory of many. With it some basic convictions were lost. For example, this story bears significant importance for how we understand the church ecumenically. It is clear that during the first century the historical development of the church entailed a pluralism of different churches in different cities. These were little communities; think in today's terms of small congregations or parishes rather than big churches. Perhaps a large city like Rome had a number of different communities. In different cities or areas the New Testament shows they had somewhat different organizational structures. In the 50s Paul complained of competing gospels. There were links between these communities: apostles (a designation reaching beyond the twelve), traveling prophets, letters, other visitors who traveled. But this was not a centrally organized movement. Rather what held the churches together in the beginning was primarily a Jesus spirituality: this is the center and the core.

This basic insight allows one to think in terms of one church and many churches. Some basic elements revolve around a Christian spirituality and form the essentials of a Christian faith that was shared across all the churches. That which differentiated the churches was considerably less important when compared with faith in God as mediated by Jesus of Nazareth now risen. Therefore, when church structures begin to divide Christians, one has to wonder about their validity, authenticity, and certainly their authority. The point of Jesus and of the salvation from God that he mediates consists in liberation and reconciliation among people and with God. If church structures begin to undermine that unifying spirituality, one has to question their authenticity.

Ecclesial Spirituality: Following Christ in Community

Let us shift our attention to the church at the present time. Can what has been learned by tracing the origins of the church help to understand the church today? The church arose from the ministry of Jesus and the slow development of a Jewish messianic movement centered in Jesus into a network of communities that gradually became distinct from Judaism and gained a separate pattern of organization. The church has always been dependent on Judaism in its roots and in its self-understanding. Only in the course of the second century did the Christian church become more distinct and autonomous. During its whole history up to the present a spirituality of following Jesus under the impulse of God as Spirit defines the fundamental substratum from beginning to end. When we take that basic principle and apply it to our church today, it generates several reflections that can help sort out how personal Christian spirituality relates to the institutional church.

A foundational principle has been stated already: Christian spirituality as a following of Jesus enjoys a priority relative to theology and the church. The sustaining force in the genesis of the church was Jesus and the spirituality he elicited from his followers. Following Jesus, in the sense of making Jesus's message of the rule of God and his life of service of people in God's name, defines the ultimacy that governs the life of the Christian. That could be developed at length of course. But the point to be made resides more simply in the recognition of this elementary structure in Christian existence, namely, the primacy of spirituality relative to theology and to the church itself. Theology consists of reflection on Christian spirituality of following Jesus and what this entails about God and human existence. The church consists of the worldly or historical organization of the group life of followers of Jesus. Spirituality is primary; the church is secondary, subordinate, and wholly functional in service of Christian spirituality.

This foundational relationship can be formulated more exactly with the following proposition: the purpose of the church is to be the medium of Christian spirituality. The church's goal is to become the historical means by which Christian spirituality is propagated and maintained in existence. At this point one can mount an argument from Christian spirituality for the necessity of the church. Without a historical institution to perpetuate Christian spirituality, it would cease to exist. This insight allows one to see that the church is not something extrinsic to Christian spirituality, something that is added on, but rather grows out of it. Personal Christian spirituality forms a part of the shared community experience. This community experience cannot withstand historical change without an institution to ensure its continuity. This formal public role should not be minimized; it is essential for the continued existence of particular traditions of Christian spirituality. As an institution, the church continues to provide assemblies of worship, sacraments, and leadership in ministry.

Another dimension of the purpose of the church is to nurture Christian spirituality in the different situations in which the community finds itself. At any given time and place the church is meant to provide support for a spirituality of following the pattern of the life and ministry of Jesus. Do the public acts of the church actually support the spiritual life of its members? The nurture that members of the church actually receive serves as a criterion for measuring the success of the church. The church has no higher historical norm by which its performance can be judged than whether it actually nourishes the spiritual life of its members.[5] If people are not being sustained in their spirituality, if people are leaving the church in large numbers because the church is not addressing their spirituality, if the church's teaching ministry is losing its spiritual authority and its leadership its moral authority, the church is failing in the very purpose of its existence. Recognition of the symbiotic relationship between the church and the spirituality of its members is needed in order to break down the idea that the institution has an autonomous existence that is prior to, independent of, and not responsible to and for its members. Such an idea presently drives much of the institutional church's leadership, but it does not hold up in terms of history, theology, or common sense. The purpose of the church is to reflect Christian spirituality and by doing so in a corporate institutional way to propagate and nourish that spirituality in the lives of its members and through them in the broader community.

There is a natural tendency in the West to think of spirituality in private, personal terms. But an important support for one's personal spirituality consists in a community of the faithful, one's fellow Christians and church members, who play the role of companions in maintaining a spiritual life even when the institutional church does not seem to help. It is difficult to maintain a private Christian spirituality, unless it is completely arbitrary and undemanding. Measuring oneself by the ministry of Jesus is certainly demanding. In the face of these high standards, when companions within the community come together mutually to encourage one another, they maintain a communitarian spirituality. From the perspective of each person who tries to follow the teaching and pattern of Jesus's life such a community can be invaluable.

Finally, Christian spirituality began as a "mission" spirituality, and this has been maintained within the church up to this time. But is it possible to retain this sense of mission in a globalized world that is conscious of national and religious boundaries, tends to think of other religions positively in terms of their particular cultural contexts, and accords them an authenticity that was unthinkable in past years? The whole missionary project seems to have collapsed in the last fifty years, except among Evangelical and Pentecostal churches.

This question is important today and needs to be clearly stated. The church preserves the Gospels, the scriptures, and the assemblies of worship in which the Gospels are read and the meal of disciples

5. This is not a contentious statement challenging the normativity of scripture. It is precisely through scripture that Christians know whether or not the church is serving them spiritually.

is celebrated. In this way the church sets the direction of Christian spirituality. That direction is drawn from the stories of Jesus's teaching about the rule of God. The rule of God can be recapitulated in the broad formula of the way the world would be if it followed the values and will of God as God is represented in the scriptures and Jesus's teaching. Being grasped by Jesus's message and also the message about his resurrection generates a mission spirituality. Christian spirituality is a mission spirituality; it bears witness by action to the values of God in society and in the world. This expansive communicative dynamism of following Jesus cannot be dissolved into a private relationship between the individual and God. But how can this be integrated with a historical consciousness that tends to appreciate the role of all religions concretely in terms of the culture and situation of those whose spirituality is shaped by them?[6]

A credible response to this question has to preserve the internal logic of Christian spirituality and, from the Christian point of view, the conviction that other religions are driven by an equally authentic spiritual experience. The key to holding these two terms together lies in a noncompetitive view of the religions and the notion of dialogue as the main quality of the active relationships between the religions. From the Christian side, the notion of God as creator allows the Christian to recognize that God is present and active as saving personal presence in all people and, therefore, through them, in all religions. This in turn can be developed into a rigorous theology of noncompetitiveness among the religions, certainly between Christianity and the other religions. Once authenticity is mutually recognized, it is relatively easy, in theoretical terms at least, to apply the rule of civil discourse in a pluralistic society to communications between religions. Missionary activity today must transpire on the basis of spiritual respect for other religions through a practice of dialogue.

A noncompetitive concept of religion and a mission to enter into a dialogue of sharing religious experience can be translated into the events of everyday life. Mrs. X of one faith meets Mrs. Y of another faith in the workplace or the neighborhood. They become reasonably close friends, and in the course of their relationship they share their religious convictions. In so doing they communicate with and in some measure influence each other quite profoundly without ever feeling or suggesting a desire that the other convert. Such an event is interreligious dialogue at the grassroots level, and it provides a picture for church policy to emulate.[7] Today the church's mission is to enter into

6. This question will be discussed further from a slightly different perspective in chapter 12.

7. Jeannine Hill Fletcher analyzes the interfaith dialogue of a women's group

dialogue with the world of secular life and the religions. A mission spirituality carries this forward according to the abilities and situation of each one. In the end, Christians play out the dimension of mission in their spiritualities by the testimony of their lives. To live a Christian life after the pattern of Jesus is to give witness to others.

To conclude, this chapter has drawn out the relationship between Christian spirituality and the church. The history of the development of the church dramatizes this relationship in unmistakable terms: spirituality is prior to the church, so that the whole purpose of the church is to serve and nurture the lives of people who want to relate to God by following the teaching and pattern of Jesus. This understanding does two things. First it relativizes the church, because it makes it functional, in service to something more important than itself, that is, the Christian life of concrete people. But at the same time it makes the church necessary, because without this community Christian life would founder amid the complex developments of history. The church is necessary, but this or that form of it is not; from the beginning and during its whole history it has been changing and existing in many different forms. That is its natural state. Therefore, if certain forms of church in particular places fail to nourish the spirituality of its constituents, they will either have to change, or they will fade away; or people will fade away from them.

in Philadelphia that met continuously after 9/11 for mutual support, healing, and understanding. See Jeannine Hill Fletcher, *Motherhood as Metaphor: Engendering Interreligious Dialogue* (New York: Fordham University Press, 2013), 145-63.

CHAPTER SIX

Following Jesus in a Scientific Age

Some scientific conceptions of reality seem to threaten the beliefs of Christian faith. Or they leave one with a vague sense that the language of faith is mythological or passé. Some people deal with this by "compartmentalization," where a person divides his or her life into separate spheres or compartments and blocks off any cross-communication. On one side, for example, the realm of Christian faith has its own inner logic, and a person of faith does not allow other knowledge to mess it up. On the other side, the businessperson does business, and religion does not enter in. But this does not work in the end, because we are one person in two relationships, with God and the world. Worldly and heavenly citizenships meet in one human consciousness, and without interchange between them a person may experience inner conflict.

The issues I wish to address in this discussion revolve around large ideas raised by science. Because I am not a scientist, the problems that I lift up are not expressed with scientific nuance. What I am reporting is more like hearsay derived from the world of science, an impressionistic account of certain aspects of the scientific story of the universe that seem to intersect with Christian faith. I am more concerned with how a broad scientific picture of reality comes to bear on the Christian picture of reality. This is what most people encounter. Exactly how do we deal with divergent worldviews? Is there a formula for approaching the deep differences in vision?

I address these questions in three steps. In the first part I isolate five basic challenges that science presents to traditional Christian faith-language. This will give the discussion a specific focus. In the second part I begin a positive response by describing the source from which it comes, namely, spirituality. Spirituality offers a ground, a starting point, and a rationale for addressing the problems. The third part draws out some ways in which Christians can overcome the problematic character of a scientific worldview by integrating it into Christian faith. The method for overcoming these problems does not contradict science but allows faith to absorb scientific conclusions into itself. I want to show that science is not an aggressive enemy of Christian faith but a friend who helps clarify faith's vision of reality.

Scientific Challenges to Christian Faith and Spirituality

Although I cannot speak from inside the intricate and complex world of science, some scientific conclusions can be grasped in the language of everyday life. They have been challenging Christian belief for some time, as the landmark cases of Galileo and Charles Darwin show. I raise up five neuralgic points for Christian imagination and understanding.

Big Bang, Evolution, and Divine Intervention

The first problem arises in a clash between the God of Christianity freely acting in the world and a scientific vision that cannot see it. In Christian language God is called Father, and this inevitably suggests a big person up there or out there. The conception of God as personal becomes translated by the imagination into "a" person to whom prayer is directed. It is true that theology has always recognized and resisted anthropomorphism, that is, speaking about God in human terms. But it is difficult not to think of God as "a" person. God in the Bible regularly intervenes in history, in person or as a voice or through angels; God acts miraculously in history; and we still pray to God for special favors. It is fair to say that Christians believe in God acting in history in what is close to overt ways.

Science presents a significantly different scenario. The age and size of the universe that is proposed by science virtually prohibits speaking of God as "a" person. How may human beings imagine or conceive the creator of a universe that is more than 13 billion years old and has been expanding at cosmic speed from its very beginning? What vocabulary can avoid the idea of a big person in the sky and still preserve the personal character of the God to whom we relate?

Generally speaking, theologians who dialogue with science are reluctant to speak of God intervening in the dynamics of the world or history and acting as a this-worldly cause to accomplish specific tasks.[1]

1. William R. Stoeger, "Conceiving Divine Action in a Dynamic Universe," *Scientific Perspectives on Divine Action: Twenty Years of Challenge and Progress*, ed. Robert John Russell, Nancey Murphy, and William R. Stoeger (Berkeley: The Center for Theology and the Natural Sciences; Vatican City: Vatican Observatory Publications, 2008), 227. The idea that God acts in the world refers either to God's universal ongoing creative activity or God's special action relative to a particular event. The idea of "intervention" may have two senses, and both of them lie beyond the ken of science. The one imagines that God's action comes from a different place or from outside the sphere of the world.

Even the origin of human life is understood in evolutionary terms as having emerged out of inorganic chemicals. All life forms have developed by an inner-worldly causality from a single primitive form of life. As Darwin stated it, "all the organic beings which have ever lived on this earth have descended from some one primordial form, into which life was first breathed."[2] This picture conflicts with a scenario in which God directly creates the human species and each single human being on the premise that spirit cannot evolve from matter.

Randomness and Purpose

The second problem subsists in a tension between the randomness of the universe and its purposiveness. Christians live in a universe created by a personal God and oriented to a specific goal. This provides a sense of a stable will of God for reality and a conception of truth that is universal and unchanging. Permanent laws of nature support a universal natural law for human behavior. Basic notions of spirituality are governed by God's having intended each person's role in history.

All of this seems to be confronted, if not opposed, by the picture of reality that is provided by the sciences. The universe is in motion. Reality is fluid, becoming, developing through time. Reality is not static; change is its default condition. Creation is still producing new forms of being.[3] Science describes in abstract terms a structure within which this process takes place as a tension between laws and random occurrences over a vast period of time. One author offers an analogy with the game of chess: rules govern the operations of the pieces, but many different moves are allowed by the regulations. In the scientific view, however, even laws can change when new forms of being arise.[4]

This cannot be because God is the power within all things holding them in being. The other imagines that God's disrupts the laws of nature, or takes them over, or acts instead of them. This idea is more contentious. See Denis Edwards, *How God Acts: Creation, Redemption, and Special Divine Action* (Minneapolis: Fortress Press, 2010), 45-47.

2. Charles Darwin, *The Origin of Species by Means of Natural Selection* (New York: Barns and Noble Classics, 2004), 280.

3. Nature is not a structure but a story. It is constituted as a narrative. This narrative adds complexities of an ascending character as evolution builds through cosmological, inorganic, geological, chemical, biological, human, social, and cultural layers. "For the 'being' of the world is always also a 'becoming' and there is always a story to be told, especially as matter becomes living and then conscious and, eventually, social too." "The process never stops and our accounts of it all are irreducibly narrative." See Arthur Peacocke, *Theology for a Scientific Age: Being and Becoming – Natural and Divine* (Oxford: Basil Blackwell, 1990), 62.

4. Ian Barbour, *When Science Meets Religion* (San Francisco: HarperSanFrancisco, 2000), 110.

Science implicitly represents a metaphysics of constant change. Being is truly open and unpredictable.[5] "The future is not simply unknown; it is 'not decided.' More than one alternative is open, and there is some opportunity for unpredictable novelty. Time involves a unique historicity and unrepeatability; the world would not repeat its course if it were restored to a former state, for at each point a different event from among the potentialities might be actualized."[6] God's providence is not in control, and there is no determined outcome within the finite world.

This deep structure of randomness, change, and new patterns of being represents on open system of being. How does it relate to a purposeful vision of the universe that has so dominated Christian conceptions of reality? This is a basic issue that may be disorienting.

Evolution and Original Sin

Christians live in an anthropocentric world. The book of Genesis witnesses to it, and Christians particularly in the West have lived by it. They assume that they are the centerpiece of creation and the masters of the universe. The world is there to be named and to be used. Yet that proud conception has been convicted of sin. Many think that the existence of suffering and death in the world is due to human sin. The language of an original sin dominates Christian understanding of the human. It appears in doctrine, theology, and ethics. More significantly, it pervades the language of liturgy, worship, and spirituality.

Science has surely complicated our understanding of ourselves. Given the age and size of the universe, it is difficult to posit that human existence occupies the place of central importance. Such a conviction has to be worn lightly and with reserve. The immensity of the universe simply dwarfs human significance. The human has been drawn into a larger narrative, so that human existence makes up "a small part of the universe, [and] we are not the whole story."[7]

Evolution has a bearing on what Christians refer to as "original sin." Evolution entails the connection of the human species to the whole history of the universe and of emergent life, including the violent struggle

---

5. The movement of reality is described as consisting of the interplay of regular pattern, or law, or "necessity" and chance, randomness, or contingency. This randomness or unpredictability can be in the very foundations of physical reality at the micro or subatomic level of being. It is more evident in the realm of natural selection in the evolution of life (Peacocke, *Theology for a Scientific Age*, 118).

6. Ibid., 69.

7. John F. Haught, "Cosmology and Creation," in *Christianity and Science: Toward a Theology of Nature* (Maryknoll, NY: Orbis Books, 2007), 127.

of life forms to hold on to existence. Evolutionary consciousness and the story of humanity rule out an original sin conceived as an event or a fall. What appeared as a defining moment in the Christian story science depicts as a natural human tendency in the light of evolution.[8] Original sin becomes a metaphor for persistent human egoism and collateral damage in the struggle for life. Attention to self persists as a part of the ongoing process of creation. The idea that this tendency is an objective condition of the human caused by an event in history that can be reversed by another event in history called redemption compounds the historical fundamentalism.[9]

Because this element in the Christian story is deeply engrained in Christian language adjustments will require careful reflection.

Jesus and Other Saviors

Over the past few centuries we have grown to respect the differences between cultures and religions. Many Christians have also come to recognize the authority and legitimacy of other religions relative to different cultures. This has led to an increasing acceptance of religious pluralism as the natural condition of the human race in history. But at the same time most churches in their official doctrines have resisted this position. The more public and prevailing view is that there is only one incarnation, one savior of all humankind, and one true religion.

It is interesting to note, therefore, that science has elicited a new challenge to the basic Christian doctrine of a single incarnation. The more science searches the universe, the more it appears that intelligent life on other planets is not only possible but also statistically probable. Given another species of intelligent life on another planet, it would be hard not to think of an analogous or parallel incarnation to that of Jesus Christ. "As incarnation is an intense form of divine love, would there not be galactic forms of that love? An infinite being of generosity would tend to many incarnations rather than to one."[10]

---

8. "In the context of natural selection, pain has an energizing effect and suffering is a goad to action: they both have survival value for creatures continually faced with new problematic situations challenging their survival. . . . It must be emphasized that pain, suffering and death are present in biological evolution, as a necessary condition of survival of the individual and transition to new forms long before the appearance of human beings on the scene. So the presence of pain, suffering and death cannot be the result of any particular human actions . . ." (Peacocke, *Theology for a Scientific Age*, 68-69).

9. This is one of the theses of Jack Mahoney, *Christianity in Evolution: An Exploration* (Washington, DC: Georgetown University Press, 2011).

10. Thomas F. O'Meara, *Vast Universe* (Collegeville, MN: Liturgical Press, 1012), 47.

The Meaning of Incarnation

The incarnation of God on other planets calls into question the present conception of incarnation. Christian faith characterizes Jesus Christ as a divine presence within the created sphere that occurred only once. In our pluralistic religious world the claims Christians make about Jesus seem exaggerated. How can we speak of the incarnation of God within our world and in Jesus in a way that is intelligible? Can doctrines about Jesus's incarnation, exalted status, and universal relevance be made in a way that recognizes the integrity of other religions?

These five problems have been stated sharply. I think most Christians are aware of them in varying degrees. So I turn to a discussion of a way that these problems can be resolved, a way that leads through spirituality.

Spirituality of Following Jesus

In this second part I propose a way of understanding how Christian faith deals with what appear to be problems raised by our scientific and technological culture. *How* does faith enter into conversation with scientific culture? This is a question of method: what is going on when a Christian entertains the data of science? In the next section I will talk about possible results of the interchange. Here I make five brief points which together essentially say this: Christian spirituality provides the basis for absorbing and integrating the data of science into faith.[11]

The first point concerns the notion of spirituality: what is spirituality? I use the term to refer to the way persons or groups lead their lives in the face of some transcendent reality. With this understanding, one can say that all persons who have an integrated life have a spirituality, because they have a transcendent organizing principle that guides their being and actions. Spirituality is thus a holistic or fully comprehensive category. A spirituality sums up the lives of persons or groups because it provides a center of gravity for all their actions in what they consider most important and worth living for.

Second, in this framework, Christian spirituality consists of following Jesus. Christians are those who have shaped their lives after the pattern of Jesus in their belief in God and God's rule. Christian spirituality usually includes a set of beliefs, an ethical code, and a number of practical spiritual behaviors such as worshiping God in Christian assembly, prayer, other devotions and good works. But the basis or ground for the whole of Christian spirituality across the many

11. I begin here by repeating definitions established in earlier chapters and then adapt the idea of spirituality to meet the problem at hand.

churches consists in following Jesus. Christianity began with following Jesus, and this is what it has continued to be and always will be.

The third point notes that Christian spirituality always reflects the historical context in which it exists. This can be factually demonstrated by a consideration of the history of Christian spirituality. It appears differently among Carthaginian Christians of the third century compared with Celtic monks of the eighth and ninth centuries, Christians in Calvin's Geneva in the sixteenth century, European Catholics under Pius IX in the nineteenth century, and Korean Presbyterians today. In other words, the common core of following Jesus, that is, living out Christian faith in God in a way that is determined by Jesus's teaching and example, takes different shapes and sizes in different historical cultures and environments. But it is also clear that a common Christian spirituality underneath the differences among Christians in different situations unites them in faith. In all cases Christian spirituality has the same ground: following Jesus as the source for the content of faith in God.

This observable fact deserves some more reflection because it holds the kernel of what I want to communicate. There are different levels to the house of Christian faith. The ground floor is the spirituality of following Jesus. This is what defines faith in God as Christian faith, the fact that it is based on and shaped by Jesus of Nazareth. All Christians share this same ground floor. But as one ascends the floors of the building one encounters differences. Different ways of following Jesus, different beliefs about Jesus, different emphases among ethical values, different patterns of worship, and different organizational structures can be found on the upper floors of the same house of Christianity. What really unites Christians across centuries and cultures is not the same set of words or practices but the same structure of the basic spirituality that defines a person or group as Christian. The fundamental orientation in living is informed and modeled by Jesus of Nazareth. This was the historical starting point of Christianity itself, and from this corporate existential basis everything else developed.

The fourth point is that Christian spirituality can absorb different cultural systems into itself and remain the same spirituality in its base of following Jesus. In other words, one Christian faith and spirituality picks up different styles, expressions, and beliefs along the way. But this means that one should not think of the relation between Christianity and scientific culture as a confrontation between two parallel sets of beliefs or ideologies of the same kind. The way to understand this relationship is not to line up doctrines and beliefs on both sides in order to compare them and negotiate between them. One should not say, "Christianity holds this truth and science holds that truth" as if two objective and propositionally defined worldviews could be compared and contrasted. Christian spirituality relates a person to God on the basis of faith mediated by Jesus; science is a way of understanding this world on the basis of empirical evidence. A better formula for this relationship is this: Christian spirituality unfolds in a scientific and technological culture and worldview; therefore it will formulate its beliefs in God, define its ethical norms, and express its worship of God in a manner that is derived from Christian spirituality but that fits this new culture in the same way Christian spirituality has always done relative to different historical cultures.

And finally, fifth, let me formulate a thesis that will be the guide for the third part of this chapter. A spirituality of following Jesus that transpires within a secular, scientific, and technological culture provides the basis for understanding Jesus as the Christ within that culture. Theology and ultimately doctrines emerge in each period of Christian history out of Christian spirituality. Spirituality, or life lived on the basis of an attachment to God as mediated through Jesus, provides the source for a constructive understanding of Christian beliefs, ethics, and spiritual practices expressed in terms of the culture at hand.

Following Jesus in a Scientific Age

I now move to the next part of this discussion and turn to following Jesus in a scientific culture. In it I follow the formula of drawing scientific culture into the dynamics of following Jesus so that Christian spirituality inserts itself into this culture.

Recognizing the Immanence of God

The first challenge of science to Christian belief that we considered arises from the reluctance to consider God entering, or intervening, into the systems of the natural world, even though few conceive of nature as a closed system. But if we think in the broader terms of God's being the inner power of being itself, as expressed in the conception of creation out of nothing, this opens up the concept of God's immanence within the world in a way that is not hostile to science and is more relevant to spirituality.

The Christian idea of creation comes from the Hebrew scriptures, and after Jesus the idea was refined with the idea that God creates out of nothing. The conception has its roots in the human experience of not possessing the ground of one's being within oneself. The absolute "whence" of our being is shared by the world of which we are a part. Creation out of nothing means that "nothing" stands between God and creatures, and this makes God the sustaining power of being itself. "God is radically immanent (interior) to all that is—but in a highly differentiated way, according to the character of each process, relationship, or object. God, then, is not an entity, like other entities—God is more like a verb, a continuing action in which everything else participates, but participates according to its own individuality."[12]

Thomas Aquinas called God's ongoing creating power primary causality; all this-worldly being and actions (secondary causality) are sustained by it. God is primary cause insofar as God causes and is the sustaining power of all being. Secondary causes are all finite agents that exist and operate only because they are themselves sustained by the power of God's active creating their being.[13] "God is unlike any other cause, is not an entity like other entities, but rather more of an all-pervasive activity or process in which all else participates, and, though present everywhere cannot be isolated as either a separate cause or force."[14] In this view, God's special action in the world is really God's universal creative action working in and through secondary or this-worldly causality. All this-worldly agency is the operation of both primary and secondary causes, both of which wholly produce the effect, but each on the basis of a different kind of causality. The so-called causal joint looked for in God's special action is accounted for by the particularity encompassed by God's creative primary causality.[15]

Living with Randomness

I turn now to randomness and purpose. A spirituality of following Jesus allows the Christian to live with randomness and rejoice in it. Purpose in the cosmos and in history does not demand that every event be programmed. Randomness within a system and movement of the whole system toward a goal are not contraries. Across or within

---

12. Stoeger, "Conceiving Divine Action in a Dynamic Universe," 229.

13. See Thomas Aquinas, *Summa contra Gentiles,* III 70.

14. Stoeger, "Conceiving Divine Action in a Dynamic Universe," 235.

15. Instead of thinking of God working in the world by a special act, God's action may be thought of as God's universal creativity at work simultaneously with secondary causes. This issue was discussed extensively in the Middle Ages in terms of grace and free will, and Bernard of Clairvaux proposed a formula resolving debates that alternatively awarded primacy to God's action or to human action: "Grace does the whole work, and so does free choice—with this one qualification: That whereas the whole is done *in* free choice, so is the whole done *of* grace" (Bernard of Clairvaux, "On Grace and Free Will," in *Treatises III* [Kalamazoo, MI: Cistercian Publications, 1977], 14.47, p. 106). The simultaneity is possible because the two agencies do not compete. God is fully the primary cause of the full action of the secondary cause. The formula used by scholastic theology in Christology describes God acting generally in the created world: all this-worldly activity is created actuation by uncreated act.

time one can notice a direction "towards increasing complexity and variety of biological forms up to the myriad intricacies of human society."[16] Although the future is unpredictable, looking backward one can read a directionality that led to the appearance of the human. When this view is combined with what was said of primary and secondary causality, God's ongoing creativity can be thought of as not working against randomness but with it as a means of fulfilling God's transcendent purposes.[17] This does not establish purpose but shows that randomness does not exclude purpose.

This, in turn, reflects back on a spirituality of following Jesus. One does not expect that God will accomplish on a historical level what God has enabled human freedom to strive for and achieve. This view entails a certain "self-limitation" of God.[18] It counsels against the idea of waiting for God to manipulate the course of history. And it emphasizes the seriousness of human freedom and the fact that through evolution God has in some degree entrusted history to human decisions.

The thrust of evolutionary history into the future rearranges how one should think of God's relationship to it. When spirituality consults contemporary science, "it is more helpful to think of God as the infinitely generous ground of new possibilities for world-becoming than as a 'designer' or 'planner' who has mapped out the world in every detail from some indefinitely remote point in the past."[19] God the creator and transcendent sustainer of history will be the ultimate principle for history's meaningfulness in an absolute future. Jesus spoke of the final rule of a personal God in an absolute future. This surrounds the cosmos with personality that remains absolute mystery. Despite the violent and seemingly vicious logic of evolution in which all life will ultimately cease to exist, one hopes for a coherent meaning that has a saving character: "There has to be a permanence in the depths of the world process that redresses the fact that nothing lasts."[20]

16. Peacocke, *Theology for a Scientific Age*, 32. See also note 3.

17. "If God works through chance, then the natural creativity of chance itself can be thought of as a mode of divine creativity in which it participates. And the gracious mystery of God can be glimpsed as the Source not only of deep regularities in the universe, but also of novelty." See Elizabeth A. Johnson, "Does God Play Dice? Divine Providence and Chance," *Theological Studies* 57 (1996): 15-16.

18. The idea of the self-limitation of God is paradoxical and intrinsically incomprehensible. It only vaguely states and does not explain how God, as the pure act of being itself, can create, out of nothing except God's self, something that is truly other than God who is being itself.

19. John F. Haught, *God after Darwin: A Theology of Evolution* (Boulder, CO: Westview Press, 2000), 119.

20. John F. Haught, "What's Going On in the Universe?" *Christianity and Science: Toward a Theology of Nature* (Maryknoll, NY: Orbis Books, 2007), 63.

Thus the scientific notion of evolution shifts the center of gravity of faith and spirituality in the direction of hope. This hope has some support within human subjectivity itself. Human beings require meaning, and meaning is often associated with purpose. Generally, human beings look for, if they do not require, purpose for living. Since human existence is not separate from the universe, but precisely that part of the universe that is self-conscious, it is plausible to look for such purpose in evolution on the basis of human subjectivity.

Rearranging the Christian Story

We saw in the discussion of original sin that science has no place in the history of evolution for an event of a fall that alienated the whole human race from the love of the creator of the universe. We cannot turn a religious myth into a historical event: not in the case of original sin nor in the case of the accompanying idea of human redemption being accomplished in a literal transaction between Jesus and God done for us behind our backs. Human existence does seem caught in a web of sin. And Jesus represents a pattern of human life led in the power of the Spirit of God that in various ways counters sin by self-sacrificing love. Jesus saves by revealing a way of life that is sustained by the Spirit of God and that leads to resurrection.

Positively, recognition of evolution in relation to sin contributes two new dimensions to Christian spirituality. One is the continuity between human existence and the patterns of life from which human existence emerged. The continuity supplies the data that explains the violence that obtains within historical human life. This, not the story of Adam and Eve, is our history. But at the same time humanity constitutes a new level of self-consciousness and freedom in evolutionary history. Human beings are called to a new set of standards of behavior above evolutionary competition.[21] Rather than struggling against other humans or other species for survival, humans are called to cooperation and solidarity. This new way of being is not aggressive and assertive against others but consists of responsible service of others, within the species, of other species, and of the planet itself. Jesus's teaching and ministry represent this.

The other dimension opens up a new vision for the role of humanity in the universe. As we saw, "One of the important implications of evolution . . . is that it allows for the transpositioning of the ideal of perfection from an imagined past to a possible future."[22] Salvation

21. See Sally McFague, *The Body of God: An Ecological Theology* (Minneapolis: Fortress Press, 1993), 144.

22. John F. Haught, "Evolution and Divine Providence," *Christianity and Science:*

is not repairing the past or restoring an idealized state of being; the universe is moving forward, and human beings now have a conscious and deliberate role in the project.[23] Evolution told Teilhard de Chardin that spirituality could not be reduced to inwardness or withdrawal from the world. "It is, in fact, in and through action that the spirit unfolds and that spirituality grows."[24] Following Jesus is transformed into an active way of life that is responsible for the world, has an eye on the future, and works toward the project of building new relationships of solidarity.

The Universal Relevance of Jesus within Religious Pluralism

Jesus is universally relevant because he reveals the creator God to whom all reality and human beings are related. But it is remarkable that the hard sciences should be a vehicle opening up the Christian imagination to recognize other religions as autonomous and authentic mediations of God's saving presence to humankind. Science opens up a cosmic horizon that makes it difficult to maintain either an anthropocentric or a christocentric view of reality. "It is not easy for an individual to see Earth as the reality for which the universe exists."[25] The size of the universe gives a better feeling for the infinity of God.[26] Cosmic thinking shifts the Christian perspective from being christocentric to being theocentric.

Once a theocentric perspective is in place, the implications of God's creating become relevant. Creation out of nothing entails God's presence within all reality, and particularly in a personal, gracious, and dialogical way within all intelligent beings. At this point all the arguments for an incarnation within the sphere of intelligent beings on other planets also apply to human history. They support incarnation in the distinctive forms of human being that are constituted by different cultures and societies. To paraphrase Thomas O'Meara, "The abilities of galactic intelligent societies [or human societies that are

Toward a Theology of Nature (Maryknoll, NY: Orbis Books, 2007), 106.

23. Denis Edwards notes these two significant principles for understanding the human that arise from the scientific story of the human: "the human person is profoundly and intrinsically interconnected with every other creature as a child of the Earth and a child of the universe; and the human person has the particular dignity and responsibility which come from being one in whom the universe has come to self-awareness." See Edwards, *Jesus the Wisdom of God: An Ecological Theology* (Maryknoll, NY: Orbis Books, 1995), 143.

24. Ursula King, *Teilhard de Chardin and Eastern Religions* (New York: Paulist Press, 2011), 211.

25. O'Meara, *Vast Universe*, 90.

26. Ibid., 92.

not Christian] and God's love toward them do not demean Jesus of Nazareth."[27] This is rather God as Spirit showing no partiality (Acts 10:34).

The insight revolves around three axioms: the supposition that cultures are deeply different, that God so wants to communicate with all that God will be incarnate to each distinctive culture, and that these incarnations of God's Spirit are not competitive. In sum, we should expect that God will be incarnate in other religions in a way analogous to how God was incarnate in Judaism through Jesus. But this requires a revision of our idea of incarnation.

Reconceiving Incarnation

I turn then to the conception of incarnation that is in place. We should not think of incarnation in the imaginary terms of the panels of a comic strip: God up there, God comes down, and God goes back up again. Incarnation refers most basically to God being the within of all things, the power and love that sustains finite being itself. God does not intervene into created reality because, as Christian spirituality recognizes, God is the "within" of all reality.

Karl Rahner works with the idea that God, as continual creator, sustains evolution. New being and new forms of being are supported by God's inner primary causality or creative power.[28] In so doing, Rahner effectively correlates the metaphysical language of primary causality in creation and the biblical language of the Spirit of God. "The Spirit can be understood as the immanent divine power that enables evolutionary emergence, continually giving to creation itself the capacity to transcend itself and become more than it is. The Breath of God breathes life into the whole process of an emergent universe. The Holy Spirit is the immanent divine principle drawing creation toward an open future."[29]

The idea of incarnation should be expanded. Incarnation should not be thought of as a past event that happened in a point of time, once for all. Incarnation expresses the intrinsic power and love of God as Spirit that encompasses existence from the very beginning. In the first three Gospels, Mark, Matthew, and Luke portray God's incarnation in Jesus

---

27. Ibid., 49. I am here pushing O'Meara's argument to a place where he does not want it to go.

28. Karl Rahner, "Christology in the Setting of Modern Man's Understanding of Himself and of His World," in *Theological Investigations* (Baltimore: Helicon Press, 1970), 9:218, 223-24.

29. Denis Edwards, *Breath of Life: A Theology of the Creator Spirit* (Maryknoll, NY: Orbis Books, 2004),48; also Denis Edwards, *How God Acts: Creation, Redemption, and Special Divine Action* (Minneapolis: Fortress Press, 2010), 44.

in these terms. Jesus is a particular representative of a "deep incarnation" that embraces the universe but has appeared "in these last days" in Jesus (Heb 1:1). This incarnation grounds Christian spirituality by expressing how God's presence and power operated within him.[30]

* * *

In conclusion, I have to ask and respond to the question of the usefulness of this kind of reflection. We all know that this kind of analysis has very little practical effect on the life of the Christian community. Moreover, those who engage in the question of how God acts in the world in dialogue with science are aware of how far their analyses fall short of the mystery that they are trying to describe. Since God's action in history is by definition hidden and unobservable, what use can these various models have? What difference do they make?

I see a twofold function and relevance of this kind of reflection. First, entering this discussion prevents naïve and anthropomorphic conceptions of God's action in the world, which frequently collapse, and thus disappoint, and sometimes occasion scandal. Second, if one enters into the question, the analyses can open up the imagination in a receptive mode to understand the world, ourselves in it, and God in relation to the world and history in positive ways that can energize spirituality. A person of faith lives out some imaginative vision of reality. Better to have a critically sensitive vision that more closely reflects reality. It will have deeper and more lasting power.

These reflections, therefore, may have some positive bearing on a given person's conception of their Christian spirituality. Here I want to dialogue with science by improvising on Teilhard de Chardin's conception of human existence supported by the two hands of God in terms of primary and secondary causality.[31]

The one hand of God is the sustaining power of God's primary causality. God holds each creature in existence by a primary causality

30. Consider another expression of this larger view of incarnation: "In this context, the incarnation of God in Christ can be understood as a radical or 'deep' incarnation, that is, an incarnation into the very tissue of biological existence, and system of nature. Understood this way, the death of Christ becomes an icon of God's redemptive co-suffering with all sentient life as well as with the victims of social competition. God bears the costs of evolution, the price involved in the hardship of natural selection." See Niels Henrik Gregersen, "The Cross of Christ in an Evolutionary World," *Dialog: A Journal of Theology* 40, no. 3 (2001): 205. There is more to be said, but the point here is not to develop a full Christology.

31. Pierre Teilhard de Chardin, *The Divine Milieu: An Essay on the Interior Life* (New York: Harper & Brothers, 1960), 47-51. Teilhard speaks of the two hands of God as the "within" and the "without" of our dependencies on God. It is not clear that primary and secondary causality inspired Teilhard's distinction.

that reaches to every being in its individuality. God as personal and loving is present to each individual being and bears it in existence from within. The other hand of God is precisely not God present to a being directly, but consists of the secondary causes that surround each being within a given system. One cannot read the intentions of God in the events that affect each one of us because, although God sustains them, God does not direct them. But God accompanies each one within both positive and negative events in the web of this-worldly causality, those that promote life and those that destroy it. These two hands of God hold the universe and each one of us in it. Christians hope that God's direct embrace will fill us and bear us up when we finally succumb to the rhythm of the evolving universe.

CHAPTER SEVEN

Personal Spirituality and Ecclesial Authority

Chapter 5 discussed a relationship between spirituality and the church; it suggested that the purpose of the church as an institution is to support the spirituality or Christian life of the members. Nothing could be clearer than that structural relationship. From the side of the individual Christian, spirituality spontaneously reaches out toward community so that the church as social organization is intrinsically part of or entailed in the common spirituality of Christians.

But after that is said, one of the sharpest problems faced by many individual Christians is the failure of church authority in their regard. Does the problem lie with the moral failure of the church member or with the inability of authority to connect? When people abandon the church, what had been offered them by the church or the leaders of the church loses its authority in their eyes. This may involve style of worship or policy on a specific issue: people cannot get past this teaching of the church or that stance on a moral dilemma. Whether it be the tension between the individual person and the common demands made by the church in this or that case, or simply the freedom of the Christian over against loyalty to a particular church, this is a perennial problem in ecclesial existence. The goal of this chapter is not to resolve this tension, for it is an intrinsic dimension of ecclesial life and plays a positive role. But it is useful to have some principles to help understand the issue and to serve as a framework for particular decisions.

The major principles are offered in the first two parts of the chapter. The first part discusses spirituality in the Christian terms of personal sanctification in everyday life with an appeal to classic Protestant and Catholic masters of the spiritual life, John Calvin and Ignatius Loyola. The second part reflects on the nature of religious authority and offers two broad examples of how that authority is conceived spiritually and organizationally in the Catholic Church and in the free church tradition. Part three responds to the question why church authority is needed, and part four underlines the kind of church authority that is needed, namely, one that can negotiate the tensions and affect the spiritual life of Christians positively.

Personal Sanctification in Everyday Life

We begin by discussing spirituality not in terms of specific religious practices, but in the terms set earlier in this book, where the whole of one's action constitutes a person's relationship with God. This conception lends itself to a conception of spirituality that includes the everyday actions of one's life, from relatively private family life to one's public behavior in the work place. Two authors who treat this subject in a classic way from the Protestant and Catholic traditions respectively are John Calvin and Ignatius Loyola.

John Calvin

John Calvin, whose theology has nourished many Protestant churches, described a spirituality of everyday life that a hundred years ago might have been called the dominant spirituality in the United States. This presentation of his ideas draws them forward through interpretation, adaptation, and paraphrase. It is important to mention that this informal description of one aspect of Calvin's spirituality sidesteps his references to the church whose presence was always foremost in Calvin's own mind.[1]

People influenced by Calvin have a strong sense of God and of God's being God, creator and sovereign, who is active in the world. They experience an obligation to recognize God, perhaps even to pray regularly, but certainly to be grateful, and to show this in their behavior.

This sense of God's providence descends to the person as an individual. God is at work in the direction of this person's life. One has a sense of being where God wants one to be, or, if not, it is because the person made some wrong turns. This sense of providence then elicits a sense of vocation, an idea of calling, so that what one does fits into God's plan for things. With these ideas one can see a groundwork for a strong spirituality that affects one's whole life, including one's work.

This spirituality is not static: one grows in holiness or union with God by one's fidelity to one's calling in life. There is no split in one's life between activities that unite one to God and other positive actions

1. For the most part I draw this material from Calvin's *Institutes*: John Calvin, *Calvin: Institutes of the Christian Religion*, ed. John T. McNeill (Philadelphia: Westminster Press, 1955). Calvin's ecclesiology is developed in book IV, but I also appeal to his views on sanctification, law, and the Christian life. See also Ernst Troeltsch, *The Social Teaching of the Christian Churches* (New York: Harper Torchbooks, 1960), 576-617, for a large interpretation of Calvin's view of church and spirituality.

that do not. Life is of a single piece before God, and one advances toward God by faithfulness in one's action. This does not amount to an argument for bypassing the church. Rather, the church is there to enable one to be united with God and grow closer to God through one's life in society.

One external measure for checking in on one's spirituality is the law, the law of God and the law of society. In some respects Luther holds up law as something negative, because it functions to show we are sinners and unable to observe it perfectly. It thus drives us to pure faith in God's forgiveness mediated by Jesus Christ. Calvin however included a more positive view of the law as a guide to God's will for those who want to draw closer to God. This has affected American culture. If we are moral people who strive to act within the guidelines of society, we are at the same time keeping close to God.

Axioms for a spiritual life. Calvin proposes a number of axioms that give some form to the orientation of a Christian to daily life. They are drawn from Calvin's treatise on the Christian life, and they regulate a life that is faithful and close to God both inside and outside the church. These are (1) self-denial, (2) use of creatures according to God's ends, (3) valuing things of this world but only relatively, and (4) stewardship.

First, a Christian should be self-disciplined. He or she has moral standards and lives by them. This person knows the difference between right and wrong, denies the self illicit gratification, and guards against succumbing to the classic temptations of greed and power.

Second, Calvin engendered a sense of God's order for things, especially in society, and a Calvinist tries to behave within those guidelines. God the creator has implanted in things a certain purposefulness, and one tries to work with it.

Third, Calvin knew the difference between an allegiance to this world and to God. Today, the Calvinist knows what idolatry is, and the attachment to God gives one leverage against things and movements in society that implicitly act as God substitutes, especially ideologies.

Fourth, one has a sense of responsibility for the world and for what is given to one's care by God. One has a sense that we will have to render an account of this stewardship, something that extends to one's social responsibilities.

It would be hard to dismiss this spirituality. It is both idealistic and reasonable, and it does not necessarily involve the church. Implicitly, this is the spirituality of many Americans because Calvinism deeply affected American Christianity. But just as American culture has changed and society is rapidly evolving at the present time, so too many who share elements of this spirituality are in a process of moving away from church membership.

Ignatius Loyola

An analogous spirituality is reflected in Ignatius Loyola, founder of the Jesuits, whose major gift to the world was his Spiritual Exercises. These are a series of considerations on Jesus from the Gospels intermingled with other principles of the spiritual life. These Exercises have nourished Catholics and others; they have left an impact on many religious orders. His ideas too are drawn forward loosely through adaptation and paraphrase. What follows is an informal description of a positive spirituality that is Catholic, but it sidesteps the church, something Ignatius could never have imagined.[2]

Ignatius roots his spirituality in the fundamental conviction learned in the catechism that the very reason for our existence is that we know, love, and serve God so that in the end we have eternal life with God. This is the goal of human life. Therefore, all our actions should be directed toward that goal or end. This simplest of Christian principles determines everything else that follows.

A pair of maxims build on this foundation. One is that Ignatius speaks of finding God's love in all things, and in the other he insists that an authentic response to God's love will manifest more by action than words.

The first maxim is based on creation. Because God is creator, God is active in all creation, all the time and right now. Therefore, one can personalize this doctrinal truth by looking at the creation that surrounds one and recognizing that God is working in it for me. In all the things that impact my life and keep me alive, one can see God at work for me out of love. It follows from this that one should respond in gratitude and love for all that God does for us, beginning with holding us in existence. The second maxim attached to this, that a response in action is more authentic and real than a response in words, raises the stakes of what is involved in this spirituality. A real response to God requires action and not just sentimental prayer. One can see in these patterns the grounds for an activist spirituality.

How does one respond? Broadly speaking, Ignatius divides the world into two camps, evil and good, or the sphere of Satan or the city

2. For the most part I draw this material from Ignatius's "Autobiography" and "The Spiritual Exercises," in *Ignatius of Loyola: The Spiritual Exercises and Selected Works*, ed. George Ganss (Mahwah, NJ: Paulist Press, 1991). See also Haight, *Christian Spirituality for Seekers*, xi-97.

of self-interest and the project of Jesus of Nazareth or the city of God. One cannot really straddle the two; bottom line, one is ultimately on one side or the other.

How does one know one camp from the other? Sometimes it is hard to tell, because Satan always poses as an angel of light. But ultimately one has the model of Jesus Christ to guide one. The side of Christ is governed by the direction that Jesus defined in his life's ministry. A Christian spirituality thus comes down to a following of Christ, not as this was defined in the late medieval period by Thomas à Kempis as withdrawal from the world but as active engagement in the world according to the values proposed by Jesus Christ. Jesus Christ is depicted by Ignatius as calling us to service under his leadership.

Service has to unfold within the context of one's place in society. Like Calvin, Ignatius recognized that people are different and have different roles in the world. But everyone can serve God within one's place in society. One works for the values of Jesus Christ within one's own milieu.

Axioms for a spiritual life. One can isolate many axioms for a spiritual life within the writings of Ignatius Loyola. The following four are basic and are chosen to run in parallel with those from Calvin. They are (1) imagining one's life in the likeness of Christ, (2) use of creatures insofar as they fulfill one's purpose, (3) indifference to earthly values compared to our final goal, and (4) the ideal to do the best we can for the greater glory of God in history.

First, one should pattern one's life on Jesus's ministry. This is a spirituality of actively following Jesus Christ; he calls each person, and to follow makes one a Christian.

Second, one should use creatures teleologically, not according to the goal that God has placed in them, but according to the goal of human life. We should use things in a way that accords with God's will for us and leads to salvation.

Third, all earthly motivation should be subordinate to the motive of serving God after the pattern of Jesus and thereby fulfilling life's course in union with God. There is a kind of single-minded purpose that governs this whole spirituality and directs each person toward the final goal. Every particular thing in life's path should be relativized in reference to the goal of existence and following Jesus of Nazareth toward it.

Fourth, the ideal human life consists of service that allows us to say that we did our best to promote the glory of God in history. This consists of helping to effect God's rule for flourishing human life over against the demonic forces that dehumanize and ultimately destroy life.

It would be hard to dismiss the integrity of this spirituality. Like Calvin's spirituality, it too comes across as both idealistic and reasonable at the same time. It still speaks to the present. But note that not one word of church enters in here. One can say that Ignatius simply presupposed the church and therefore did not have to mention it. But it is striking that his Exercises do not stress the sacraments,[3] which is the usual place where the church is drawn into discussions of spirituality. Can one live this spirituality without the church?

In sum, Calvin and Ignatius represent two activist and potentially socially engaged Christian spiritualities that, although they were designed in the sixteenth century, share a certain classic character. They have been presented here, against the grain of each author's attachment to the church, as spiritualities that might attract people independently of the church. This sets up an artificial but instructive tension with the religious authority of the churches.

Religious Authority

We now turn to religious authority. Because of the subtlety of the notion of authority in our time, we begin with a conception of religious authority that tries to take into account a postenlightenment Christian culture. A loose description of two different forms of church authority, one Catholic and the other Protestant, are put into play in order to bring the abstract notion of authority down closer to Christian earth and the tensions that are found in the actual exercise of Christian authority.

The Idea of Religious Authority

It will help to begin with a working definition or conception of what authority is. A working definition may not be the best, but the point is not to defend this conception but to work with it. Recognition that authority refers to a human relationship constitutes a crucial component of what is being referred to. Enumeration of the factors involved in genuine religious authority helps to gain some clarity on a subtle topic.

First, we begin with the following general definition of authority: authority is the ability or power to influence, direct, command, or move another person's thought or way of acting.[4] What are the compo-

3. Ignatius refers to Mass, the Eucharist, confession, and communion, but they are not essential or intrinsic parts of the logic of the Spiritual Exercises (SE). The Exercises are always adapted to those who are making them. It is not that Ignatius is hostile to confession and communion (SE, 44). Rather, if they are available, and people want or need them, they should take advantage of them.

4. I take as a guide for my remarks Joseph Komonchak, "Authority and

nents of this straightforward conception, especially in a religious and Christian context?

Second, not all kinds of authority are the same. Religious authority is not military, police, legal, parental, or professional authority. One has to be attentive to the kind of authority being imagined. A good way to start that discussion is to be clear what religious authority is not. If one confuses religious authority with parental authority, it would mean that the leaders of the church should deal with adult members of the church like children. Drawing out the comparisons in each case reveals a number of possible distortions of religious authority.

Third, and more positively, we can define religious authority as in some measure representing God's authority. This way of speaking refers specifically to Christianity and does not refer to the way other religions represent transcendent reality or this-worldly mediations of religious authority. What makes religious authority religious is that in one way or another God is implicitly involved in its conception and exercise. It is important to be careful about how this is envisaged because it is vulnerable to anthropomorphic views of God exercising authority within history.

Fourth, to begin to think about how God's authority gets drawn into the exercise of religious authority, one should note that God's authority always reveals itself in worldly vehicles: Jesus, scriptures, church, tradition. In other words, because God is God, and thus not directly available to human beings, God has to become known in the world through the things of this world. This is true of all religions and, on close analysis, even of mysticism. All human encounters with God occur in the world, and we cannot escape our place in the world in the way we experience God and God's authority. That provides a context for what all Christians accept: Christians are those who meet God in Jesus of Nazareth. Christians meet Jesus in and through the scriptures. Christians also meet him in the church that preserves the scriptures and the memory of Jesus. And this church has a long tradition that accounts for its present identity, so that this history helps to define how and where Christians encounter God and God's authority. So far, then, Christian religious authority is founded upon a manifestation of God's authority encountered in Jesus, scripture, and church. Using this as a foundation, points five and six propose two necessary qualities for a genuine religious authority.

Magisterium," in *Vatican Authority and American Catholic Dissent: The Curran Case and Its Consequences*, ed. William W. May (New York: Crossroad, 1987), 103-14. But one should not ascribe to Komonchak all the views expressed here.

Fifth, the first of these two necessary qualities for a genuine religious authority is the competence of the one possessing authority. To illustrate the point with extreme examples, no one who appeared to be a bumbling idiot could claim genuine religious authority. To have the ability in our culture to move us to act, a person with authority has to be and appear to be competent. But one should note that competence is not enough by itself to ensure authority. Authority is not reducible to competence because many competent people do not possess authority. Authority needs something more than knowledge and ability.

Thus, sixth, the second of the two necessary qualities of genuine religious authority requires that it elicit a free commitment of trust on those subject to it. Religious authority cannot be coerced; if it were, it would not be religious authority, but police or military or terrorist authority. The forum of freedom for religious authority is quite fundamental; it explains why Vatican II declared the freedom of religion. The inner relationship between a human being and God transpires in the intimate space of one's freedom and conscience; it cannot be coerced by any outside agency, including the church.[5] But at the same time, authority cannot be reducible to the inner commitment of people to some authority figure because it may be that what is taken as an authority is not true, authentic, or real. This would not then be a response to authority but an illusion. The fifth point, on competence, and fourth point, on the integrity of God's worldly vehicles, ensure its religious authenticity.

Finally, in the seventh point, we are able to put these reflections together and define religious authority more fully as a social relationship or covenant between the one possessing authority and those who are free persons who accept this authority. Authority then needs both competence in the one with authority and trust on the part of those who accept it.[6] Everything that follows is guided by this conception. Authority consists of a relationship: it is not the same as competence; it cannot be reduced to possession of knowledge or truth, because this frequently does not command obedience. As a relationship, authority demands competence and free acceptance on the part of those who submit to it.

---

5. Vatican II, "Declaration on Religious Liberty" (*Dignitatis humanae*), I.2-3.

6. Does this mean that those who freely assent to religious authority create it? Do they bestow it on church leaders and pastors? In some respects this may seem to be the case. But more deeply they are responding to God's authority, revealed in Jesus Christ, and communicated through the community which is the church. Their assent to authority does not create authority out of nothing, but freely responding to authority formally constitutes it.

Authority in the Church

The following descriptions of church authority in Catholicism and in the free church will help make the abstract idea of religious authority more concrete.[7] Christian churches have different organizational structures and thus systems of authority. After being socialized into a given structure of the way authority works, individuals will still relate to it in different ways. These broad characterizations of religious authority in two different churches should not be taken as normative. The point is simply to show that authority is mediated differently in different Christian traditions.

Authority in the Christian churches comes from God to the community through Jesus Christ. The historical contact point between the church and God's purposes is Jesus Christ; the churches recognize the continuing influence of God as Spirit in Jesus's name within the church. This authority from God through Jesus may be viewed in two different ways: it may be given to the church from outside itself by Jesus, or it may be given to the church from within its relationship to God. The differentiation describes different theological perspectives and doctrines.

Churches like the Catholic Church see the authority of God in Jesus being handed over to leaders during his lifetime; they then formed a church. Those who see authority bestowed "from within" and from the perspective of the congregation see authority based on the work of the Holy Spirit within those who have faith in Jesus Christ. These communities in turn bestow authority on their leaders. These major differences in conceiving the lines of authority became visible in the sixteenth century and live on today in large churches such as Roman Catholicism as distinct from smaller congregational churches. In one, authority is exercised by people occupying objective offices; in the other, authority resides in the congregation and is bestowed on ministers by the congregation. Many churches stand between these extremes and share the values of both sides. In all cases, however, authority comes from God through Jesus and scripture.[8]

Authority in the Catholic Church. In the Catholic Church this authority is structured in a hierarchical organization of ministries. Parishes have pastors. The authoritative leaders of regional groups of churches

7. The term "free church" refers to churches that have a congregational polity and relate back to the left wing of the Reformation. I trace two such ecclesiologies in Roger Haight, *Christian Community in History: Vol. 2, Comparative Ecclesiology* (London: Bloomsbury, 2014), 219-60.

8. Haight, *Christian Community in History*, 2:276-88.

are the bishops with their helper priests and deacons who lead the parishes or congregations. The pope sits at the top of the pyramid. This is a "sacred" organization because it is taught that God set it up through Jesus. Although critical history does not support this view, it is important to note that it does not support any other single view either. The fundamental rationale for these organizational offices is to provide ministry; their whole purpose is to enable the community to nurture the faith of the members.

Authority works on the premise that those appointed to office are competent and aided by God as Spirit. This responds to the question: where does the authority of those who hold these offices come from? What gives them their authority relative to the people in the church? This authority comes from God through Jesus Christ and more directly through the community or church itself. The officeholder shares in this authority for two reasons: first, because the person has been duly appointed to the established office; second, because the community of members is encouraged to trust that the person so installed in the office is competent. In short, authority is "bestowed" with the office, and it is frequently said that competency is supported by the grace that accompanies the office. But if a member of the hierarchy or a priest demonstrates incompetence, he will lose his religious authority even when he retains his juridical authority.[9]

All authority does not reside in members of the hierarchy or priesthood alone. Vatican II insisted that the whole church is animated by the Spirit of God, so that all members are actively responsible for the church's mission and in that measure share authority. If the church is by nature missionary and ministerial, so that all have a responsibility to witness to the faith, then all must also have some authority in affirming what they witness to. One cannot be a witness without having some potential authority in one's witnessing. The activity of ministry and witness of all the laity implies some kind of correlative role in the exercise of authority. One cannot have responsibility without some correlative share in authority. The problem here is that currently there are very few vehicles in the Catholic Church for the exercise of this authority of the priesthood of all the faithful. This is why Catholics are continually trying to create some vehicles for exerting their rightful authority, and bishops by and large resist them.[10]

---

9. The ideal situation consists of religious authority and juridical authority coinciding in one person or agency. But that does not always happen. On the one hand, a person who holds an office of authority may lose religious authority and still exercise juridical authority. On the other hand, some people exercise charismatic authority without holding office.

10. No one has written more clearly or forcefully for the baptismal rights of the

Authority in the Free Church. It would not be unfair to authority in the free church tradition to describe it as operating "from inside out," if this is properly construed. The designation sets up a contrast of type with the authority that works through an objective hierarchy of offices. That which holds the free church together is the internal principle of a common faith that each member shares. This church relates less to Jesus of Nazareth's setting up of an original structure of the church and more to the Word of God preserved in scripture. The Word of God validates any given church congregation assembled in his name. The members of the church can experience the life-giving Spirit of God. The external structure of the church flows from the community that is established in faith. The community of faith has authority over any given church office. The title of a significant early work of Luther captures the idea well: "That a Christian Assembly or Congregation Has the Right and Power to Judge All Teaching and to Call, Appoint, and Dismiss Teachers, Established and Proven by Scripture."[11] The Word of God of course is transcendent and objective, but it is appropriated by the congregation and empowers it.

The principle of the authority of the congregation as a whole lies in the Spirit of God at work within it. This stands as an almost direct antithesis to an external structure controlling the inner life of the congregation. The head of the church is Christ, and the church stands in a vertical relationship to the Word of God. The external structures of the church flow out from the inner life of the community animated by the Spirit of God. "One finds no official hierarchical structure in the congregation, certainly no vicar of Christ on earth that mediates the lordship of Christ over the members of the church. The church is simply the community gathered in Christ by the Spirit. The church then is entirely lay; it is the *laos* or people of God."[12]

The authority of the minister, therefore, is derived first of all by the delegation by the community of the minister to the office. In effect, reception of the minister's authority is given by this appointment. But the minister validates this authority charismatically by performance. Being installed in an office bestows authority, but this is construed in functional terms rather than gaining an inherent objective power. In

laity and the neglect of their ministerial talent in the Roman Catholic Church than Paul Lakeland. See, for example, Paul Lakeland, *The Liberation of the Laity: In Search of an Accountable Church* (New York: Continuum, 2003); Paul Lakeland, *Catholicism at the Crossroads: How the Laity Can Save the Church* (New York: Continuum, 2007); Paul Lakeland, *A Council That Will Never End: Lumen Gentium and the Church Today* (Collegeville, MN: Liturgical Press, 2013).

11. Martin Luther, *Luther's Works*, vol. 39, *Church and Ministry*, I (Philadelphia: Fortress Press, 1970), 305-14.

12. Haight, *Christian Community in History*, 2:280.

the free church, the objective sanctity of the institution is replaced by an existential holiness and effectiveness of the minister. The minister will reflect an authority that belongs to the Word of God and is supported by the Spirit working within the minister and the congregation.

The Catholic system combines theology and organizational structure to give the ministers a great deal of authority in a descending order; in the free-church tradition, the congregation as a whole enjoys authority given it directly by Christ and the Spirit that is within the community. But the minister can offer authoritative prophetic critique in the measure in which he or she brings the power of the Word of God in scripture to bear on the church in any given situation. "Anabaptism rests ultimately on perpetual spiritual re-creation which derives its authority from the work of the Spirit among men thereby united, and not from ecclesiastical structure."[13]

These two examples rest at opposite poles of a spectrum of ecclesial structures that channel God's authority into Christian life. Between these two types of church authority exists a wide variety of distinctive combinations of the themes that have been outlined. These structural differences do not account for the degree of strictness in enforcing authority. In the end, authority in the church assumes many different forms and styles.

Why Church Authority Is Needed

The question why church authority is needed arises out of a libertarian culture where institutions claiming authority are not respected. An adequate response to the question has to include a healthy view of religious authority that appeals to freedom. That will be described in the next part of this chapter. But it may still be useful to offer common-sense reflections on personal and social needs for religious authority.

Spirituality is too important a matter to be left to individuals.[14] It is surely true that many who have given up on the Christian church design their own views of human life and of their own trajectory. But we are a large human race, and the chances of individuals figuring it all out for themselves separately from all the rest are slight. The idea of a private worldview and spirituality seems paradoxical. By contrast, the church, like religious traditions generally, supplies a community with a common language and a tradition of experience. It has been tested by time and continues to support an impressively large body of people across cultures. In a pluralistic world, this does not overcome

13. Paul Peachey, "Anabaptism and Church Organization," *Mennonite Quarterly Review* 30 (1956): 217.

14. Schneiders, "Religion vs. Spirituality," 177.

the particularity and singularity of this meaning-giving framework, but it surely bears a gravitas and depth that lend it authority relative to any given individual.

Ordinarily, spirituality that is deep, operative, and successful tends to share itself. It looks for like-minded expression in a community's worship and its corporate expression of gratitude to God. It gains authority by not being locked up but shared among others. A spirituality shared in community takes on authority when it provides a framework that buoys up the drowning human spirit, keeps it afloat, and carries it along. Rugged individualism works for some but not for most. The authority of an internalized spirituality may begin to make sense to individualists if they feel coherent meaning slipping away.

Besides the nourishment of the spirituality of individuals, there are social reasons why religious spirituality calls out for authority. Christian faith needs an institution to have an influence on society by its corporate witness. The spiritual life of Christians is something that is relevant for all people. It is conceived as having come from God by revelation, as true, and as destined for all people. This way of life needs a public face and a social embodiment in order to have visibility. A Christian spirituality is not in the end a private affair but a way of life that is proposed to all human beings. It is not something cobbled together by a particular individual. The fundamental logic of Christian faith and spirituality bears a religious authority rooted in its universal relevance.[15]

A community held together by a common authority enables more effective service in society. An individual activist spirituality would be less effective without a social movement to channel it into society. Authority is needed to direct individual spirituality into a corporate movement that is intended to have effects on society and the world. These reasons do not encourage Christians to leave the church, and they explain why some people are still very deliberately, not as a mass movement, joining it.

The Kind of Authority That Is Needed

In a libertarian culture, authority is resented because it is perceived as competing with personal freedom. Libertarianism does not distinguish an authority that supports individual freedom from an overbearing authoritarianism. But in the abstract ideal picture of what authority and especially religious authority could be, authority looks nothing like the imposition of power on freedom but precisely some-

15. These statements are not made from an exclusivist standpoint. Other religions may also make such claims.

thing received in and by freedom. What follows are some projections that stem from the nature of religious, Christian, and in particular genuine ecclesial authority. These fairly straightforward qualities can be verified in each one's own experience.

Generally, every exercise of authority should be competent and intelligent. Negative and positive instances illustrating each of these qualities abound. For example, Pope Paul VI's decision to forbid what is called "artificial" birth control, against the advice of his own commission of experts and pastoral agents who studied the matter together, was motivated more by fear than by intelligence or competence. The ruling was too closely aligned with a particular understanding of papal authority and not concerned enough with people's lives. The positive side of this is that authority always has to be pastoral, and it must appeal to people interiorly as did Jesus. Vatican II firmly insisted that authority in religious matters transpires in the inner conscience of each one and is a matter of freedom. This means that religious authority is effective only if people receive it by saying "Yes, this is true and right."[16]

Authority is exercised in matters of different levels of importance. It is crucial for all concerned to know the degree of seriousness at stake in the exercise of authority. The following three distinct types of subject matter exemplify different degrees of engagement with authority.

Sometimes the church teaches or commands or legislates in matters that are simply disciplinary. Prescriptions may concern the way things are done; they are purely practical. In this case, the authority being exercised is disciplinary authority and is not religious in the sense of affecting one's relation to God. Posture at a liturgical event, whether one fasts or not, whether the clergy dress one way or another, and so on are not religious matters that affect people's relationship with God.[17]

In deep matters of truth and goodness, church authority strives to represent God's will as shown by Jesus of Nazareth in his teaching. It is not obvious how this can be achieved, and it always needs testing. Such claims of religious authority have to be measured by Jesus, the scripture that presents Jesus to us today, and interpretations of the tradition. It also requires theological reflection on whether these interpretations of the revelation of God are intelligent and comprehensible. Such exercises of authority always have their ground in the revelation and faith of the community in God that is focused by Jesus Christ.

Then there are matters between these two, when authority seems to

16. This does not mean that an exercise of authority cannot interrupt human freedom. I will bring up the example of excommunication further on.

17. This sphere extends further than these obvious examples indicate. A whole array of differences among Christians appear to be no more than culturally and socially mediated matters. Some, like sexual mores, take on more importance than they merit.

be commanding something that is not a strictly religious matter but does relate to the whole life of the church community. Here authority enjoys a bias, and John Calvin explains why. Although something may appear relatively unimportant, still God through Jesus wills the well-being of the community, and this requires obedience and respect for church leaders. Thus, indirectly, these acts of authority appeal to God's general will that each member respect this level of church authority for the well-being of the whole community.[18] Breaking off from the main body of the church over trivial matters makes no sense. Yet there is another side to this question: from a social perspective religious institutions are generally conservative. Inertia is hard to overcome, and change is always threatening. But if authority does not attend to the changes in society, it may be lost by attrition.

How does the church decide what can be authoritatively taught? It has all the resources through which God is revealed in the Christian economy. Generally, the external sources and criteria for a legitimate exercise of religious authority lie in scripture's account of Jesus's ministry, scriptural comment on it, the history of the community, and the discipline of theology. When controversy arises over a particular exercise of church authority, there may not be any obvious way of solving the issue immediately. There will always be differences in how to read both the documents of our past and the exigencies of the present situation. Controversy is not always bad, if it is aimed not just at winning but at the well-being of the whole church. Here are some further maxims for appreciating controversy in the church.

In a dispute within the church no party can claim the exclusive support of the Holy Spirit. This particular counsel is necessary because all parties think that the Holy Spirit is on their side. And it may be that the Holy Spirit is on many sides at once. But no one can claim the Holy Spirit against another's claim, except on the basis of objective discernment and reasoning, because a priori the Spirit is the exclusive possession of no one.

Authoritative closure of a still legitimately open question damages church authority by its sectarianism. This is a constant danger in the churches. For example, in the face of external threat from science or from critical history, church leaders overreact and assert a narrow, restrictive sense of identity over against culture. Science and the authentic content of faith cannot be in conflict with each other; one can believe in God as creator and recognize the new story of cosmogenesis and the evolutionary picture of the rise of life on our planet. Religious

18. Calvin, *Institutes*, IV.10.4-5.

authority strays and weakens itself when it wanders into the domains of the sciences. Scientists embarrass their disciplines when they use them in polemics against the spiritual core of religion. But in the end, religious authority has to enter into a culture that is itself influenced by science. Authority has to proffer intelligible positions.

Church authority also has to adjust to the de facto pluralism within the church at all levels. Pluralism does not describe a situation containing purely different views, nor does debate imply that nothing is shared in common. It does not mean relativism. Pluralism means differences within a wider context of common exchange and shared values. The United States is a good example of political pluralism: shared common values, broadly represented in the Constitution, but differing political strategies and parties. We are gradually coming to recognize that pluralism describes the natural human condition. No nation, society, or organization lacks diversity among its members and constituents. Thus, uniformity is not a value, and authority should always reckon on diversity within larger convictions held in common.

One way in which church authority can honor this pluralism consists in presenting its teaching and direction in more open and less specific terms. For example, the language of scripture has wide appeal but requires interpretation that always yields differing views. Teaching authority can use the language of principles and values that are deliberately vague and invite different applications. Such language entrusts to those who receive this teaching the task of responsibly appropriating it within their own particular concrete circumstances. In this way pluralism is allowed to work with and enhance authority.

All this does not take excommunication off the table. Excommunication is an act of authority that becomes necessary in extreme circumstances. At certain times excommunication is needed to protect the identity of the church against something that might seriously compromise it. When, during the Marcos years, a Jesuit bishop in the Philippines announced in all his churches that anyone who tortured others in his diocese was excommunicated by the very act of so doing, he acted with genuine religious authority.[19] Excommunication does not ultimately determine one's relationship with God; it is a disciplinary declaration cutting one off from the public life of the church. But torturing people does affect one's relation to God.

19. An account of his action is given by Bishop Francisco F. Claver, *The Stones Will Cry Out: Grassroots Pastorals* (Maryknoll, NY: Orbis Books, 1978).

Responding to Church Authority

How should members of the church respond to church authority? On the principles that have been outlined here, one can formulate a few guidelines.

Christians should not respond to the authority of their own church as they would to military leaders, that is, by a spontaneous or automatic command–obey reaction. The church is not an army. Nor would it be at all appropriate to respond as children to parents. Such an idea is demeaning and theologically wrong. A response to those with professional skill comes closer, but the sheer pragmatism of a good doctor's or lawyer's first or second opinion does not capture all that goes on in a response to a religious authority. Passive compliance with whatever those in authority say amounts to a misguided rejection of religious responsibility. How, then, does one respond critically, freely, responsibly, and authentically to equally authentic authority?

Many Christians "pick and choose" what they receive at the hands of religious authority. The phrase usually designates a negative practice: it suggests a lack of respect for authority because it winnows out whatever does not fit one's tastes, leaving no obedience at all. This view implies that to question absolute authority in one single respect undermines a genuine response that should respect the absoluteness of religious authority by obeying its every suggestion. But that resembles a parent–child relationship; it also fails to recognize possible distinctions in the subject matter at hand. No thinking person accepts any earthly authority in every respect. Instead of a negative designation, the idea of a "pick and choose" Christian can positively represent mature and responsible church membership. Many people respect authority generally, but in this or that instance feel required to try on other options. The metaphor of "trying on" draws an analogy with wearing a new pair of shoes. One has to walk around in them for a while to see how they fit, how they work, how in this case they make sense in one's everyday life of faith. Social and cultural pluralism makes this possible.

Some may object that "respecting authority" and "trying out other options" cannot be coherently coupled. But this common practice has to be understood in human terms. On the one hand, a person recognizes the good faith and the positive intent of a given prescription by authority. The spirit in which it is proffered and the goal it promotes are well intentioned. But, on the other hand, this person may also recognize its inapplicability in a particular case. There are other ways of accomplishing the same end, and so one chooses another course of action. For example, in Western Catholicism, pastors of parishes are supposed to be priests, and priests are supposed to be unmarried. But in the United States today many women run parishes in various dioceses, and many Catholic priests today who converted to Catholicism after their original ordination and marriage remain married. Is not the church trying these arrangements on? Authority always has built into it exceptions when the practical pastoral result is not achieved by the letter of the law. In time the exceptions become the law.

In sum, a healthy Christian community would integrate genuine authority into a wider self-conception and practical identity. Such a community would bear a respect for an authority that was not self-serving but always looking to the needs of the community and the people in it. This authority should be able to hear criticism, as the kings of Israel were supposed to attend to the prophets who spoke in God's name. This church authority should not be polemical, always looking to criticize positions that are not shared by another church or party in the larger church. This church authority will be positive and constructive. It will promote a culture of holy conversation. Hostile debate in religious matters is unseemly; sharing religious convictions with others and listening to theirs is appropriate Christian behavior. Christian authority should be understood in a way that does not shut down dialogue but promotes it.

* * *

In conclusion, what is to be said of Christian authority? Authority is a fact of social life even though many rebel against it. If one does not respect one authority, it is usually because one respects another. There is no doubt that church authority leans toward being authoritarian. Its main temptation is to wrap this authoritarianism in sanctity and to appropriate to itself God's authority instead of opening up God's authority as a transcendent sphere. The church cannot really claim this sphere as its own, but it should try to communicate it. God as Word and Spirit judge the authority structure of the church and are not controlled by it. Once these basic principles are understood, Christian authority can follow the pattern of Jesus Christ. True religious authority appeals to freedom. Only rarely is it coercive in the name of the whole community. The assurance that authority remains authentic lies in the community's sense of ownership and responsibility for their own church. The best and only real guarantee that Christian authority will function correctly is a mature and responsible church membership on the part of the laity.

CHAPTER EIGHT

Liberation and Spirituality

These reflections on liberation and spirituality respond to a precise question. There is no better way to begin than by stating it clearly. People committed to action in behalf of liberation need a spirituality. What spirituality does Christianity offer them? The issue is not why Christian spirituality needs to be attentive to the demands of the poor and other victims of discrimination. The reasons why Christian spirituality must be liberationist have been made convincingly over the past forty-five years. It should be taken for granted that Christians are to be concerned with liberation. A slightly different issue is at stake in the question of what spirituality, present in Christianity, is summoned forth when people who are dedicated to the project of liberation turn to Christianity and ask about its spiritual resources. This question comes from a different audience, one made up of those who are not sure that Christianity or religion generally has anything to offer to the commitment to human liberation. In addressing that question the aim is to present some clear convictions about what Christianity has to offer and how it may affect the lives of liberationists.

Because this has to be done in a short space, the response will appear more like an outline than an argument. But both those familiar with Christianity and those less so will be able to understand the basic elements of the spirituality that is proffered. The presentation moves forward in three parts. The first explores the language of liberation and spirituality. The second and substantive part brings forward four classic witnesses to Christian spirituality and allows each to highlight a particular element of an integral Christian spirituality. And the third emphasizes the dimensions of ultimacy and finality within Christian spirituality.

Liberation and Spirituality

The words "liberation" and "spirituality" are familiar to everyone, but they do not bear the same meaning in everyone's usage. The discussion, then, has to begin with a brief definition of the meaning of these terms as they are used here. These definitions do not have to be developed at length. What follows simply stipulates aspects of these terms that are crucial for the logic of the position presented here.

Liberation

The term "liberation" is used very broadly because human repression takes many forms. In these reflections "liberation" refers to the process of attaining or assisting others to attain freedom from various obstacles to human flourishing. There can be no doubt that since the nineteenth century social oppression has provided a focal point for understanding liberation. Humanity in the West has gradually become more and more conscious of the social and historical conditioning of individual human beings. We have learned that societies are human constructions, that they favor some and neglect, marginalize, and positively subjugate others, that no society has to be the way it is, that it can be changed, that some people encourage and others resist change, and that human beings can have a less or more conscious role in the process. We have the potential to be agents of social liberation. But other forms of liberation need not be excluded from the concept. It makes no sense to neglect some forms of repressed human freedom in favor of others, even though some forms of human deprivation are more serious than others.

One problem with such an open view of liberation is that it seems to give every liberationist concern an equal voice. It may even open a door to competitive interests. It is one thing to say that every human diminishment requires attention. But in a limited economy of human energy, time, and resources we cannot, either as individuals or societies, attend to all problems with equal vigor at the same time. We need some criteria for measuring importance. To this question a scale of values offered by Bernard Lonergan has some relevance. He begins to rank from below in an ascending scale the needs and values that lie open to human commitment.[1] The systemic denial of basic human requirements like food and shelter calls out for immediate attention. But a scale of other values measures relative importance of various human needs and opportunities for freedom's development.

The first level of values relates to biological needs and pertains to existence itself; this is the sphere of the necessities of food, clothing, and shelter that sustain existence. Without attention to these vital goods life itself is threatened. Other ascending values pertain to the expanding scope of freedom and the values that can fulfill it. In ascending order are social, cultural, personal, and religious values.

---

1. Bernard J. F. Lonergan, *Method in Theology* (London: Darton, Longman & Todd, 1971), 31-32.

Social values include the order of the community that assures the distribution of the necessities of life and thus are close to vital values. Cultural values presuppose vital and social values and address intellectual and artistic potentialities. Personal and religious values define spheres of human fulfillment through love and commitment to transcendent meaning.[2] This scale of values, which arguably is a transcultural anthropological constant, provides a rationale for directing the moral imperative to resist human suffering toward an option for the poor. It states something obvious: "that if vital material needs are not fulfilled no other needs can be fulfilled. The destitute are furthest removed from full humanity, having not even the means for survival, much less the social, cultural, personal, and religious expression of humanity."[3]

In sum, although the demands of liberation are many, those who barely exist on the threshold of life justify a preferential option for the poor.

Spirituality

Rather than argue for a single proper understanding of spirituality, which is not possible, I simply recall here the notion of spirituality described earlier in this work. *Spirituality refers to the way persons or groups lead their lives in the face of transcendence.* In this view, spirituality does not refer to an esoteric sphere: everyone has a spirituality insofar as they have a more or less integrated and coherent lifestyle. That around which it is organized or centered, that which one lives for, may be called transcendent because of the role it plays. Implicit in this view of spirituality is that it resides most deeply in action or patterns of behavior, so that the clearest window into its nature or character consists of the way a person lives. This insight draws on the truism that the real commitments of persons lie embedded in what they do and not necessarily in what they say.

Another set of distinctions is important for this proposal: spirituality may be *unconscious, conscious,* or *cultivated.* An unconscious or not fully conscious spirituality is common enough for all to recognize. Many people just live and do not reflect deeply on their lives; they do not dive below the immediate consequences of decisions that transpire on the surface of life. Others seem to have a reflective hold on themselves; they are aware of who and what they are and what they are doing. But there is a third level of spirituality that can be called

---

2. Ibid.

3. Patricia McAuliffe, *Fundamental Ethics: A Liberationist Approach* (Washington, DC: Georgetown University Press, 1993), 55-59 (56-57).

cultivated. The religions often call for this and offer ways of shaping and attending to personal and group spirituality through various reflections and practices. The point of these distinctions is that the third level of spirituality is not the whole of it; unconscious and simple conscious self-appropriation and action also constitute spirituality. Everyone has a spirituality, and generally it is better to be aware of it than not.

This leads us to the following question: what spirituality can Christianity provide persons or groups looking for a cultivated spirituality that will support an already spiritual human life committed to engendering liberation? What explicit form of spirituality does Christianity hold out to liberationists?

Four Witnesses to Christian Spirituality

The question is large and the resources for a response stretch from Jesus of Nazareth to the present. The history of Christian spirituality is as full as Christian tradition itself. A feasible way of providing an answer, not the answer, to the question may be found by turning to classic spiritual writers. The response that follows summons four witnesses and allows each of them to contribute just one element from his own elaborately cultivated Christian spirituality. These witnesses are John Calvin, Martin Luther, Ignatius Loyola, and Meister Eckhart. They are chosen for no other reason than to contribute to the response to the question themes that are rooted in the classical Christian tradition. Because they cannot speak at length, in each case a single insight is chosen from their spiritual writings, a point that in some measure characterizes the spirituality of each one. Together these four dimensions present a constructed package that is at once ecumenically eclectic but coherently responsive to the question.

John Calvin

John Calvin (1509–1564) had a sense of the awesome reality of God, creator of heaven and earth. God is God and complete sovereign over all reality. Many are aware of Calvin's views on predestination and cannot get past that. But the positive side of Calvin's sense of God's providence easily became a view in which God's particular will was at work in all the events of nature and history. These objective positions of Calvin are the subject of much discussion that interprets him in his context and retrieves what it can in our significantly different culture.[4]

4. For a present-day retrieval of Calvin see Henk van den Belt, ed., *Restoration through Redemption: John Calvin Revisited* (Leiden: Brill, 2013).

That God positively wills every particular event seems extreme today; but God's presence in an accompanying way to each person all the time can be defended. It reflects the primary causality of the creator who constantly creates. The symbol of God as Spirit converts the same idea into personal presence.

A positive retrieval of divine providence in our evolutionary world of process can still incorporate Calvin's sense of God. God is personal, and, standing before God, every human being should have a sense of calling and purpose that is as particular to each one as are the codes of his or her DNA and genetic structure. At this point Christian spirituality offers each one the grounds for a sense of identity that, by being related to God, shares in the absoluteness of the creator's intent. In our world, Calvin's call loses its static and deterministic character; it becomes a unique openness to do what no one else can do. Each one has a particularly valued place that is his or her own in an incomprehensibly large process of creative becoming. God has "appointed duties for every person in his particular way of life," so that every single task one performs will "be reckoned very precious in God's sight."[5] As Troeltsch put it, in Calvin's spirituality a person is "filled with a deep consciousness of his or her own value as a person, with the high sense of Divine mission to the world, of being mercifully privileged among thousands, and in possession of an immeasurable responsibility."[6]

Martin Luther

Martin Luther (1483–1546), as a man of the sixteenth century, had many ideas that are not transportable into our century. For example, he drew some sharp lines between Christian spirituality and participation in the affairs of this world that liberation theologies usually resist. But he also had a conception of the individual's relationship to God that was personally freeing and provided each one with leverage over the powers of this world.

Most are familiar with Luther's doctrine of justification by grace through faith. People do not possess within themselves the resources for their own salvation. Human beings, in the face of guilt and death, have to rely on an ultimately divine power to rescue them from their moral failures and the implications of actions that have demeaned or injured others. Sometimes sin penetrates so deeply into a person's

5. John Calvin, *Calvin: Institutes of the Christian Religion*, ed. John T. McNeill (Philadelphia: Westminster Press, 1955), III.10.6.

6. Ernst Troeltsch, *The Social Teaching of the Christian Churches* (New York: Harper Torchbooks, 1960), 617.

being that only God can forgive it. Only God can overcome the power of death. Faith consists of accepting this dependence on God.

Luther conceived this relationship with God as happening through the mediation of the person of Jesus Christ. It can also be conceived through a relationship with the living creator God. In each case, the bond between a person and God transforms the individual. Within such a relationship, a person receives an internal power over the world by being freed from ultimate fear of the world. Luther expressed this freedom as making people "lords of all" and yet "servants of our neighbors." This spirituality "is lord over sin, death, and hell, and yet at the same time it serves, ministers to, and benefits all people."[7] Herein lies a truly transcendent and spiritual source of power in the sense of freedom. The true witnesses to this power are the martyrs, and liberation movements have quite a few Christian martyrs. But there are many martyrs outside Christianity. The question is whether Christian spirituality could be a resource for such conviction.

Ignatius Loyola

Younger than Luther and older than Calvin, Ignatius Loyola (1491–1556) developed a spirituality that adds another essential element to the mix. In 1521 Ignatius underwent a prolonged conversion that transformed his spirituality of loyalty to the Spanish crown to militant loyalty to Jesus Christ. During a two-year period of asceticism he began putting his experiences into a form that could be shared with others called the Spiritual Exercises. One central feature of this spirituality releases transcendent meaning for liberationists in our time.

The generic essence of Ignatian spirituality in the Exercises is "following Jesus." But this following of Jesus completely transforms the *Imitation of Christ* of Thomas à Kempis that was influential at the time.[8] Following Jesus for à Kempis meant withdrawal from society; in Ignatius it meant engagement with society. Ignatius depicted Jesus as a leader, one who is about to launch a crusade against the forces of evil in order to replace them with the values of the rule of God. Jesus is like an earthly king looking for followers who says to each person: "My will is to conquer the whole world and all my enemies."[9] The following of Jesus thus becomes an activist spirituality committed to a life of being

7. Martin Luther, "The Freedom of a Christian," in *Martin Luther: Selections from His Writings,* ed. John Dillenberger (Garden City, NY: Doubleday, Anchor Books, 1971), 76.

8. Thomas à Kempis (1380-1471) wrote or compiled *The Imitation of Christ,* which consists of a compendium of brief reflections on various themes of Christian spiritual life that are noted for an emphasis on a practical everyday asceticism of withdrawal from the world of distracting superficial events.

9. Ignatius Loyola, *The Spiritual Exercises,* #95.

instruments of God's will for human flourishing. Within a late medieval imaginative framework one finds a structure for active participation in the cause of God within human history. The fundamental structure of this spirituality readily correlates with the project of social liberation.

Meister Eckhart

One might not expect to find liberationist themes in a fourteenth-century mystic, but Meister Eckhart (1260–1327) is full of surprises. Behind his spirituality lie Thomist metaphysical conceptions of being. God is not a being, God is no thing, but the pure power of being itself. As such God is the inner ground of being of all that is. Of each thing and of every person, God is the empowering source of being who is always actually operative within. When one consciously ascends the mystical ladder to union with God, God will ultimately be found within the self as the power of one's own being.

These metaphysical and mystical heights get translated into some astonishing practical conclusions, one of which is found in Eckhart's reflection on the Gospel story of Mary and Martha (Luke 10:38-42).[10] In the traditions of spirituality, Mary and Martha are symbols of contemplation and action, or, in liberation spirituality, of mysticism and politics. Traditional spiritual interpretation holds that Mary the contemplative represents the higher-valued activity compared with Martha's being busy about many things. A progressive interpretation of the two forms of activity calls for alternating phases of life, one person going back and forth between action and spiritual contemplation so that each informs and nurtures the other.

Meister Eckhart's interpretation of this passage contributes a fourth element to a spirituality for liberationists. Martha, he says, has reached the pinnacle of spirituality. Mary, in his view, by doting on the words of Jesus, shows that she is still striving for union with God; Jesus's teaching captivates her, showing that what he is referring to still eludes her. Martha, by contrast, spontaneously takes up the role of service from a position that shows that she has already attained union with God. That mystical achievement of interior union with God gives Martha the resources for ready service in action; she is not striving to achieve anything, but acting out of a union with God that gives her an exalted freedom to serve others. "Martha was so grounded in being that her activity did not hinder her."[11] Martha acts out of a permanent interior

10. Meister Eckhart treats this in *Meister Eckhart: Teacher and Preacher*, ed. Bernard McGinn (New York: Paulist Press, 1986), Sermon 86.

11. Ibid., 343.

moral disposition that reflects a consciousness of being empowered by union with God that releases her freedom into service with absolutely no distraction from the bond with God. Here the antithesis of God's will and human will have been overcome. God's grace cooperates in human freedom in a noncompetitive way as one will to accomplish the rule of God within human affairs. Human freedom becomes the vehicle of God's fashioning in fragments a new liberated society.

Toward a Synthesis

What does Christianity offer liberation spirituality? If a person committed to human liberation embraced Christianity, what would this Christian liberation spirituality look like? The four witnesses together offer a possible composite portrait.

This liberationist would stand self-possessed with an identity that bears an absolute quality because of his or her relationship with God. This person has a position within the history of the human race, in the world, and even within the cosmos. As an individual and as a member of the human race this person would feel mysteriously enveloped by God's accompaniment if not a providence that suggests an already-determined future.

This same relationship would allow this person or group an inward spiritual freedom of being. This can be measured against all the hostile powers, impersonal or social, that threaten human existence. Paul called this a freedom from powers, principalities, and death, a freedom that is real even when it is tinged with psychological fear. God as creator and ground of being becomes a transcendent source of courage.

Jesus of Nazareth supplies a more concrete but still open direction to this spirituality because at bottom a Christian spirituality consists of following Jesus. Jesus is regarded as the revealer of God's rule, the way the world would be according to the intention of the creator God. Jesus is also regarded as the leader who has shown the way. His interpretation of the rule of God is flexible within each human situation but always constant in willing the flourishing of human beings, especially those whose elementary freedom is suppressed.

Finally, this Christian liberation spirituality contains a formula for a style of life, a broad conception of how to budget one's freedom and energy relative to God and God's mission of liberation in history. It is not a budget that puts conscious attention to God and God's mission in competition with each other. Rather, union with ultimate reality and existing in truth, which are the aims of all spirituality, manifest themselves in fundamental moral dispositions that spontaneously overflow in service to God's love for all human beings and all creation. To work for the liberation of God's beloved is to love God.[12]

The Eschatological Meaning of Liberation

We are dealing with a conversation between liberationists and Christians on spirituality. Thus far these reflections have shown how, when they are interrogated by liberationists, Christians can retrieve from their spiritual traditions convictions that have a direct bearing on liberation spirituality. This final section takes up the specifically transcendent and eschatological dimension of Christian spirituality and shows what it adds to "temporally bound" liberation spirituality. This effort follows a classic Christian impulse to represent Christian spirituality as respecting, transforming, and in the end guaranteeing and fulfilling human desires and aspirations.

This will become apparent in three points. First, the question of the whither of any spirituality is a spontaneous and legitimate secular question. It arises from within all spirituality insofar as it is a way of life; the question is not imposed from outside spirituality itself. Second, one can provide in broad Christian terms the material content of what will constitute final liberation. Third, in all of this one has to be attentive to the character of the hope that generates goals and how it in turn relates to the promise of God revealed in Jesus.

Teleology and Eschatology

To begin, it is important to notice the source of the teleological or eschatological dimensions of liberation. The question of where movements of liberation are leading comes from within the movement itself. The question of ends, or goals, or final outcomes is not foisted upon immediate desires for liberation. These questions accompany secular this-worldly endeavors. They are not the same as "will we succeed in this drive for liberation?" They cannot be reduced to "will we overcome?" The questions about temporal outcomes reflect questions of a deeper kind that have more to do with the comprehensiveness of the movement itself and the deeper desires and expectations that fuel it. No

12. This simple statement expresses a large idea. It represents one of several points that are not worked out theologically. The path to a theological rationale might proceed in two steps: the first would endorse Karl Rahner's transcendental analysis of the inner identity of love of neighbor and love of God (see Karl Rahner, "Reflections on the Unity of the Love of Neighbor and the Love of God," *Theological Investigations* [New York: Seabury, 1974], 6:231-49). The second step would be to shift the imaginative framework of Rahner's reflection from an interpersonal to a social context. One loves the neighbor socially in the struggle for social justice.

one can participate in liberation movements without being attacked by frustration. Only occasionally does dedication to the cause of liberation celebrate small successes, not enough to make earthly fulfillment a realistic expectation, only enough to show that some triumphs are possible and to act as a symbol for an absolute future. Eschatology and teleology deal with the final outcome of the concern and efforts at liberation.

Are the symbols of an absolute eschatological or teleological future enough to make the commitment to liberation worthwhile? Such a question runs parallel to life itself. Spirituality defines what one lives for. If a life's commitment to liberation is worthwhile, then one has to have a rationale for it. That is the exact function of eschatology and teleology: they propose a relationship of spirituality to ultimacy.

Imagining the End Time

The content of the end time in Christian spirituality cannot be described in material terms, but only in formal terms that are drawn from life together in this world and projected into the future.[13] This has yielded a number of different Christian conceptions of what is held out in front of human life. The scriptures offer many images of human fulfillment, from the heavenly banquet to utopian or heavenly conditions of justice and peace. Is there another more analytical language about an ultimate future that can preserve the mystery and still provide metaphors for our hopes?

One of the simplest, clearest, most comprehensive, and profound definitions of ultimate liberation from a Christian perspective has been provided by Gustavo Gutiérrez. Liberation consists of being in communion with God and with one's fellow human beings.[14] This conception has to be understood in a way that is both personal and social at the same time. It is not possible to have an integral personal liberation while other human beings are suffering and unfulfilled. It also has to refer to something now and not only in the future. This ultimate transcendent condition can be understood in both this-worldly terms and eschatological or teleological terms. Also, each concept, eschatology and teleology, adds something that the other needs. An eschatological view understands the end of the human project as something

13. This is a somewhat literalist statement, for the human imagination travels where we cannot in this present life. Thus, once called up, the end time cannot not be imagined and has generated an expansive history of images. See John E. Thiel, *Icons of Hope: The "Last Things" in Catholic Imagination* (Notre Dame, IN: University of Notre Dame Press, 2013).

14. Gustavo Gutiérrez, *A Theology of Liberation* (Maryknoll, NY: Orbis Books, 1973), 151.

that God alone constructs, but it is essential that human freedom be involved in that process. A teleological understanding of the end time refers to human activity, but it sometimes suggests deterministic or organic necessity. The process of liberation must be integrated into an absolute dependence on God and the openness of evolutionary randomness. Nevertheless, few short formulas capture so concisely in a contemporary paraphrase the logic of human desire and the dependence on God's efficacy for its fulfillment: human beings in a right relationship of communion among themselves and with God.

The Character of Hope

A spirituality that bears some conception of a transcendent outcome does so in hope. Like faith, hope is not knowledge but a positive disposition of openness to the future in a conviction that the end, like the origin, will be grounded in God. There are reasons for such hope, but they do not add up to anything like a demonstration. One such impulse is instinctual and part of the nature of human existence. A drive toward life and life to its fullest underlies existence itself, and it pierces through the inevitable evolutionary cycle of death. This basic trust in existence reaches for transcendent fullness of being. But this basic trust really constitutes a question about the future rather than a possession of it. In response to this question the God of Christianity promises resurrection. Faith in Jesus's resurrection is hope for the future. Finally, life is full of fragmentary signs of peace, justice, and well-being that hold out a promissory note to human imagination. These signals come together in the Christian hope for resurrection and eternal life.

This hopeful and realistic projection of transcendent life has a bearing on this-worldly spirituality. It bends back and offers a rationale for fixing certain values as the transcendent lure of one's spiritual commitments. But the conception of relationship between human action now and the construction of the end time should also validate the meaningfulness of people's activity in this world. One must be able to say that human action and what it creates in this world somehow count, that they make a difference in the final construction of reality. If the transcendent outcome of reality is not affected in any way by human activity, the material content of human spirituality is rendered ultimately meaningless or irrelevant. In the Christian conception of things human freedom is not deception. Its creativity is itself a gift of God, and that which it creates well will become an integrated part of the end time.

* * *

We began this reflection with the question of what Christianity had to offer in response to questions that might be posed by liberation spirituality in matters of the depth of spiritual grounding and the transcendence of outcomes. Can Christianity enhance liberation spirituality?

Gustavo Gutiérrez, with his differentiation of levels of meaning contained in the symbol "liberation," offers a framework for a comprehensive response to this question. This means that the term "liberation" is used to recapitulate the transcendence that measures the human commitment and action that is spirituality. When it is so used, it has three distinct but integrated senses that show the full scope of human spirituality and liberation.[15]

On a first level a Christian spirituality of liberation describes a commitment to the flourishing of human freedom in history. Humanity's distinctive kind of being is defined by its inner or spiritual freedom. A liberation spirituality is committed to the service of human freedom or self-determination as a primary this-worldly object that is worthy of this commitment. It also pinpoints those most in need of assistance, those deprived of freedom at the most basic level of existence, as the primary subjects of human concern.

Second, this human freedom is materially constituted in and by social relationship, by the actual social conditions in which it exists. Freedom may be diminished by society, or it may be more fully actualized by benign and nurturing social structures. The Christian commitment to the social flourishing of human life attends to and promotes liberating social structures.

Third, liberation accurately translates in our period of time the meaning of the term "salvation" in Christian tradition. "Liberation" subsumes into itself the earthly meanings of liberation and realistically hopes that in an eternal sphere the questions of meaning will be answered and the debts of innocent suffering will be repaid in justice and peace. It is important to see that this third explicitly transcendent dimension of hoped-for liberation draws the first two into itself. Existential participation in this third meaning of liberation is utterly ungrounded and empty without the first two dimensions. At the same time, without it, it is hard to see real ultimacy in exclusively personal or social liberation here and now. Thus, Christianity does more than accommodate liberation spirituality; it offers it transcendent ratification.

15. Gutiérrez, *A Theology of Liberation*, 149-87, discusses the levels of salvific liberation that are instructive for spirituality.

CHAPTER NINE

The Logics of Liberation and Spirituality and Ecospirituality: Two Facets of Creation Spirituality

This chapter seeks to isolate an inner core that is shared by liberation and ecocentered spirituality. The term "logic" points to this basic rationale. These spiritualities can take many different forms when faced with various local situations and mechanisms of human and ecological degradation. But if these two spiritualities are looked upon as distinct species that fall under the umbrella of a common genus or family, we should be able to find an essential structure that analogously aligns them in a critical reformist genus. I aim first of all to capture the inner logic of these two spiritualities and, by laying them side by side, implicitly to compare them. On this formula, this could be called an essay in comparative spirituality.

Liberation and ecocentered spiritualities extend beyond Christianity. One needs to be neither Christian nor religious to take up either one of these spiritualities. From different perspectives one could say that Christian faith was either grafted on to these spiritualities or they were absorbed into it. In either case, one can both distinguish them from Christian faith and, on that assumption, one can ask what specifically Christian faith contributes to this secular commitment. I will offer this analysis in the third part of the discussion. It will show that these spiritualities relate as two species that fit under the genus of creation spirituality and that both enrich Christian spirituality and are enriched by Christian faith.

Before moving forward, however, I should recall the meaning of the term "spirituality" as it is being used in this book. The analysis depends on this conception of spirituality. Spirituality refers to the way persons or groups lead their lives in relation to what they consider ultimate, transcendent, or of all-embracing importance. This is a secular definition; all human beings who live consistent lives have a spirituality that is essentially defined by the way they live. What is ultimate for them appears in the consistent patterns of their action.

This may or may not exactly correspond with their stated purpose in life. But on the premise that we are what we do, that our real commitments are those born out in our actions, ultimate reality for us manifests itself in the way our lives actually unfold.

This conception of spirituality so defined always unfolds on two levels: one is the existential level of actual life, and the other is the reflective level of analysis. The one level is lived out in action, with or without explicit analysis. The intellectual analysis, the other level, can be simple or highly developed according to different religions, worldviews, disciplines, schools, and so on, that serve as the matrices for understanding human life. It should be clear that what follows is a highly abstract examination of what can be compelling ways in which human beings direct their lives on the ground.

The Logic of Liberation Spirituality

I begin with an attempt to schematize the logic of liberation spirituality. There is no single way of doing this; what is going on in a corporate human commitment can be depicted in any number of ways.[1] To represent this spirituality without a historical account of one or other of these movements compounds the abstraction. But I suppose that readers are familiar with liberation movements and liberation theologies. The point then is not to contribute new knowledge about liberation spiritualities but to set up a framework that can be used to enable a comparison between both of these forms of spiritual commitment. Thus, both spiritualities are considered according to a structure with three dimensions: first, a negative experience of contrast; second, a categorical imperative that urges a moral response to the situation in a purely formal way; and third, a positive moral commitment or fundamental option that constructively guides responsive action and even programs.

Negative Experience of Contrast

I draw this category of a "negative experience of contrast" from Edward Schillebeeckx, who borrowed it from neo-Marxian critical social theory.[2] The term indicates an experience that something is radically and intrinsically wrong. This is in varying degrees a direct intuitive experience, whether beginning with a vague sense or devel-

---

1. I have described the spirituality of Latin American liberation spirituality in Roger Haight, *An Alternative Vision: An Interpretation of Liberation Theology* (New York: Paulist Press, 1985), 233-56.

2. Edward Schillebeeckx, *Jesus: An Experiment in Christology* (New York: Seabury Press, 1979), 621-22.

oped into an absolute conviction. The feeling or perception indicates that a certain social situation or action or an event is more or less radically wrong: "this should not be!" This experience has roots that are deeper and prior to the explanation of why something is wrong. Such perceptions can be occasioned by situations or events that are personal and limited, but it also applies to convictions that accepted social behaviors are wrong and that the social conventions that sustain them are corrupt.

Some kind of negative experience of contrast lies beneath all liberation movements. Some social situation is widespread and scandalous, one that causes repugnance or outrage, not only in those who are its victims, but also on the part of anyone who becomes aware of it. The experience does not depend on analytical understanding: one can be shocked by gratuitous injury to a child before as well as after understanding why it happened. Historical and social explanations frequently intensify the moral reaction. I do not need to recite the statistics of hunger in the world, the greedy politics that engender poverty, or the lack of concern that supports massive deprivations of what are considered fundamental human rights by most peoples. There are too many situations that summon forth a negative experience of contrast between an existing situation and what should be.

In Latin American liberation spirituality, the conditions of poverty in which such large percentages of citizens of various countries exist provide the contrast experience that fuels the demand for liberation. In North America, black liberation movements react against the racism that remains long after the institutions of slavery have been officially dismantled. It is deeply engrained. Women who are protected by law are still openly discriminated against in a culture that allows institutions to continue to practice what law and morality forbid. Other communities such as gays have mobilized to represent their situation and their cause. Wherever groups form a collectivity that is consciously aware of patterns of human oppression, one has the seeds for a liberation movement and spirituality.

Categorical Imperative

A negative experience of contrast gives rise to reflection both on what is wrong and what should be done. The language of a "categorical imperative" comes from the moral reasoning of Immanuel Kant. It has the merit of rooting moral response in the essential social structure of human existence. The demand to act morally is not imposed from outside a person or society. As a formal structure it can be experienced within the self in a most rudimentary sense of duty. The idea that such an inner command is "categorical" means that it is absolute and unconditioned; it is a structure of being human. A categorical imperative transcends particular situations so that it is not dependent on certain particular cultural or social conditions but forms part of conscious existence itself. To achieve this status it must be a formal or structural demand rather than a material course of action.

Kant formulated his view of the categorical imperative in different ways, but the gist of all of his formulas is that the human person enjoys an inalienable value; a person should never be used merely as a means to another end.[3] No human person should be treated in a way that would be unacceptable as a common standard for all, including oneself. One can see that this absolute norm has a direct bearing on life in society. Any social system or institutionalized pattern of behavior that does not respect the absolute value of the human person is objectively wrong. This absolute moral rule cuts through relative secular or religious ideologies that are used to rationalize social injustice.

Fundamental Option

If the categorical imperative provides a formula for discerning why an action or a situation departs from basic moral standards of humanity, a fundamental option more positively points the direction of negating the negation and righting the wrong.[4] I use this term in a nontechnical way to distinguish an all-encompassing orientation of a person or group, as distinct from a concrete choice of this or that object. It refers to a deep orienting commitment of the will toward certain values that influences concrete decision making. A fundamental option consists of a commitment to channel behavior in a way that counteracts the prevailing negative situation in its personal, social, political, or cultural form. A fundamental option remains quite distant from strategy or policy for social change. Everyone sees the common good from the perspective of their own interests. Any complex social situation will require a good deal of concrete planning and negotiating. But all

3. Immanuel Kant, *Fundamental Principles of the Metaphysic of Morals* (Buffalo, NY: Prometheus Books, 1988), 58.

4. The term "fundamental option" is drawn from Karl Rahner's theology of freedom. It means the combination of the intentional commitment of a person's whole life and all the concrete decisions that together actually constitute a person's total commitment. Rahner's view here describes the existential self-disposition and being of a person and not the character of an individual act. See Karl Rahner, "Theology of Freedom," in *Theological Investigations,* Vol. 6, *Concerning Vatican Council II* (Baltimore: Helicon Press, 1969), 183-87. I am using the category in an analogous way to capture a fundamental moral disposition or habit, broadly differentiated, from which positive actions flow in a certain direction.

of them take place within the context of a shared moral disposition. Without a fundamental commitment to the task, prior to agreement on specific goals, there will be no action at all.

The "preferential option for the poor," formulated by Latin American liberation theology, provides one of the best examples of a fundamental social option directed against massive poverty and generally dehumanizing conditions of life. It is important to notice that the poor spontaneously buy into an option for the poor because it is in their interests. This is true even though the masses of the poor may not agree on what will truly ameliorate their situation. Still, much more interesting is whether a cross section of society can be attracted by a common good that embraces all in society. This requires that those who fully participate in society and the economy have a sense of social responsibility that is not satisfied with a fundamentally unjust, or racist, or sexist community. The preferential option for the poor, therefore, is an example of a response to a negative situation that tries to engage everyone in a society where all have a stake in what is truly a common good. In short, the option for the poor is most evidently moral when it is an option *of* those who are more advantaged. It is true that the goal of liberation theology is to give poor and oppressed people their voice so that they can perform as subjects of history. But it is also clear that without buy-in from the powerful the goals of liberation theology will not be achieved.

In sum, the inner core of liberation spirituality consists of an experience of some mixture of scandal and compassion that elicits an outrage at human destitution, a moral critique of the status quo, and a positive and pervasive commitment to a course of action that will ameliorate the situation.

The Logic of Ecocentered Spirituality

This second section offers an account of the most rudimentary logic of ecospirituality. I use the same pattern of analysis as the one used in liberation spirituality. This provides correspondences for comparison between the two spiritualities. There is a good deal of interpretive contrivance in the setting up of these patterns of analysis. These analytic structures are not meant to be restrictive but to open up a fuller descriptive and imaginative conception of what is going on in these spiritualities.

A Negative Experience of Contrast

The negative experience of contrast that supports an ecospirituality can be simply aesthetic. Consider a sweeping landscape of low-ranging wooded mountains with their tops leveled and bared by strip mining for coal. Picture beautiful lakes and rivers that are actually polluted and dangerous. Imagine the stories of the development and the intricate lives of the thousands of species of plants and animals that are yearly becoming extinct. A human project that appears beautiful and constructive loses its aesthetic substance and may cause revulsion when it systematically destroys life. How many large projects around the world today illustrate this principle?

But the negative contrast experience that underlies ecospirituality penetrates more deeply when it is mediated against the background of an appreciation of the scientific story of the formation of the universe. This story begins with an unimaginable explosion of energy at the beginning of our universe about 13.7 billion years ago. From that moment the universe has been expanding in all directions and forming millions of galaxies of stars analogous to the Milky Way, each containing innumerable stars that may have local systems of planets like our own. Our planet was in existence for billions of years before it first generated life. Organic living things emerged from one primal ancestor that gradually evolved into the millions of species of life now found on the planet and millions more that came into being and have gone extinct. *Homo sapiens*, our own species among the mammals, is rather late in the whole story of the universe and in the story of life.

Several features of this story make it more than a bundle of scientific information. First of all it is a story: reality came into being and developed over time. Because of its size and age, the story has an awesome, mesmerizing character; because it is our story, we are engaged in it; because it binds all reality together in a temporal causal connection, it communicates a sense of solidarity with all creation. That is the case chemically. As individuals we are constructed of the material of the universe, and we bear the history of its coming to be within us. In other words, the world of nature and especially of life is not merely an external context of our autonomous rational lives. Rather, we *are* that part of the physical biosphere that has become conscious of itself. This sense of an inner bond with other creatures is a part of ecospirituality.

The destruction of life on the planet leads to a negative contrast experience that grounds an ecospirituality at a level of consciousness deeper than the aesthetic. Long-range, the perception senses the destruction of our own habitat and with it the extinction of human life as well. But the essence of ecospirituality is not anthropocentric. One can distinguish three phases of evolution on the planet Earth after its initial formation: the gradual geological rearrangement of the planet, the rise and development of plant and animal life forms, and the appearance of human beings. The prehuman biosphere has had a spectacular history of development and interconnectedness within itself before the emergence of human self-conscious freedom. The intricate, dynamically interrelated existence of so many species of life, the integrity of the whole sphere of plant and animal behavior, especially as manifested in local systems, together forms a biosphere that is valuable in itself and not simply because it is our prehistory. The destruction of species on a mass scale, not just by "natural" extinction but simply by "clearing away" in order to "make room for" human activity, appears as something massively wrong. The statistics of this destruction are just as stunning in size as the statistics of human hunger, and they are often interrelated. In other words, there is an enormous violation and degradation of nature going on here.

Categorical Imperative

The categorical imperative that condemns wanton destruction of life forms is, like Kant's, also unconditional. But it does not lie on the surface of consciousness. It has to be mediated by premises and always needs discussion in its application. First of all, this categorical imperative is founded on the ontological value of various forms of life. Ontological value refers to the intrinsic importance of a form of being and its individual instantiations. One could easily design scales of value among the intricacies of life along various spectra. But each species has a value in itself. This means that its value cannot be reduced to its usefulness to human beings. Construing them in a one-way relationship to the human, as beautiful, entertaining, and useful for human consumption, health, and recreation, easily overlooks the "in-itself" or ontological value of other beings

This introduces a contentious area that is intrinsic to ecospirituality and frequently rises to the surface of discussion. It has to do with the place of the human in the spheres of planetary existence. To oversimplify, on one side an anthropocentrism regards the emergence of the human as the vanguard of evolution. As the highest form of life, a life that broke out of subaltern forms into self-conscious freedom, the human dominates creation and has assumed responsibility for its development. On the other side of the equation lies not biocentrism, which would assume in its turn dominant rights, but a conception of integral interconnected life on the planet that recognizes the ontological value of species that is independent of human assessment and usefulness. Ecospirituality depends on a transition from reliance on "instrumental reason," operating within an anthropocentric bias, to a form of "embedded reason," which thinks within a broader horizon of human life constituted in an integrated matrix of many interconnected forms of life. Without this conversion against the grain of anthropocentrism ecospirituality will not be convincing.

The categorical imperative for ecospirituality may be expressed in different formulas, but one of its moral philosophers is Thomas Berry. He articulates the eco-categorical imperative in this way: "The one thing necessary is to appreciate that the Earth itself and all its living and nonliving components is a community, that the human is a member of this integral community and finds its proper role in advancing the well-being of this community. There can be no sustained well-being of any part of the community that does not relate effectively to the well-being of the total community."[5]

Fundamental Option

It is much more difficult to construct the fundamental option of ecospirituality in concise language than it is in the case of the various forms of liberation theology. Of course it may be an option for a definite plant or animal that is threatened in a specific ecosystem. But the individual cases, even when they are piled up, do not convey what is at stake in ecospirituality.

Perhaps the best approach to this dimension of ecospirituality will be through a contrast and an adjustment of a point of view that most would accept. One can find a general resonance with John Calvin's principle of stewardship. He formulated it this way in his *Institutes*: "all those things [creatures] were so given to us by the kindness of God, and so destined for our benefit, that they are, as it were, entrusted to us, and we must one day render account of them."[6] All would agree with this implicit charge and resultant commitment to care for the Earth. The religious form that Calvin gives it finds resonances in a naturalist anthropocentrism: human beings are in charge, and even ecospirituality has to make its appeal to human beings. But the problem is that responsibility for care easily slides into domination: what is good for humanity is good for the world.[7]

The fundamental commitment of an ecospirituality has to be elicited out of an "embedded reason," one that thinks ecologically in terms of respect for all forms of life and harmony of the species within their

5. Thomas Berry, "Teilhard in the Ecological Age," *Teilhard in the 21st Century: The Emerging Spirit of Earth*, ed. Arthur Fabel and Donald St. John (Maryknoll, NY: Orbis Books, 2003), 63.

6. Calvin, *Calvin: Institutes*, 3.10.5.

7. Elizabeth A. Johnson, *Ask the Beasts: Darwin and the God of Love* (London: Bloomsbury, 2014), 265-67.

environments. This form of consciousness is both lord and servant; it has to admit that the ontological value of other forms of life makes a claim on moral decision making. To call this a fundamental option for social and cultural patterns of behavior or laws that respect the varieties of life in their specific differences does not have much rhetorical punch. But it describes the fundamental desire, option, and commitment of ecospirituality.

In sum, ecospirituality rests on an epistemological appreciation of the autonomous value of life forms other than the human and a respect for them. On this basis it is shocked by the wanton destruction of the planet's systems of life, apart from self-interested concern for the survival of the human species. The categorical imperative of this spirituality is the intrinsic demand that the human be fitted into the communitarian web of life out of which it was generated. And the fundamental option of this spirituality consists of a commitment to promote policies and behaviors that respect the interrelational integrity of life.

What Christian Faith Adds to These Spiritualities

The object of Christian faith is God as God is revealed in the person and ministry of Jesus of Nazareth. The doctrines of this faith are presupposed here. The question I raise pertains to the influence Christian spirituality may have on each of these two spiritualities and how they in their turn influence Christian spirituality. One does not have to be a member of any religious body or a believer in transcendent reality to be a liberationist or to have an ecocentered spirituality. But being a Christian injects into these spiritualities new depths and relevance, and drawing these spiritualities into Christian faith transforms it. The impact is felt in both directions. There is surely a space for these spiritualities within Christian faith, and when they are absorbed, the experiences behind them and their languages affect the shape of Christian belief. They force faith to expand its vision under the pressure of these imperatives and fundamental options, and they give it contemporary relevance. And when Christian faith merges with liberation and ecospirituality, it instills in them new breadth, depth, and height of meaning. I offer only a line sketch of these transformations in keeping with the restraints of this statement. Each of the points that are simply stated here could be expanded by descriptive historical examples.

God, as Personal Creator, Injects Intentionality into the Universe

Faith in God as creator of heaven and earth lies at the foundation of Christian faith. This creator God is personal. Christian faith goes further and describes the character of God as good, as friendly, and as the lover of what God creates. At the center and very heart of reality is divine goodness and love. Faith supports and confirms a deep inner bond of unity to the whole of creation. All human beings share more than a common descent: they are a community of persons under a single loving God.

But one must understand that God cannot be construed as an individual person because of the limitations that are inherent in the image. To be God, God must be infinite being, the power that creates, out of no preexisting stuff, all finite reality other than God's self. Such a God cannot be imagined accurately, and therefore cannot be designated as *a person*. But we affirm an infinite source and ground of being that incorporates within God's "self" all that we know of personal being. To imagine God as an individual, as the term God inevitably suggests, creates enigmas that cannot be resolved. But once that has been said, the conviction that the source and permanent ground of being itself is personal transforms all reality by informing it with intentionality. The attributes of personhood applied to God—intelligence, will, feeling, desire, intention, and purpose—will always be subject to anthropomorphic distortion. Nevertheless, criticism of that inherent tendency opens up the human spirit to a transformed view of the evolutionary world, the whole biosphere, the phenomenon of the human, and its place in this overwhelming scene or space. Acceptance of a personal creator paradoxically introduces profound intimations of intentionality and purpose into a system that runs on the basis of contingency and randomness mixed with the steady patterns of energy and matter.

God Is Present to and Accompanies the Unfolding of Evolution and History

The first point entails this second aspect of Christian faith when it is brought to bear on liberation spirituality and ecospirituality. The first point displays God as encompassing all reality by creating power; this second point emphasizes how this involves God's personal presence within all of reality as the power of its being. In other words, because creation is an ongoing action of God, God constitutes the "within" of all being as the sustaining cause of its being. To put this in personalist terms, God does not remain "up there" and "out there"; such "physicalist" language distorts the transcendence of God as well as God's suffused presence within created reality. God's transcendence is precisely that which allows God's immanent presence to all reality. To communicate this idea Christians used the language of the Jewish Bible and spoke of God as Spirit: God as Spirit is no other than transcendent God at work within the finite world of spirit and matter.[8]

Faith's conception of God has implications for the existential character of spirituality. It means that God accompanies reality in its evolutionary and historical development. God sustains the becoming of reality; God empowers it; and God is present to it in a personal way. Human beings are accompanied in their spiritual quest, in their making their way through life and in their commitments. Human beings are not isolated or alone in the universe.

The description of the Christian faith through the lens of liberationist and ecocentered spiritualities brings out another dimension of its character. It is not the case that God is a known object whose existence is threatened by the suffering caused by human oppression or the violence of the evolutionary process. It is rather that these are the givens of the natural world and history. Human suffering does not undermine religious faith but may be its point of departure. God appears within these processes as the constructive power of actual being, and thus in some measure as revealed in or by these negativities as the ground of a positive standard of what should be. In both cases God "appears" within the negative contrast experiences as a source of empowerment to resist what liberationist and ecospirituality confront. God gives meaning to both spiritualities by being a God who is the basis of justice, of compassion, and of life.

God Encompasses and Sustains Reality and Offers a Promise of Permanent Value

Christian faith brings a third dimension to the spiritualities of liberation and ecocenteredness, namely, a promise that the processes of evolution and history have permanent meaning and value. This conviction marks the significance of faith in the resurrection of Jesus through the power of God. Jesus is not an isolated individual phenomenon but a revelation from within a religious tradition that has universal import. His ministry and his destiny reveal both the character of God and of human existence. The story of Jesus as a mediation of a revelation of God tells not only of his destiny; it reveals what has always been going on within the dynamics of ongoing creation from the beginning. The inner Spirit of God who raised Jesus out of death and into the eternal life of God bears witness to the permanent ontological value of what evolution and history constructively create. From a secular point of view the destiny of the evolving universe and life in this world is death and a return to nothingness. The promise of resurrection transforms

8. Ibid., 134-43.

that death into life. Faith mixed with hope bestows on the evolving universe, the human history in it, and each individual person an ultimate value.

* * *

Liberation spirituality and ecospirituality are both secular spiritualities that respond to scandalous negative experiences of destruction that are perpetrated by human beings against other human beings and against the natural world. The massive negativities of social suffering and destruction of nature's web of life evoke committed resistance. And this in turn becomes an authentic and coherent secular spirituality. The value of oppressed human persons in themselves and the besieged biosphere in itself are worthy objects of the commitment of individual persons and the social movements sustained by them. Both are from different perspectives liberation movements; and both address forms of destruction of the creation that has evolved up to this point in time.

The thesis of this chapter is that Christian faith enhances these spiritualities and is enhanced by them. Christian faith in the God of life, creator of heaven and earth, revealed in the Jewish prophets and in the ministry and person of Jesus of Nazareth, gives these spiritualities a qualitatively new transcendent depth, height, and meaningfulness. Nothing positive in these spiritual ways of life is lost; but new dimensions of permanent meaning and fulfillment transform them. In absorbing these spiritualities, Christian faith too is transformed; it is given a new language for understanding itself and new relevance for life in the present moment. It would be an absolute mistake to read these two distinct spiritualities as competing for human investment. Read in the context of a larger creation spirituality that is revealed in Jesus's ministry, they can only be understood as enhancing each other. They not only coexist but also at certain points overlap and complement each other, because so much of the despoliation of the earth serves the interest of certain groups at the expense of others.

CHAPTER TEN

Four Gifts of the American Church to the Universal Church

Is it the best of times or the worst of times for the Catholic Church in the United States? I want to propose that, while things could be better, the American church is in relatively good shape in terms of its resources to solve its current problems and to contribute something to the universal Catholic Church.[1]

More specifically, the thesis I want to offer is that at this stage in history the American church has four gifts to offer to the universal church. The first has already been written into universal church doctrine, whether or not it has been internalized around the world. That is the doctrine of religious liberty. Three other extended experiences in the American church may develop into doctrines for all. The first concerns the place and role of women in the church. The second has to do with the place and role of the laity in the church. And the third will define the grounds for an open and positive evaluation of other religions.

To elaborate this grand vision of the vocation of the American church briefly and schematically, I will proceed in four stages. First, I will set up the model of how the doctrine of religious freedom came to be experienced in the American church and, chiefly through the agency of John Courtney Murray, became a Catholic doctrine at the Second Vatican Council. With that experience as an example I will ask whether these other typically American experiences might also be channeled into doctrine for the whole church.

In all of this, I grant that I project a vision of a possible future that is idealistic, perhaps overly so. But, given the experience of Vatican II, we should not underestimate the power of God as Spirit within the community. I want to probe beyond the flagrant crisis that the American church is currently undergoing and urge a deeper historical role with

1. The term "church" obviously refers to the Roman Catholic Church in this essay. Although it was written over ten years ago, I have kept it in its original form. For many in the church after the sexual abuse crisis was first exposed it was the worst of times.

which our church has been charged and from which we should not be distracted.

Religious Freedom

I begin with the doctrine of religious liberty that was taught at Vatican II in order to show how it made complete sense in the context of the American Catholic experience. The doctrine of religious liberty of Vatican II says all human beings enjoy freedom in their religious commitments. Assent to religious doctrines or membership in a specific religious group cannot be required or enforced by an outside social agency. Each person has a natural, inner right to self-determination in his or her religious commitments.

Murray's role in shepherding this doctrine through the council is well known. He was of course an American, familiar with the Enlightenment principles on which the United States was founded, and a scholar of the history of church–state relations. Murray had collaborators at the council, and not all reasoned in the same way. But Murray's own position had its roots in the American experience, and in some measure this is reflected in the conciliar decree.[2] Let me describe in general terms how this came about so that I may use it as a model for what is to follow.

The American Constitution

I begin with the American Constitution and its First Amendment. Often this amendment is referred to as positing a wall of separation between church and state. It is no wall, but rather a twofold guarantee that the government will not establish and not interfere with religion. It reads as follows: "Congress shall make no law respecting an establishment of religion, or prohibiting the free exercise thereof. . . ." We all know how difficult it can be to interpret the application of this simple idea in concrete cases. But all Americans can delight in the benefits of the exercise of religion in freedom, not only without interference from the government, but with protection by the government.

American Catholic Experience

The American Catholic experience in the course of the nineteenth and early twentieth centuries is a dramatic success story. I'll not tell that story here, but I want to highlight a couple of aspects of it. Catholic

---

2. Herminio Rico, *John Paul II and the Legacy of Dignitatis Humanae* (Washington, DC: Georgetown University Press, 2002), 38-41.

immigrants arriving in the nineteenth century both did and did not experience the separation of church and state. In fact, the United States in many ways appeared to be a thoroughly Protestant nation. For example, elementary schools were often fundamentally Protestant in their ethos. But Catholics were free to build a parallel Catholic society and culture, with schools, aid to the poor, health care, and in the end associations for almost every profession. After World War II, a fairly established Catholic population, newly educated at government expense (through the G.I. Bill) continued to enter the mainstream of American public life. The result was an educated, public church made up of a modern and even postmodern laity that was also believing and practicing. American Catholics experience a government that is friendly, supportive of religious freedom, and protective of the right to develop religious-based institutions, which have in turn been put to the service of the wider public. The Catholic Church in the United States has thrived in a modern industrial nation structured by enlightened rational principles often associated with natural law.

Confronting the Obstacles

The European experience of church and state has not been so benign. The very topic arouses memories of different national experiences. Sometimes national governments had to free themselves from the influence of the churches: they may have taken over what had been the functions of churches, or expropriated church property, or persecuted the church. The process of the secularization of governments in Europe, therefore, undercut many of the privileges enjoyed by the Catholic Church. From the church's side, convinced that Catholicism was the one true religion, theology maintained that when a nation was Catholic, other religions had no clear right to exist; when a nation was not Catholic, a nation was bound to tolerate and extend basic rights to the Catholic Church.

Distinctive Contribution of the American Church

What the American church communicated to the universal church was its positive experience of the so-called separation of church and state. In the American experience secular society means a religiously pluralistic society. America is neither a Protestant nor a Christian nation; the nation is not a religious union but a civic union. The religious liberty of all citizens constitutes one of America's most basic premises. It has resulted in religious pluralism and a belief that freedom in religion is an unquestionable birthright. Any American can test the depth of this conviction by looking out at various religious conflicts and finding them incomprehensible insofar as they are purely religious. Religious freedom represents a completely positive doctrine, not against Christianity, but one discovered to fit neatly with the Christian revelation of the nature of God as creator. The doctrine of religious freedom will enrich the whole church and humankind generally as it gradually becomes internalized. To the extent that this gift has firm roots in the American experience, the American church can be proud.

Women in the Church

A second potential gift of the American church to the universal church concerns the place and role of women in the church, in society at large, and in the world. I do not have to document the degree of oppression experienced by women throughout the world, nor the fact that women are barred from official leadership positions in the Catholic Church. This is a serious problem for the church, for women in the church, and for the mission of the church to the world. But it continues to be addressed in the church in the United States. What are some of our resources and experiences?

The American Constitution

I look back at the founding documents of the nation not as proof texts but as bearers of basic values to which Americans consistently appeal. It is good to recall the limitations, fears, prejudices that constricted the founding vision. For example, in the beginning, the American experiment was elitist: voting rights were limited to a tenth of the male population with land or money. Citizenship was thus stratified and graduated. The social fabric of the south was racist, and so was the almost universal treatment of black people in the white North. More generally, by our standards, the whole nation was sexist. But counterbalancing these limitations of the age were a number of fundamental principles from the Enlightenment that were reinforced religiously with Christian doctrines such as creation. The Declaration of Independence affirmed, "We hold these Truths to be self-evident, that all Men are created equal, that they are endowed by their Creator with certain unalienable Rights." Despite its actual, historically limited meaning, the term "men" syntactically meant all people. Like a subversive worm in a computer's main drive, this religious and anthropological principle worked its way into general consciousness, and is still doing so, for it has not run its course of completely destroying the racist and sexist dimensions of the American program.

American Experience

This is not the place to review the historical growth of the women's movement or movements which blossomed into a more general ethos and critical theory in the last half of the twentieth century. Gradually, after the demonstrations for voting rights and rights in employment, through the experience of World War II and in the explosion of the feminist movement, the idea that all human beings are created equal gradually took on its intrinsically true meaning. Despite this progress, however, women still experience socially structured oppression in the five areas underlined by Serene Jones: exploitation, marginalization, powerlessness, the prevalence of masculine cultural norms, and violence.[3]

Confronting the Obstacles

Where is the Catholic Church in America relative to the question of the role of women? Consider the church sociologically as an organization: the task of the official leadership of the church belongs to the clergy. But women are excluded from orders, the ranks of the clergy, and official leadership roles because of their sex. Therefore the church is officially and according to its current doctrine a sexist institution. In fact, women make up the majority of ministers in the American church, and this has been the case since the growth of women's apostolic religious congregations in the nineteenth century. But the five areas of social oppression of women continue to be reflected in the church. The failure of the American bishops to recognize these areas of oppression in the church and to correct them decades ago shows how deeply the roots of this sexism reach into the structures of the church.

Distinctive Charge to the American Church

American women in the church have responded positively and constructively to this impasse in a massive movement of Catholic feminist theology. Many such theologians are well known: Mary Daly, Rosemary Radford Ruether, Elisabeth Schüssler Fiorenza, Anne Carr, Margaret Farley, Elizabeth Johnson, Sandra Schneiders, Susan Ross, Mary Catherine Hilkert (I could expand the list); womanist theologians Shawn Copeland, Diana Hayes, and Jamie Phelps; mujerista theologians such as Ada María Díaz and María-Pilar Aquino. These

---

3. Serene Jones, *Feminist Theory and Christian Theology* (Minneapolis: Fortress Press, 2000), 79-93.

theologians have developed various feminist interpretations of God, Jesus Christ, the church, sacraments, ethics, and spirituality that are distinctively American. But this feminist theology is universally relevant. It will continue to ride the tide against a universal oppression of women. The case of women is being made on the ground in a women's movement, and these theologians are formulating its implications. They follow St. Paul at his deepest: "There is no such thing as . . . male and female; for you are all one person in Christ" (Gal 3:28). I believe that it is only a matter of time until these theologies widely take hold in the American church, and that the American church has the special role to midwife these values into the consciousness and then the doctrine of the universal church.

Laity in the Church

One of the most remarkable developments in the Roman Catholic Church since Vatican II has been the development of lay ministry. That development has been astonishing in the United States. In making my case here let me begin by recalling some foundations of American and recent American Catholic experience.

The American Constitution and Vatican II

The founding impulse of the United States is democratic. By that I mean that the source of legitimate authority of a government of this people comes from the people. Thus, the Declaration of Independence says that to secure the citizens' inalienable rights, "Governments are instituted among Men, deriving their just Powers from the Consent of the Governed, [and] whenever any Form of Government becomes destructive of these Ends, it is the Right of the People to alter or to abolish it, and to institute new Government. . . ." And thus the Preamble of the Constitution of the United States says, "We the people of the United States . . . do ordain and establish this Constitution for the United States of America."

With these predispositions, American Catholics were open to the strong language of Vatican II on the laity found in its Dogmatic Constitution on the Church (*Lumen gentium* [LG], ##30-38) and in its Decree on the Apostolate of the Laity (*Apostolicam actuositatem* [AA]). With a theology of baptism in the background (LG, #31), it says that "by its very nature the Christian vocation is also a vocation to the apostolate. No part of the structure of a living body is merely passive but each has a share in the functions as well as in the life of the body. . . . the member who fails to make his or her proper contribution to the development of the Church must be said to be useful neither to the church nor to himself or herself" (AA, #2). "The apostolate of the laity is a sharing in the salvific mission of the church. Through Baptism and Confirmation all are appointed to this apostolate by the Lord himself" (LG, #33, and AA, #3). It is clear that these ministries come under the supervision of the clergy (LG, #37; AA, #24). But it is also clear that the competence of lay ministry extends "both in the Church and in the world, in both the spiritual and the temporal orders" (AA, #5). This is forceful conciliar language concerning the active ministerial role of the laity.

American Catholic Experience

It is common to divide the historical experience of the Catholic Church in the United States into three quite distinct periods: the precolonial period up through the American Revolution and the founding of the nation, the period of the immigrant church of the nineteenth century up to the mid-twentieth, and the post–World War II church, energized as it was by the Second Vatican Council. World War II was a watershed: after it American Catholics became more educated and affluent, moved to the suburbs, imbibed suburban values, and became more like Protestants in terms of individual decision making, so that Catholic parishes became voluntary organizations. Catholics today are the most educated Christians in the United States. Consider too these factors related to the internal life of the church that occurred over the past forty years: the virtual disappearance of nuns, the decline of priests, laity filling the breach, the growth of a more differentiated ministry, complexification of parish life, and the new highly motivated, educated, and skilled laity functioning at all levels in many parishes.[4]

What I am pointing to with all this empirical data are "the signs of the times." One can make some generalized judgment on the basis of these two sets of data: on one side are the statistics of the decline of sisters and priests; on the other are the statistics of lay people in ministry, of over 300 training centers for laity in ministry. It is true that, if the criteria for ordination to priesthood were changed, some of the pressures on sacramental ministry would be addressed: circuit-rider priests, parish closings, parishes without the Eucharist. But that would not address the other distinct problem of the new equation in the relationship between clergy and laity which has already arrived in the American church.

4. See Philip J. Murnion and David DeLambo, *Parishes and Parish Ministers: A Study of Parish Lay Ministry* (New York: National Pastoral Life Center, 1999).

Confronting the Obstacles

At the present time, one can find in many parishes a superb balance and collaboration between clergy and laity. But it is not firmly institutionalized: it depends on the parish, the pastor, the staff. Any given parish with a healthy and productive formula can change overnight with the appointment of a new pastor. In other words, deep institutional patterns of clericalism remain resistant to the collaboration of laity. I will simply mention two manifestations of this.

One was a decree of the Vatican issued two decades ago that outlined all the pastoral activities or ministries that were reserved for priest and that could not be assumed by the laity.[5] The decree seemed to fear that lay people participating in ministry were competing with priests. In a situation where the number of priests was decreasing and lay ministers were increasing, it sought to bolster priesthood by carving out anew the activities and ministries that are reserved for priests. The result was a thoroughly negative document that listed all the things that the laity could not do.

Another manifestation of the confrontation between clericalism and the rise of the laity in the American church consists in the lack of communication between laity and higher clergy in the diocese. Whereas the American church intermittently manifests good communication on the parish level, this does not extend to the diocesan level. This lack of communication was dramatically displayed over the years marked by the sexual abuse crisis.

Distinctive Charge to the American Church

There is a revolution going on in the Catholic Church in the United States. Although we are too much in the middle of it to grasp its dimensions, we should be able to read the signs. I characterize the revolution as "the rise of the laity." Unlike other quiet revolutions in other countries, this is not the current of disaffection and abandonment, but a new kind of engagement and participation that is distinctively American. The proper corporate reaction to this revolution is captured in the maxim that I associate with Theodore Hesburgh and Andrew Greeley in the context of Catholic education but applicable here: "trust the laity."

The positive significance of the development in the American church since Vatican II can be read in some measure as a weakening

5. See "*Ecclesiae de mysterio*: On Certain Questions regarding the Collaboration of the Non-Ordained Faithful in the Sacred Ministry of the Priest," by Eight Dicasteries of the Holy See, Vatican, August 15, 1997, http://adoremus.org.

of the clerical system as we have known it. The "open system" of the most progressive parishes, whether in suburbia, rural areas, or among the poor in cities, is something new and valuable. Lay people are participating at all levels in the actual running of the parish. In them one finds diversification in ministerial expertise together with lateral communication and collaboration. The challenge now is to implement this sharing of responsibility and openness on the diocesan level. If the American Catholic Church can design administrative structures that preserve priesthood and lay collaboration in a noncompetitive way on the diocesan level, we may help revise the canonical structuring of clerical and lay responsibility into new patterns of authority and corporate responsibility for the universal church.

Religious Openness to Other Faiths

The issue here is the last to arise in consciousness. In a way, the issue concerns the practical fallout from the doctrine of religious freedom. The doctrine on religious freedom is a political doctrine. But political freedom in religious matters raises a theological question. In fact, theological questions are constantly being raised by the new interaction of Christians with people of non-Christian faiths. These questions pertain to our understanding of ourselves as Christians relative to other religions. This issue has been discussed heatedly among Christian theologians over the past forty years, and that discussion is far from over. But I am less concerned here with this theological discussion than with the common experience of educated American Catholics. Some serious things are going forward here that are particular to the church in the United States. Our attitudes relative to other religions are being changed for us by concrete events.

The American Constitution

Let me go back briefly to the American Constitution and its First Amendment, which deals with the nonestablishment of any religion in the United States. Catholics have benefitted from the implication that this is not a Protestant nation. But with the last period of new immigration policies begun during the 1960s, new arrivals in the United States have included many people who practice other religions of the world. In the past, the civic union that was the United States could tacitly presuppose some Christian substructure and conventions, and Jews were forced to go along with it. Little by little those Christian underpinnings and supports of what many still take to be a Christian nation are being removed.

American Experience

The American Catholic Church was allowed to grow because of nonestablishment. We had our experience of anti-Catholicism from outside, and we had our own private doctrines of no salvation outside the Roman Catholic Church. But we grew and flourished *because of* the deeper and constitutional value of religious pluralism. In the current American experience, what happened for Catholics in the nineteenth and early twentieth centuries is happening for members of other religions. Muslims, Hindus, Buddhists, and constituents of other religions are bringing their religions with them in an organized form. Historically, that is, concretely and actually, the United States is passing from being a largely Christian nation, in terms of numbers and rhetoric, to one that is more and more explicitly multireligious. This expresses itself in language, visibly in architecture, dress, and patterns of behavior, and in demands for new religious exceptions to rules. It is reaching into all phases of public life and, through intermarriage, into private family life as well. The United States is being called upon to become a political and social union embodying a religious pluralism that extends well beyond Jewish-Christian pluralism. Is this happening evenly and smoothly? One can read all sorts of negative anecdotes. Organized resistance exists on local levels, some of it clearly racist and bigoted; reactions against other religions often accompany various forms of fundamentalism. But one also finds some solidly positive signs, and the future looks good because American history and the American mythos support a positive valuation of religious pluralism as such.[6]

Confronting the Obstacles

There are obstacles to religious openness within the church that do not ring true to the American Catholic experience. For example, *Dominus Iesus* is a Declaration of the Congregation for the Doctrine of the Faith published in 2000 that asserts that the Roman Catholic Church is the only fully authentic Christian church. It also preserves the supersessionist status of Christianity relative to other religions. It was signed by the Prefect of the Congregation, Joseph Ratzinger, who went on to become Pope Benedict XVI. The way *Dominus Iesus* was received by the Catholic Church provided insight into how Catholic consciousness changed on these matters. Like a weather vane, reaction pointed in the direction of broad, strong resistance to Catholic supremacy on the part of embarrassed Catholics and showed how far an evolution of

6. See Diana L. Eck, *A New Religious America* (San Francisco: Harper Collins, 2002).

pluralist consciousness had progressed among the ordinary faithful, no matter what theologians said.

The problem consists in the absolutist form of classical doctrine, not its message. On the one hand, American Catholics believe that there is salvation outside of Roman Catholicism and even outside of Christianity. On the other hand, Catholics strongly believe that Jesus Christ is a real mediator of salvation from God. This last doctrine has to be affirmed and taught with clarity, but in a new pluralist context and a noncompetitive spirit. We are learning that religious freedom is a religious doctrine besides being a social doctrine. Its explanation must accommodate in principle the theological grounds for religious freedom and not simply the political principle that people have a right to be wrong.

Distinctive Charge to the American Church

Like the movement from the American experience to religious freedom mediated by Murray, the growing American Catholic experience of openness to other religions needs a movement from actual developments to the level of reflection and self-understanding. The reaction to *Dominus Iesus* shows that Catholics need a new theology and then a new doctrine that preserves the Christian commitment to God in Jesus Christ and at the same time guarantees the intrinsic validity of other religions in principle. Respect of peoples who have long histories of religious experience and practice demands in part that we acknowledge the autonomous truth and value that constitute their religions. This process is, I believe, going on in the mutual reinforcement of the work of theologians and the *sensus fidelium* of American Catholics. The point at which this experience will pass into doctrine is still far off, but one can see it on the horizon.

* * *

We cannot let the present crisis in one area of the church, namely, in its clerical leadership, distract attention from the enormous gains that have accrued to the Catholic Church in America through a natural process of historical inculturation. Apart from the inexcusable betrayal of young people by abusing priests and betrayal of their families by bishops, we have witnessed enormous positive gains in almost every area of Catholic life: parish life, quality of schools at primary, secondary, and college levels, lay ministry, the development of American theology, especially feminist theology, a wide variety of social ministries in the areas of health, the elderly, battered women, the imprisoned, the poor, new immigrants, ethnic groups, and world out-reach through missionaries and Catholic social agencies. American Catholics know the value of religious freedom, affirm the equality of women, experience energy and responsibility for the church's mission, and recognize the value of other religions. These are lessons for the universal church, and I hope that gradually they will find a theological rationale that is so convincing that these truths will pass into universal doctrine as four gifts from the American to the universal church.

CHAPTER ELEVEN

The Spiritual Exercises as an Ecumenical Strategy

The ecumenical movement, which for quite some time proceeded by comparison of the doctrines and ecclesial structures that divide, has foundered. This chapter suggests turning to what all churches share in common as a new starting point for ecumenism, namely, an ecclesial spirituality of following Jesus. The Spiritual Exercises of Ignatius Loyola can help bring this bond of unity to the surface. Negotiating on the basis of this common possession will allow the ideal of a pluralistic unity to take hold and encourage ecclesial structures that protect rather than exclude different church traditions. Such is the thesis of this chapter.

I begin with the stipulation that the word "church" refers to the great church, the whole Christian movement, and not exclusively to any denomination.[1] This discussion unfolds within the idea that beneath the church as a collection of institutions lies its foundation in what may be called an ecclesial spirituality in which all participate. Once one becomes convinced of the expanded significance of this elementary structure, it can become a source of leverage for shifting basic perceptions and understandings of the church as it is today. Because Ignatius Loyola's Spiritual Exercises directly relate to ecclesial spirituality, they affect assumptions about the foundations of the church. This makes them relevant to theories and practices of an ecumenical nature.

Developing this thesis in a relatively short space requires a crisp didactic style. I set up the discussion with a series of presuppositions that may seem controversial in the blunt oversimplified form in which they are stated. Whether or not one agrees with these on the whole or in part, they at least define the imaginative framework that lies behind the argument. Once the context provided by those premises is set

1. This usage requires a conversion from regarding one's own church as the norm for the true church. That latter view effectively blocks the impulse of the ecumenical movement.

out, the proposal moves through four points. The first posits a broad understanding of spirituality as the foundation of the church. The second further develops the first and offers several reasons showing how this foundation is prior to, and the constant source of, the church's institutional structures. Third, the Spiritual Exercises directly address the ecclesial spirituality that all Christians share in common, and this makes them directly influential in how we conceive the unity of the church. The fourth section gives examples of how the Exercises could become actually relevant to ecumenism in theory and potentially in practice.

Presuppositions

I begin with a presupposition that sets the context for this reflection. Each of the following points should be argued at greater length. But these considerations have been proffered often and by many over the past decades. They are headlined because each one of these descriptions is significant its own right.

Decline

Christianity in the West is in decline as measured by people abandoning the churches. Protestant, Catholic, and Orthodox churches are experiencing this; increasingly Evangelicals, Pentecostals, Fundamentalists are beginning to feel it. The phenomenon is recorded and analyzed from many perspectives; it cannot be understood as a result of a single cause, and therefore the church cannot mount a single strategy to reassert itself. The decline has been going on longer in Europe than in North America, and even though rates of change do not predict the same proportion of alienation from the church in the United States as in Europe, we seem to be headed in the same direction.[2] It would be difficult to maintain that division among the churches is the main reason for Christianity's losing its traction in technologically advanced societies. But neither does the failure of a common effort to appropriate and address the problem forecast a more favorable future for the church in the West.

Historical Consciousness

Historical consciousness, consciousness of unmitigated pluralism, and global awareness are marks of contemporary Western culture. These

2. Robert D. Putnam and David E. Campbell, *American Grace: How Religion Divides and Unites Us* (New York: Simon & Schuster, 2010), 76.

attributes used to mark an elite intellectual culture, but rapid communication and extensive travel have accustomed almost everyone to social change and deep cultural differences throughout the world. One no longer needs to study to learn that different groups of peoples have their own ways of looking at things and of understanding in ways that fit their interests. This pragmatism of everyday life in society and among nations changes one's perception of the unity of churches. No one expects the church to look the same in different places and cultures. Western Christians can understand the postcolonial desires of other peoples to develop their own inculturated Christianity: historical consciousness demands it. It is no longer difficult to imagine one church with many branches that are really different from one another. This is a major shift in a framework for thinking: it overcomes Christian tribalism and the intrinsically competitive views of the churches that have been a Christian legacy for centuries.

Pluralistic Church

The natural state of the large church's existence entails pluralism. Pluralism does not refer to a formless set of differences but to unity amid differences, or to differences within an overarching and unifying field. Sometimes sharp differences coexist within one particular church; this condition is not anomalous but normal. Pluralism appears at all levels of the church. The New Testament, which may be considered the constitution of the church, reflects multiple incipient church polities and theologies, making some measure of rich diversity normative for ecclesiology. The history of ecclesiology demonstrates diversity through constant development and change. It also shows that pluralism describes the church at any given time across peoples and cultures. With the sixteenth-century Reformation, pluralism became dramatic. Today the churches take their divisions for granted. But the forces of fission threaten serious damage to the coherence of the Christian tradition. Christianity, therefore, absolutely needs an ecumenical movement.

The movement back toward unity, however, cannot transpire on classical principles of uniformity within a single universal institutional form. Lack of change, stasis, and immovable institutions make no sense in an evolutionary world and cannot succeed in human history. The whole church ideally is comprised of living, interacting, and noncompeting communities that have their particular traditions, customs, and practices. Prior to creating institutions that unify, the great church needs mutual recognition of different traditions. This may lead to communion among churches with their own traditions. Some time down the road, as with different ethnic churches in a single large urban denomination, multiple ecclesial traditions will not need to challenge one another on less-than-essential issues but can enrich the church as a mosaic of churches, each of which contributes something distinctive to the whole. The language and law of the whole will stay close to the foundations of the New Testament constitution, which allows pluralism.

Essentials and Peripherals

There is a hierarchy of truths. This common-sense principle says that everything that Christians profess or do is not of equal objective value or existential importance. The distinction became important in sixteenth-century Reformation ecclesiology.[3] It is a working supposition of the World Council of Churches.[4] It became a formal principle in Roman Catholic ecclesiology at Vatican II: "In Catholic doctrine there exists an order or 'hierarchy' of truths, since they vary in their relation to the foundation of the Christian faith."[5] Accepting the principle does not automatically resolve different perceptions of how important this or that feature of church life really is. But taking the hierarchy of truths seriously entails forcing the question of what is truly at the center of the church and not allowing lesser issues to obscure the essence of a shared Christian confession.

The image of a large, full tree, with a thick trunk and a thicket of leaves at the crown, opens up the imagination to various ways of conceptualizing what is basic and what is subsidiary and therefore not church dividing. This image suggests a dynamic center of the church through which its life energy is channeled to the many diverse branches that stretch out in gradually less important, individual details. The image would be falsely construed by a conclusion that the leaves of a tree are really not necessary and that the tree could live as a bare trunk.[6] Such a reductionist interpretation destroys the tree.

---

3. The principle of *adiaphora*—from a Greek word meaning things that are indifferent—became important during the Reformation period. It distinguished in principle between things in the church that are essential and others that are less important.

4. For example, the principle is the basis of the Faith and Order Commission's document *Baptism, Eucharist, and Ministry*, Faith and Order Paper 111 (Geneva: World Council of Churches, 1982); and *The Church: A Common Vision*, Faith and Order Paper 214 (Geneva: World Council of Churches, 2012).

5. Vatican II, *Unitatis redintegratio* (Decree on Ecumenism), no. 11.

6. Liberal theology's ecclesiology was accused of reducing Christianity to a bare essence and thereby pruning away the historical fullness of Christian life as a worshiping community. But the idea of an "essence" of Christianity or the church can be understood in a more subtle way as the inner foundation of ecclesial existence

Rather, the image allows the many leaves to fill out the whole tree: it is an image of inclusion and acceptance of many different customs and practices and beliefs. It guides discussion toward a language that describes the inner core of being a Christian and thereby does not allow things at the extremities—things vital to some churches but not others—to occlude what is more central and common to all.

Where We Dwell in Common

This phrase comes from a chapter in a book in which I try to show how much the ecclesiologies of the many churches share with one another.[7] All churches already enjoy the essentials of Christian faith. Paul enumerates what those essentials are when he urges the Ephesians "to preserve the unity of the spirit through the bond of peace: one body and one Spirit, as you were also called to the one hope of your call; one Lord, one faith, one baptism; one God and Father of all, who is over all and through all and in all" (Eph 4:3-6). There is no better concise definition of the essentials of the Christian faith shared by all. Very little falls outside the range of this definition of what it means to be a Christian. This statement of our common faith unites Christians so firmly that almost nothing else should be allowed to divide them. In other words, within the circles of the bonds that Paul lays out, we can discuss all other differences as members of the same church and even as friends in the Lord.

This perception of the depth of unity that can absorb differences and engage them together shows how deeply historical contextualization, pluralism, and a global perspective have worked their way into our corporate consciousness. A few decades ago, the differences between the churches seemed to be simply unbridgeable despite ecumenical optimism and good will. Today, as if we were seeing Christianity anew from a different vantage point against the massive background of history and innumerable other religions, all Christians begin to look alike in their essentials. Given the depth of their commitment to God as mediated through Jesus and what that means, what could divide them? It is difficult to formulate today the cataracts that were able to cloud over recognition of our common faith. Only something truly momentous should so alienate churches that they give up on a faith that really binds them together.

---

that supports the whole church. See Roger Haight, "Comparative Ecclesiology," *The Routledge Companion to the Christian Church*, ed. Gerard Mannion and Lewis S. Mudge (New York: Routledge, 2008), 393-94.

7. Haight, *Christian Community in History*, Vol. 3, *Ecclesial Existence* (New York: Continuum, 2008), 3-27.

Nonexclusive Institutional Forms

Pluralism in the church means that a unified corporate body contains differences within itself that are so absorbed by a common sense of belonging that they are not allowed to divide the church. Such differences are found in individual church congregations, denominations, and the whole church. In the context of the ecumenical movement, pluralism sets up the goal of ecumenical activity: the main ecumenical question is how to create some kind of institutional unity or alignment out of an existential, social, and spiritual unity that already lies beneath actual divisions. If the inner life of a particular church community is pluralistic in the sense of containing a variety of vibrant, authentic traditions, the institutional structure of the church should protect and nourish all of them. The church needs structures that protect traditions rather than choose between them or create some alienating synthesis. Once Christian communities become convinced that other Christians of different traditions are truly Christian, resentment at including them in one's own family will disappear. Yet there is always a proviso here: a truly pluralistic community has to recognize that different traditions in a unified community do not set up hostile competition between them but actually enrich a fuller and denser ecclesial spirituality. The principle that any institutional unity that is forged between churches must preserve distinctive traditions rather than compromise them has become a cliché in ecumenical discussion. But this principle remains radical and neglected.

Leadership in the Churches

The ecumenical movement began in the nineteenth century and had a focusing event in 1910.[8] The story of its development through the first half of the twentieth century culminating in the World Council of Churches in 1948 tells of gifted leaders who would not quit in the face of tremendous difficulty. If the impetus to ecumenism that was felt when the Catholic Church joined the movement with Vatican II has since died—many testify that it has—this points to a crisis of leadership. After so much ecumenical conversation and the production of such impressive documents by churches in dialogue and the Faith and Order commission—with relatively little ecumenical decision

---

8. The event was the World Missionary Conference held in Edinburgh. The inspiring story of the ecumenical movement leading to the creation of the World Council of Churches is told concisely and with fitting tribute to its leaders by W. A. Visser't Hooft, *The Genesis and Formation of the World Council of Churches* (Geneva: World Council of Churches, 1982).

making outside of several Protestant and Anglican churches—one has to notice an almost absolute void in publicly recognized leadership on the part of the churches. Although many church leaders will say that they cannot lead where no one will follow, one may rightly respond with the question, "What is leadership?" The movement from below among people who lack power in the church is palpable; but it manifests itself chiefly in attrition. The present division of the churches is mainly political and organizational rather than theological, and the leaders of the churches bear the burden of the responsibility for perpetuating division.

These seven presuppositions may serve as an introduction to this discussion. Most people are familiar with some or all of these observations and may even take them for granted. But when they are gathered together, they mark off a distinctive moment in history, a historical context that calls for genuinely new appreciations of the church in our time. The thesis of this essay is that the road toward a new impetus for the ecumenical movement must lead through ecclesial spirituality. And the Spiritual Exercises of Ignatius Loyola offer a way of focusing and thinking about the problem. They also suggest a program that can address the issue. I will develop this program in the next four parts of the discussion.

Spirituality as the Core of Christianity

In some ways the idea that the core of Christianity or the church is the spirituality that it nurtures is obvious. But the point here is to isolate this idea and use it as an operative principle that will affect ecumenical interchange. That role largely depends on how one understands what spirituality means.

There are many valid ways of understanding spirituality. People usually associate spirituality with religion, although today the range has expanded greatly to include all sorts of techniques of self-care and the quest for well-being. In religious usage, spirituality frequently consists of a distinct domain of life that consists of various sets of practices that nourish the inner life: prayer, worship, devotions, meditation, or bodily practices. Spirituality may consist of that inner space of a person's reflective presence to the self where the affects generated by life's many relationships, both activities and passivities, are assimilated and digested. Spirituality is a vast area of interiority that affords many working definitions and approaches.

In this discussion "spirituality" has a distinctive meaning that is open and inclusive, one repeated several times in this volume. It refers to *the way persons or groups live their lives before transcendence.* A comment on the two main elements of this view will help reveal its potential.

First, this expansive view of spirituality as the way people live shifts the notion of spirituality to a framework that is wider than religious belonging and deeper than any particular set of practices. Spirituality is something that all persons have if their lives are organized around some center of gravity. The notion is close to the way Paul Tillich defines faith as "ultimate concern."[9] In this case, then, spirituality refers to a person's ultimate concern as it manifests itself in action. Spirituality, as faith in action, means that people's consistent behavior actually carries their deepest faith commitment. Without such an expansive view of spirituality a large part of life that has spiritual relevance will be left out of one's sphere of attention. This is an activist view of spirituality because even human *passio* or suffering elicits reactions, and without them our passivities have no spiritual value.

Second, spirituality involves more than a style of life; ideally, it is intentional. On a functional level, spirituality takes the form of the transcendent value to which it responds. It is true that many spiritualities are dedicated to objects that are less than transcendent. But in each case what provides the overriding value and centering object of a person's life may be called transcendent because it functions as the consuming interest that organizes his or her life. Nevertheless, proportionality should govern the relation between a human response and its object. In Jewish and Christian traditions, idolatry has a simple logic: something that performs such a transcendent role in shaping a human person should itself be truly transcendent. For Jews and Christians that transcendent and ultimate reality is God, and making anything else the object of one's ultimate concern is idolatrous.

What distinguishes Christian faith and spirituality as Christian from all other faiths is Jesus of Nazareth. Christian spirituality is centered on God, as God is revealed in Jesus Christ. The definition of "Christian," referring to one whose faith in God is mediated through Jesus Christ, also defines the essence of Christian theistic spirituality. Christians find God as given to them through the person and ministry of Jesus of Nazareth. All Christians share this spirituality; in defining

9. "Faith is the state of being ultimately concerned" (Paul Tillich, *Dynamics of Faith* [New York: Harper & Row, 1957], 1, 4). It is important to note that Tillich also describes faith in a passive voice that highlights the priority and initiative of transcendence "breaking into" human consciousness: "We have used the metaphor 'being grasped' for describing the state of ultimate concern. And being grasped implies that he who is grasped and that by which he is grasped are, so to speak, at the same place" (ibid., 99).

Christianity, this spirituality describes what all Christians possess in common.[10]

Placing Jesus of Nazareth at the center of the Christian's relationship to God makes this spirituality of following Jesus the substance of the ecclesial spirituality that is shared by all Christians and all the churches. In ordinary language the word "church" almost automatically refers to the visible church and the public institutional churches that make it up. We spontaneously notice that churches differ from one another. Objectively, Christians have grown accustomed to differences among churches, to what distinguishes and divides them. But beneath all of them lies the same substantial ecclesial spirituality of connecting with God through Jesus and living according to that principle.

If the essence or heart of Christianity can be conceived as spirituality, then one must think that this shared ecclesial spirituality will provide the basis of the unity shared by Christians. In other words, the basis of unity does not lie in institutional structure but in unity with God mediated through Jesus of Nazareth and the way of life that embodies it. Although this seems elementary and clear, the next section pursues this corporate Christian spirituality further in order to give it existential prominence.

Christian Spirituality as Foundation of the Church

The corporate spirituality of following Jesus plays a constitutional role in the very being of the church. This principle states the major premise of my argument. The spirituality of following Jesus grounds the church; the institutions of the church are drawn from it; ecumenical relationships depend on it. That ecclesial spirituality is the source and ground of the church appears in three distinct approaches to the relationship between spirituality and the church; they converge to show why the spirituality of following Jesus should represent a consensus in any quest for church unity. These approaches pass through history, social anthropology, and ecclesiology.

History

The early historical development of the church shows how Christian spirituality is prior to organizational development and is the source of it. Schematically, that historical development progressed through

10. Some Christians will insist that it is the risen Christ that defines their faith. But the risen Christ is Jesus of Nazareth, and we know nothing about a risen Christ apart from Jesus or from one who is not identical with Jesus.

stages. It is important to note that the scarcity of historical sources and the uneven development of the Christian movement during the first century make any close description of various stages problematic. The picture of how the movement of disciples developed in the two decades after Jesus's ministry remains unclear. Did the movement begin principally in Galilee where Jesus's ministry for the most part unfolded, or in Jerusalem? But development from embryo to institutional forms did happen. Thus, even possible or probable patterns of development help us form some imaginative narrative of how the church evolved over the course of the first century.[11]

Several clues indicate that after Jesus's execution the disciples were left in confusion. With the Easter experience and the consciousness of mission that the resurrection of Jesus instilled, a Jesus movement gradually formed within Judaism. It was initially attached to and housed within the synagogues. But it is also likely that the disciples of Jesus continued to gather together for meals, and that what became the eucharistic meal was an early institutional form for the assembly of disciples.[12] In Jerusalem and perhaps in Rome, Elisabeth Schüssler Fiorenza imagines the Jesus movement simultaneously belonging to the Jewish community and gathering together for meals, thus forming something of a parallel community.[13]

In mid-century, tensions developed between the followers of Jesus and the synagogue in Antioch around the year 49. Paul directly testifies to the event, and it has echoes in Luke's Acts of the Apostles (Gal 2:1-14; Acts 15:1-35). In Luke's telling the dispute began when some people from Judea came to the Gentile-Christian-Jewish community in Antioch and declared that no one could be saved who was not circumcised (Acts 15:1). Delegates were sent to Jerusalem, where the matter was discussed. Luke gives the impression the matter was resolved when the Jerusalem church sent back a letter saying that Gentile Christians did not have to be circumcised, but the community should maintain some dietary norms and refrain from "unchastity" (Acts 15:28-29).

This is a paradigmatic event in several ways, not least in showing a tendency of the young Jesus movement to seek some autonomy relative to its parent.[14] In different communities and locales and according

11. For a review of the recent literature on the origin of the church, see Hal Taussig, "The End of Christian Origins? Where to Turn at the Intersection of Subjectivity and Historical Craft," *Review of Biblical Literature* 11 (2011): 1-45. The use of the term "embryo" should not be taken to suggest an organic development.

12. See Hal Taussig, *In the Beginning Was the Meal: Social Experimentation and Early Christian Identity* (Minneapolis: Fortress Press, 2009).

13. Elisabeth Schüssler Fiorenza, *In Memory of Her: A Feminist Theological Reconstruction of Christian Origins* (New York: Crossroad, 1983), 177-79.

14. The controversy in Antioch is subject to various interpretations. Is it mainly

to different timetables well into the second century, these tensions gradually led to more independence of the newly named Christian communities until they began to look like a church.

In this development, on the Christian side, the constant is a spirituality of following Jesus. Out of a corporate following of Jesus grew the various interpretations of him found in the New Testament and the different institutional structures that were employed to hold the communities together, thereby ensuring the continuity of the movement. The historical development of the early Christian churches illustrates, if it does not demonstrate, how the spirituality of following Jesus precedes and is the source of the historical foundation of the developing church: its teachings, its institutional structures, and its ethics. When these organizational forms were borrowed from the various options that presented themselves in the first and second centuries, the spirituality of following Jesus gave them their new specific identity.

Social Anthropology

The distinction between "structure" and *communitas* is recognized in sociological literature.[15] Structures refer to "the patterned arrangements of role sets, status sets, and status sequences consciously recognized and regularly operative in a given society and closely bound up with legal and practical norms and sanctions."[16] *Communitas* by contrast refers the spontaneous character of the full life of the group that overflows structures and more freely responds to stimuli within the community and to the world outside it. In this sense, *communitas* transcends the structured life of the group, transgresses its boundaries, and at certain points may threaten the ordered life; it has a primal energy of its own. Structure orders the energetic life of the community. *Communitas* is the origin and empowering source of all structures as precisely that which is structured. This tension describes an intrin-

---

about circumcision, thus allowing Gentiles to be Christians without it? Or is it about table fellowship, thus allowing Jewish Christians to remain Jewish while eating with Gentiles? See Esler, *Community and Gospel*, 105-9.

15. This distinction is developed by Victor Turner and Edith Turner, *Image and Pilgrimage in Christian Culture: Anthropological Perspectives* (New York: Columbia University Press, 1978). Karl Starkloff, "Church as Structure and Communitas: Victor Turner and Ecclesiology," *Theological Studies* 58 (1997): 643-68, applies these categories to the study of the church.

16. Starkloff, "Church as Structure and Communitas," 649. For example, the role of the pastor of a congregation is to serve the community by providing preaching, sacramental ministry, and leadership; this position is established by various kinds of ecclesiastical law or custom; and the pastor and the congregation operate within those parameters. The whole community is organized and structured with various office holders; wider forms of unity would require higher-level office holders.

sic dimension of the church; it is something good, a dynamic, tensive and catalytic source of the church's life. Hence the ideas of *communitas* and corporate or ecclesial spirituality are virtually synonymous.

Behind this analytical distinction of reciprocally related tensive forces in the church one can discern what may be called the principle of functionality in the development of church structures. This principle refers to "the manner in which something gains its value from its relation and service to something else on which it is dependent."[17] The principle can be understood in terms of the dynamic relationships between means and ends. In ecclesiology it describes how ministries developed when needs arose in the community, people responded to them, and a persistent need generated an institutionalization of a ministry to ensure that the need was consistently met. For example, when the Twelve were overworked and needed help in the overall ministry of the community, they asked that a set of ministers be chosen to share the labor, and those chosen were formally commissioned (Acts 6:1-6). Sociologically, this commissioning resembles a creation and routinization of a ministry needed at the time. What is scripturally normative here is less the actual ministry and more the practice. One has a sense, after reviewing how the church developed through history, that it has within itself the power to create whatever ministries and offices are needed for the health of its corporate spirituality. The New Testament shows how the authority for this creativity comes from the ministry of Jesus and the power of the accompanying Spirit.

Ecclesiology

The relationship between structure and *communitas*, the dynamic principle of functionality, and tradition occupy prominent places in ecclesiology. They consistently reappear in the development of the church across history. A particularly noteworthy example of structure/*communitas* and functionality is found in the work of Dietrich of Niem, a constructive and mediating conciliarist writing in the early fifteenth century. He implicitly gave prominent attention to the distinction in his understanding of the basic structure of the church.

Recall the basic problematic of the Western Schism (1378–1417). It began when two popes were canonically elected and their papal lines continued. In 1409 a third pope was elected in an attempt to break the stalemate; it did not work, and so there were three popes. The problem consisted in finding a way to restore the papacy, which was dividing

---

17. Haight, *Christian Community in History*, Vol. 1, *Historical Ecclesiology* (New York: Continuum, 2004), 63. I develop the principle of functionality at various junctures in all three volumes of this work. It is a highly relevant historical process.

the church, to its proper role of unifying the church. Where were the authority and the leverage to resolve this colossal historical tragedy?

Dietrich of Niem resolved this problem ecclesiologically with a distinction between what he called the "universal church" and the "apostolic church" and the relation between them. One dimension of the church, the universal church, is the whole movement of people with Christ as its head; this is the existential, living mass of Christians living their faith in the churches. The "universal church" correlates neatly with the category of ecclesial spirituality, the whole church viewed existentially. The other dimension, the apostolic church, consists of the institutional offices that hold this body together historically. These are the pope, the cardinals, the bishops, and clerics. They hold the church together by performing their official functions or roles of various kinds of ministry.[18] The priority of the universal church to the structure that functioned to hold it together allowed the council that represented the church to depose dysfunctional popes and elect a new one. Brian Tierney has shown that this distinction can be traced back historically through the tradition of the canonists to the High Middle Ages.[19] But one can also see this principle, analogous to the sociological distinctions, as consistently operative in the church in less dramatic circumstances.

Another ecclesiological concept that recognizes the role of spirituality in the church is "tradition," when it is understood in a modern social existential sense. Early in the twentieth century, Maurice Blondel described tradition in a coherent way that most churches could accept. Instead of being a memory of undocumented statements or facts, tradition refers to the whole life of the Christian community as it passes through time. Tradition refers to the lived corporate experience of the church manifested ultimately in its action: its activities and its religious practices. The tradition of the whole church and of the churches "supplies the verification of what it believes and teaches in its age-old experience and its continuous practice."[20] As the corporate practice of the church, the everyday living of its people, tradition preserves the past because it embraces within itself "the facts of history, the effort of reason and the accumulated experiences of the faithful."[21]

18. Dietrich of Niem, "Ways of Uniting and Reforming the Church (1410)," in *Advocates of Reform: From Wyclif to Erasmus*, ed. Matthew Spinka (Philadelphia: Westminster, 1953), 150-52.

19. Brian Tierney, *Foundations of the Conciliar Theory: The Contribution of the Medieval Canonists from Gratian to the Great Schism* (Cambridge: University Press, 1955).

20. Maurice Blondel, "History and Dogma," in *The Letter on Apologetics and History and Dogma*, ed. Alexander Dru and Illtyd Trethowan (New York: Holt, Rinehart, & Winston, 1964), 219-87, at 269.

21. Ibid.

All churches have their particular traditions in their familiar, motivating sets of experiences and practices. These possess an inner authority, an internal self-justification that has to be respected. This notion of tradition refuses to contrast the category with life normed by scripture. Tradition refers precisely to the body of the church carrying the norm of scripture forward through existential history. Tradition is the corporate ecclesial spirituality of the church; it functions at the level of *communitas*, and the role of structure is to preserve vital traditions.

In sum, structure (or institution) and community are not separable; together they make up one church at various levels. But in an ecumenical context one cannot think of the church only as institution without differentiation. The key to Christian union begins at the place where God as Word and Spirit is effective within the lives of the Christians who constitute the church. From there, distinctive churches, whether denominations or free churches, can recognize the spirituality that Paul described working in ecclesial bodies other than their own. This shared platform can be described as ecclesial spirituality, as the developmental life of the whole church, as *communitas*, or as tradition. It opens up a perspective for recognizing a common basis that authorizes different forms of ministry and organization. There is no direct route to the creation of a unifying structure of the church as a whole. But neither should the unity of the churches be described as "purely spiritual," whatever that could mean. The way toward more comprehensive structure must pass through mutual recognition and communion among churches. And ecclesial spirituality, conceived most fundamentally as a following of Jesus, provides that possibility.

The Spiritual Exercises Nurture What Christians Share in Common

I turn now to the Spiritual Exercises of Ignatius Loyola as an example of a spiritual practice that can nurture a common ecclesial spirituality by appealing to all Christians. Earlier I told the story of how Ignatius Loyola (1491–1556), a Spanish Basque, soldier, and royal assistant, was wounded, had an extended conversion experience, and then successively became an ascetic, a pilgrim, a spiritual director, a student, a priest, and the founder of the Society of Jesus.[22] Over an extended period of time after his conversion he gradually compiled what is known as the Spiritual Exercises. The key point in that story at this juncture revolves around the evangelical character of his Spiritual Exercises. Essentially they consist in meditations on and contemplations of the stories of Jesus's ministry that are found in the Gospels.

22. Chapter 1, pp. 11-12.

Ignatius adds other considerations that give the stories a distinctive "Ignatian" character, but the constitutive core of the Exercises consists of the Gospel stories. The Exercises were finally published in 1548 and are now surrounded by a 450-year tradition of literature amounting to a large body of theoretical and practical commentary. I will highlight distinctive characteristics of this Christian spirituality that make it particularly appropriate to ecumenical discussion: its nondenominational, pretheological, and universally applicable essence as distinct from certain particularities of their origin. These comments are directed toward showing how the Exercises can be understood not as a Catholic or Jesuit preserve, but as a Christian possession that is in fact readily accessible to all people and capable of nurturing a common ecclesial spirituality.

Many aspects of the Spiritual Exercises combine to make them open to all people and especially all Christians. In the first place their basic structure is evangelical. The fundamental building block and substance of the Exercises are contemplations of the stories of Jesus in the Gospels. For various reasons, they lack a clear denominational bias. For example, as a Catholic spirituality, it is remarkable that the Exercises do not unfold in a highly sacramental framework and that the sacraments do not play an essential role in this spirituality. Insofar as Jesus of Nazareth provides the focal point of this spirituality, all Christians can share the Exercises.[23]

The genius of the Spiritual Exercises lies in their fixation on the ministry of Jesus of Nazareth and not on his divinity. One can hardly dispute that Ignatius had a high Christology and could even refer to Jesus as the Divine Majesty. But according to the "Call of the King," one of the contemplative exercises and the linchpin of all the contemplations on Jesus's ministry, the focus falls on Jesus of Nazareth as a human being. Ignatius presents Jesus as a leader to be followed. As a

---

23. At the end of the Spiritual Exercises Ignatius included a set of rules that are called by interpreters "Rules for Thinking, Judging, and Feeling with the Church" (*Spiritual Exercises*, nos. 352-70). These rules have a pointedly Roman Catholic and sacramental reference. The focus of the imagination on Jesus in the contemplations allows one to distinguish the core of this spirituality as *following Jesus* from the particular sixteenth-century Catholic ecclesial spirituality that is enshrined in these rules. The rules had a rationale of their own. Within the Catholic Church today, some of these rules are still relevant while others are obsolete. More importantly, taken together, the rules are meant to communicate a sense of commitment and loyalty to the church. And most importantly, they have to be appropriated in the Catholic Church of Vatican II, which is committed to an ecclesiology of the people of God and the ecumenical movement. Pope Francis explicitly interprets Ignatius's thinking with the church today as thinking with the whole people of God. See Pope Francis, "A Big Heart Open to God," *America* 209, no. 8 (September 30, 2013): 20-22.

human being and a public figure, Jesus is available to all Christians no matter what their doctrines about him might be.[24] In other words, Jesus of Nazareth is not a source of division, as various doctrines about him may be; rather, he is the historical person who holds all Christians together.

The goal of the Exercises is to develop a spirituality of following Jesus and making his ministry the guide of one's decision making and living. The basic logic of the Exercises may be construed in a variety of ways.[25] But all Christians implicitly are followers of Jesus, and they all can explicitly go back to the stories of Jesus and appropriate them by the two basic practices of the Exercises. The first is imaginatively to enter into the historical concreteness of Jesus's unfolding ministry as it is represented in the vignettes of the Gospels; the second is, by a fusion of narratives, to allow Jesus's ministry, person, and values to impact one's own life and to offer new possibilities and horizons. "Fusing narratives" means holding in conjunction the narrative of Jesus's ministry and a person's own story in a way that fosters an exchange of meaning and ideal. Such is the program of the Exercises.[26]

Beyond a program, the Exercises provide a school in the sense of a common method. They offer a technique by which a person can continually take the stories of the Gospels and, by internalizing any given story, use it as a method of praying the scriptures. At both levels, program and school, they support an ecumenical spirituality. Christians of every stripe can come together to "make" or "do" the

24. This does not involve a "separation" between Jesus's humanity and divinity but refers to the perspective in which Jesus is presented, that is, to the sensible observer. The divine identity of Jesus is always necessarily mediated by his human vocation and earthly ministry. In this contemplation Ignatius actually refers to Jesus as Lord and "Eternal King." But the point of this meditation is the turn to Jesus of Nazareth. The issue is not the absolute status of Jesus, but how he is approached in the Exercises. Jesus is treated "empirically" as a person of history whose divinity was not an overt datum, but something recognized later through corporate inference and interpretation. A contemplation uses the senses to allow the human Jesus to make an impression on one's imagination and, through it, one's affections. In the Exercises, an Ignatian approach, as keynoted in this contemplation, stands for the turn to Jesus of Nazareth.

25. See Haight, *Christian Spirituality for Seekers*, 46-69, for a typology of three different interpretations of the fundamental logic of the Exercises.

26. The metaphor of a "fusion of narratives" operates in the sphere of practical life in a way that is analogous with an intellectual appreciation of conceptions from the past as depicted by Gadamer. He writes that a horizon of consciousness means "the range of vision that includes everything that can be seen from a particular vantage point." (Gadamer, *Truth and Method*, 269.) A fusion of horizons, in which understanding and interpretation of the conceptions of the past take place, consists in drawing things understood in a past horizon into a present-day horizon of consciousness. The impact of a past figure on the life of a person today operates by an analogous process that is equally subject to critical appropriation.

Exercises with little adjustment beyond what is necessary to make a sixteenth-century text intelligible to a twenty-first-century audience of a given culture. The Exercises have an activist accent, but they are so essentially evangelical that, rather than compete with other Christian spiritualities, they augment them.

Finally, the Spiritual Exercises are pre-ecclesial but lead directly toward an ecclesial spirituality. The Exercises in the form that Ignatius gave them end with the fourth part, which is given over to contemplations of the apparitions of the risen Jesus and culminates with an exercise in creation spirituality and finding God in all things. But they are clearly open to the continuation of the story in the disciples' encounter with God as Spirit (Pentecost) and the development of the church outlined earlier. It is quite appropriate to extend the contemplations that Ignatius provides to include stories from the Acts of the Apostles in order to draw the imagination of those who make the Exercises into the continuing development of the Jesus movement of which he or she is a participant.[27]

In sum, the basic structure of the spirituality of the Exercises, as distinct from some of the Ignatian tropes, makes the activist following of Jesus appeal to all Christians. It even reaches across the boundaries of different faith traditions at very fundamental levels because it overtly presents Jesus's ministry in a way that can be appreciated by all on a historical level. On the basis of this insight, we can now turn to ways in which the Spiritual Exercises may be used, either as inspiration or as a practice, to foster the quest for Christian unity.

Ecumenical Uses of the Spiritual Exercises

If the Spiritual Exercises are so directly relevant to the spirituality that is shared by all Christians and that binds us together, that is, an ecclesial spirituality of following Jesus, are there ways in which they might actually be deployed in the service of Christian unity? Two uses, one theoretical and the other practical, come to mind. There may be others.[28]

The first way the Spiritual Exercises can be used ecumenically is theoretical and strategic. On the basis of an understanding of the priority in importance of spirituality to doctrine and church structure, and in a context of the hierarchy of truths, the Spiritual Exercises

---

27. I do this in *Christian Spirituality for Seekers*, 261-77.

28. It should be clear that the relevant point in this discussion is the return to scripture with a special emphasis on the ministry of Jesus. Spiritualities other than the Spiritual Exercises that return to Jesus as the source of Christian faith and ministry could perform the same function.

help focus the attention of all Christians on the core of Christian faith. They display the trunk of the tree and not the thousands of leaves that have developed over time and sometimes distract attention from what is essential.[29]

This positive strategy shows by contrast what may be a faulty method of ecumenical interchange. If the direction for ecumenical interchange suggested by the Exercises is correct, it implies that the ecumenical movement should not proceed by comparing different doctrines, or institutional structures, or religious practices as though these will somehow become bonds of uniting the churches. These institutional elements are what divide the churches. It is certainly true that one cannot ignore all differences, but the idea that exploring them will lead to unity is fundamentally mistaken.

Ormond Rush alludes to a different approach to church unity that has been growing over the past two decades, one largely mediated through the World Council of Churches. Instead of fixing on explaining and comparing differences among the churches, the parties would do better focusing on the apostolic tradition that each church professes to maintain, that is, that which they share in common. "Instead of comparing and contrasting traditions, both parties attempt to interpret together the apostolic tradition. If each can recognize in the other's interpretation 'the apostolic faith,' then surprising agreement and common ground can be achieved."[30] As an addendum to the norm of the apostolic faith, I suggest that churches also strive to articulate the spirituality that underlies the apostolic faith that they carry forward. The apostolic faith that is lived in each church supplies a common foundation that supports the differences in church superstructure.

The way toward unity has to proceed by nurturing pre-existing commonalities that bind Christians together: one faith, in one God, mediated by one historical figure. These are the things that Paul raised up so clearly. And a transparent way of entering into that sphere is to nurture the spirituality of following Jesus that is common to all Christians. This will engender not only talk about Jesus but also about the different ways of following him and the different ways of appreciating the world that encompasses the church from the perspective of following Jesus. When the core Christian spirituality of following Jesus and that which directly expresses it are in place, differences may not be ignored but may actually be promoted in a pluralistic church.

---

29. Note that the priority of spirituality to doctrine does not demote or minimize doctrine. The relationship is not competitive. The distinction merely situates doctrine in a larger religious and epistemological framework.

30. Ormond Rush, *Still Interpreting Vatican II: Some Hermeneutical Principles* (New York: Paulist Press, 2004), 67.

As a theory for getting back to the unity that we actually share, this understanding replicates, *mutatis mutandis*, the original formation of the church during the early centuries. It is also the only way forward. "We must walk united with our differences: there is no other way to become one. This is the way of Jesus."[31]

Seminaries can implement this theological position by gradually broadening the parameters in which they teach the subject matter "church." There are wide variations in ecclesiology between narrower denominational seminaries that teach "their own" ecclesiology and multidenominational seminaries that may have nothing like a normative view of the church. Just as missiology has lost some of its status in Western seminaries, in open seminaries ecclesiology as a critical and normative discipline seems to be yielding its place to denominational administration. Can a noncompetitive ecclesiology, as an inclusive-historical and a normative-ecumenical discipline, provide the groundwork for the training of ministers prior to the study of a particular tradition and ecclesial polity and ministry? The history of ecclesiology and documents from the Faith and Order Commission of the World Council of Churches can provide irenic views of the whole church that we share together.[32]

The second way the Spiritual Exercises can help the ecumenical movement is by gathering ecumenists or ecclesiologists from different traditions together to make the Exercises as a group. This will help drive home the depth and comprehensive character of the Jesus spirituality that the churches already share in common. The goal would be to stimulate an understanding of how inclusive a Jesus spirituality is; it contains *in nuce* all that Paul intimates with his phrase referring to being "in Christ."[33] This mystical identification with Jesus Christ, when it becomes the ground of a corporate spirituality of the church as the body of Christ, is precisely that which allows for a pluralism of church traditions. If the New Testament displays a pluralism of church

31. Pope Francis, "A Big Heart Open to God," 28.

32. For examples, see n. 4 above.

33. According to Joseph A. Fitzmyer, the phrase "in Christ" is used 165 times in Paul's letters. "The most common use of *en Christō* is to express the close union of Christ and the Christian, an inclusion that suggests a symbiosis of the two" (Fitzmyer, "Pauline Theology," in *The New Jerome Biblical Commentary*, ed. R. E. Brown, J. A. Fitzmyer, and R. E. Murphy [Englewood Cliffs, NJ: Prentice Hall, 1990], 1409b). A good example is the following: "Therefore, if any one is in Christ, he is a new creation" (2 Cor 5:17). There is a mutuality implied in the phrase, so that if one is in Christ, Christ is also in the person (e.g., Gal 2:20). In other words, attachment to Jesus, the historical figure who is now risen and called the Christ, is something deep and profound that transcends exemplary influence. It gives rise to the idea that the members of the church make up the body of Christ.

polities, and the New Testament is normative for the church today, different church traditions should not be approached as a negative. The pluralism of churches demonstrates how Jesus can and should be appropriated differently, personally and corporately.

It will be particularly important for leaders of the churches to make the Spiritual Exercises with other leaders. Ecumenical theologians have been negotiating doctrines and practices for a century and from the Catholic side, since Vatican II, for 50 years. Whereas there have been tangible results among some Protestant churches, the Catholic Church has little to show for the effort invested. Leaders of the churches are still isolated and timorous relative to the positions already held by the faithful and by theologians. The leaders of the churches who are not leading should assume responsibility for their inaction.

The presentation of the Spiritual Exercises should be attentive to the way they stimulate responses to the dilemmas that are raised by secular life today. These are the questions that are driving people out of churches and that leave those inside churches confused. Frequently these are questions that are simply ignored in the insistence on using formulas from the past. What should not preoccupy ecumenical discussions are the questions and problems of past history. Many are based on premises that no longer obtain. Virtually no one today is interested in whether people are justified by faith alone or in the exact way in which the practices of faith relate to final salvation. Close association with Jesus of Nazareth shows quickly that he clearly knew the difference between basic religious truths and matters that did not matter. He spontaneously differentiated the essentials from the oppressive religious practices of his time. Jesus's freedom from outdated traditions in the name of the rule of God should stimulate the ecumenical movement the way no other impetus could.

* * *

Let me draw together the threads of this argument into a summary statement. Conversation about the church has to be contextual; the social and cultural situation of the speaker and the subject matter have to become an intrinsic element of the proposals set forth. I have stipulated a set of considerations that prompt these reflections; those who disagree with these have their own. Together, the premises enumerated here indicate a situation that helps to explain ecumenical indifference and also opens up possibilities of new understanding and initiative.

Within this context the constructive reasoning begins with the position that the foundation of the church consists of what I have called spirituality, and then more precisely ecclesial spirituality. Building on the premise that spirituality refers to both a personal and communal way of life, ecclesial spirituality at bottom consists in following Jesus. Of course everyone agrees that Christians are followers of Jesus, but few ecclesiologists or ecumenists make their proposals on the explicit basis that following Jesus defines the substance of Christian faith and that following Jesus is the foundation of the church.

In order to draw out that conviction, the argument turned to the history of the development of the church, which in effect demonstrates that following Jesus is prior to the church. To solidify this position, we considered a view of the church from the perspective of organizational sociology, a traditional distinction in ecclesiology that was represented most clearly in the crisis of the Western Schism, and a social-existential conception of tradition. These considerations reinforce the foundational character of ecclesial spirituality. They support the major premise of the argument. The proposition is not that ecclesial spirituality is a specific Christian spirituality, but that the spirituality of following Jesus forms the existential basis of the church as such.

Building on this premise, where can we find a public spiritual practice that is ecumenically open and at the same time focuses in on the substance of the church? Ignatius Loyola's Spiritual Exercises can play this role because they are essentially a spirituality of following Jesus that directly nurtures ecclesial spirituality: the church is the community of the followers of Jesus. In the beginning, the church came into existence by development out of a Jewish spiritual movement of following Jesus. Thereafter, the narrative structure of the Exercises can be represented in a way that recapitulates that development. The Exercises move persons through the narrative of Jesus's ministry, death, and resurrection in order that they might shape, redirect, or strengthen their Christian lives of following Jesus.

This view of the church, which simply describes what is going on in the church in social terms, and its conjunction with the Spiritual Exercises, which foster an ecclesial spirituality of following Jesus, should generate forms of action, both theoretical and more practical, that will be ecumenically fruitful. I offered only a couple of suggestions; concrete situations will elicit more. Theoretically, the church has to appropriate and internalize deeply what all the churches share in common. Then, on that basis, as a human collective the church may develop various kinds of institutional structures appropriate to its vocation as a sign to the world of the union and reconciliation of human beings. Those structures have to develop out of the church's common spiritual life; they will never be created by mere organizational bartering and compromise. The whole church requires institutional assurances that vital and authentic Christian traditions will be protected and not compromised. Practically, churches have to find ways of nurturing together the spirituality they share in common. The Spiritual Exercises can be very useful here because they cut through less important matters to the essential following of Jesus.

CHAPTER TWELVE

Truth in Other Religions

All people of good will hope for interfaith harmony. But not everyone believes it possible. I am speaking here not of religions "getting along" with one another but of deeper questions that almost necessarily lead to elementary antagonisms. For example, most religions teach their faithful that their faith is the highest or truest among them all. People do not ordinarily profess a faith they regard as inferior to others. Religions tend to promote the view that other religions are inferior to themselves and may even teach that their religion is the only true religion. In an interdependent world, these are grounds for distrust and unrest. The question addressed here is whether it is possible for religious persons to become convinced that other religions can be as true and authentic as their own. Without attitudes that approach that norm, there can be no religious harmony, only interreligious subordination, which almost inevitably supports some kind of conflict. Is it possible for religions to transcend tolerance and a social-political guarantee of religious freedom and speak well of other religions on deep metaphysical grounds?

How is it possible to believe that other religions are true and valid? It is one thing to feel a certain way and another to be able to justify the feeling. One has to be able to respect other faiths not by weakening one's own personal religious faith but precisely by appealing to it. The ability to do that requires some explaining. Such an explanation will not be able to show that all religious are the same or equal, because they are not. And it will not help to establish that all religions are relative, so that their truth remains local and only applies to single groups. By and large religious people do not accept the radical relativity of their own faith. If something is true in the sphere of transcendent ultimacy, it must be true for all. The goal, then, is to explain how it is possible that the more passionately people are committed to their own faith, the more they can affirm that other religions are also true and to the same degree.

Many who approach this topic will expect a closely reasoned theological argument. But theology rarely decides this issue. Attitudes toward other religions are formed less through the intellectual sphere of theology and doctrine and more as spontaneous attitudes of appreciation stimulated by a host of cultural factors. Of course, one cannot write about such basic attitudes toward the religious "other" without intelligent analysis of the issues involved. These include facts about belief and practice and theoretical questions about the nature of truth. Nevertheless, people of good will harbor hopeful images of peacefully living with people of other faith traditions and being open to and interacting with them at various levels. On the basis of this hope they will appreciate reasons that promote unity and establish bonds that may actually hold people of different faiths together.

The argument here, if it is correct to call it that, draws from and refers back to spirituality. Spirituality in this instance refers to disciplined reflection that studies the way people should live their lives before ultimate reality according to the norms of a given community or religion. This reflection takes into account the pressure of contemporary exigencies, including those raised by religious pluralism. The aim is to try to understand the spreading spiritual conviction among Christians today that other religions, even though they are very different from Christianity, participate in what can be called religious truth. Other religions have an autonomous validity. Because this is an essay in Christian spirituality, my language is drawn from lived Christian faith. My hope is that the logic may apply by analogy to other faiths.

The discussion moves forward along the path of four considerations. The first is that religions should not be understood as being in competition with one another. Second, arrival at that conclusion requires a reflective assessment of what is entailed in religious diversity. From there the discussion turns in the third place to a conception of the kernel of Christian faith in order to find an openness to other religions. The last point then situates Christian faith within a larger context of human history in order to arrive at the conviction that religious pluralism is not one of the deficits of human history but its positive natural condition.

No More Competition among Religions

In Europe during the High Middle Ages, leaders of the church could stir up a great deal of religious enthusiasm for going into battle for the faith. In Europe today, by contrast, one would find a general embarrassment among Christians about the Crusades and other missionary efforts that are associated with invasive force. Today's ethos includes a complete rejection of religious war and a recognition that nothing positive is gained by religiously motivated violence. If war itself is evil, religious warfare contradicts the very content of the faith of the religion that is drawn into it. Many have a strong sense of religious autonomy and resistance to anything like proselytism. This prompts a first proposal: religious faith traditions have to be understood today in a way that sets them into a relationship with one another that is noncompetitive.

Behind every interreligious antagonism there lies at some level a competitive instinct that one's own religious faith is superior to another. Competition rests on a comparative perspective that elicits considerations of higher and lower, superior and inferior, and true and false. The comparison becomes competitive when a characteristic of one religion is regarded as something lacking in another. The object of faith becomes in some manner a definable quantity or a set of contents or beliefs that some have and others do not. Within this context, when one party is richer, the other who lacks a certain datum of faith must be poorer. Truth and moral character become objectified into things that have been acquired and are regarded as possessions.

By contrast, a noncompetitive view of religious faith may be found in attitudes and behaviors that lie beneath or behind institutional forms. They are the subjective qualities of an existential spirituality. This is the response of faith as distinct (but inseparable) from the beliefs that give it expression.[1] In much of Christianity, these attitudes have grown friendlier toward other religions during the course of the twentieth century. On the one hand, all human beings are seekers; each faith tradition, by engaging transcendent reality, does something that is common to if not in solidarity with all other traditions. On the other hand, a reverent attitude toward the beliefs of other people recognizes that all religious faith engages a transcendence that cannot be reduced to clear conceptual forms. The transcendent object of faith is infinite, neither definable nor measurable, always exhibiting an aura of mystery. No religion can enjoy a comprehensive hold on ultimate reality.

From a social point of view everyone has a fundamental human right freely to enter into a relationship with transcendent reality. This freedom stems from the recognition that religion rests on a truly spiritual relationship of persons to transcendence, and this must be inherently free. This interior contact and relationship with transcendent reality constitutes the substance beneath organized religion, and it cannot be subject to coercion and be authentic at the same time. By

1. This is not the place to expand on the epistemology of faith. The structure of faith, its grasp of transcendent reality, and the relation of these to the propositions of faith are topics that have to be presupposed here. See Roger Haight, *Dynamics of Theology* (Maryknoll, NY: Orbis Books, 2001).

extension, the internal experiential core of organized religions cannot be judged by criteria from outside them, with exceptions that relate to obvious antisocial behavior patterns and beliefs that are spontaneously condemned by all. We seem to be able to extend to other cultures an internal, coherent, and autonomous validity. What is required for religious faith to attain such a noncompetitive respect for other religions?

Assessing Religious Diversity

Finding grounds for a noncompetitive view of religions may begin with reflection on the phenomenon of religious diversity. We live in a new situation in which the many major religious faiths are socially present to one another in the major cities of the world. It is hardly possible under these circumstances not to ask questions such as these: How should the religions relate to one another? Is one's own religion the true religion among the many? How do the other religions relate to one's own? How should we formulate a realistic and fair understanding of the diversity of religions? Is religious plurality a good thing? If it is good, why is it so threatening? In a former time these questions were rarely asked by Christians because the answers were presupposed. They are certainly asked today, and the answers are by no means the same across churches and among individual Christians but are the source of much debate.

Some years ago, Edward Schillebeeckx pointed out that when these questions are asked from a competitive point of view, they compound the problem.[2] For example, the question "Which religion is true?" or "Is there one true religion?" is almost always entertained from the perspective of one of the religions. The implicit supposition is that there is an answer, so that the question is framed in an intrinsically competitive way: if one religion represents the truth, then others either do not or do so in a less than adequate way. Because the question becomes appropriated from the perspective of the religion of the one asking the question, the norms for what passes as true are spontaneously derived from the perspective of that one faith tradition out of the many. Truth in other religions is measured by the truth of one's own tradition. But by the measure of each religion, other religions never measure up. Is there a way to open up the narrow competitive character of the way in which each religion relates to others in order to find a better and noncompetitive way to address religious pluralism?[3]

2. Edward Schillebeeckx, *Church: The Human Story of God* (New York: Crossroad, 1990), 164-65.

3. John Hick has proposed and defended a philosophical theory of religious

Before directly responding to that question one should bear in mind that the object of religious faith must remain hidden in mystery. Because religions revolve around faith in transcendent reality, they do not have an objective, comprehensive, descriptive, or conceptual grasp of the object of their faith: it remains elusive in its transcendence. For this reason, religions appear to be more authentic in proportion to their admission of their transcendental ignorance. This fundamental premise drawn from the philosophy and epistemology of religion gives theoretical grounding beyond historical fact for the legitimacy of religious pluralism. It also opens up space for each religion to be humble enough to respect other religious traditions.

On that premise, a more sympathetic way of broaching the question of truth in a situation of religious pluralism is this: how can we understand our own faith in a way that affirms and validates other religious traditions? Schillebeeckx phrases the question this way: "How can Christianity maintain its own identity and uniqueness and at the same time attach a positive value to the difference of religions in a non-discriminatory sense?"[4] This question is designed as a way of entering into the relationship between religions with a bias that other religions bear truth and that we bear some responsibility to be open to it, to find it, to acknowledge it, and appreciate it. Once we become convinced that other religions form their adherents in positive moral ways and appreciate their engagement with transcendent reality, we have some grounds for mutual religious recognition. The question accedes to the demand that other religions have to be understood on the basis of their own origin, history, and self-understanding. They cannot adequately be judged by criteria imposed on them from outside themselves. At the same time, they will in fact be judged wanting in the light of practices that attack human flourishing and ignore commonly accepted human values.

Schillebeeckx's formulation of the question intends to protect the legitimate autonomy of all religions. It does not presume that people abandon their own faith when they ask about other religions in positive terms. On one side, each religion has to provide for itself a rationale that opens up the possibility of other religions appreciating their legitimacy. On the other side, each religion will be able to recognize

---

pluralism that examines religions from a neutral point of view. Such reflection is exceptionally valuable and should not be discounted. At the same time, the actual encounters between religions force appreciations that are practical and proceed from below. The question posed here envisages some level of actual religious encounter. For John Hick's theory of religion see his *An Interpretation of Religion: Human Responses to the Transcendent* (New Haven: Yale University Press, 1989).

4. Schillebeeckx, *Church*, 165.

the legitimacy of the other only on the basis of its own vision of reality. In the end, the new form of the question of other religions simply removes the competitive assumption that for one religion to be true others have to be less so or simply false. It seeks the precise point at which the competition is dissolved.

To sum up here: a noncompetitive strategy of interrogating the grounds of religious pluralism and entering into a positive relationship with other religions asks this question: how can I understand my own religion in such a way that it opens up recognition of truth in other faith traditions? This formula tries to remove two obstacles to genuinely inquisitive interfaith dialogue that may lead to harmony. Negatively, it tries to eliminate competitiveness in the very asking of the question of truth in religion. And positively it accepts an implicit desire of our time to understand other religions sympathetically and to provide a basis in one's own faith for respect for the other's. In other words, it does not contradict people's own faith in trying to appreciate other religions, but precisely looks to the fundamentals of their own faith tradition for reasons to receive positively what other faith traditions say about themselves.

The Kernel of Christian Faith

Is it possible under these conditions to develop an answer to the comparative question about other religions in a way that is noncompetitive? On the assumption that people of other faiths could find an analogous logic, we ask Christianity whether there is something that belongs to the central logic of the faith that would allow Christians to appreciate the autonomous authenticity, truth, and value of other religions. The question looks for an appreciation of the fundamental logic of Christian faith in a way that opens up from inside that faith an expectation of the authenticity and truth of other religious faiths. Such a question could generate a variety of responses. The following formula provides an answer that is direct, simple, and laden with further consequences: *Christianity consists of faith in God, creator and savior, as God is revealed in the ministry of Jesus of Nazareth and in his death and resurrection. By revealing the mutual relationship between God and human beings, Jesus calls forth a way of life that follows certain fundamental principles illustrated in his ministry.* This representation of the kernel of Christian faith gives it a noncompetitive character and opens up a receptive attitude toward other religions. This can be illustrated in a schematic way in the following three points that will then be expanded in the next section.[5]

---

5. It should be clear that these three points are not meant to be reductionist. One

First, the object of Christian faith is God, the transcendent creator of heaven and earth and of all things. This creation was not a single act in the beginning; God is constantly creating and preserving reality at all times as its ground and the sustaining power of its being. God loves what God creates, and this guarantees the value of everything created. God is savior because God's very love of creation overflows itself to become the source and power of eternal fulfillment.

Second, this God, as the object of Christian faith, is revealed in and through the ministry, the death, and the resurrection of Jesus of Nazareth. Jesus spoke of God as loving father and preached what the world would be like if God's rule were followed in history; faith in his resurrection is hope in a promise of eternal life for all.

Third, authentic Christianity entails a following of Jesus, which has traditionally been called the imitation of Christ. People are authentic Christians or followers of Jesus Christ in the measure in which they internalize and try to live by the values of Jesus. The authenticity of a religion has to be regarded as a living or existential movement and not a notion or an idea. If another religion promotes values that are analogous to Jesus's depiction of fundamental moral attitudes, it offers plausible grounds for the truth of its message.

Religious Pluralism as a Natural Condition

Reflection on the three essentials of Christian faith will show that they provide Christians with the reasons why they can accept the possibility of the validity of other religious faiths.[6] And this provides the rationale for relating to other faiths in a noncompetitive way that is the condition for religious harmony and cooperation. Other religions may be regarded as autonomous groups of authentic and true religious brothers and sisters through their different faiths. Notice that the reasoning here does not measure the validity of other religions by Christian faith, at least in their details, for these faiths have their independent and autonomous groundings. Rather, the idea is to show how Christians can recognize and accept how other religions may be considered valid on the basis of a noncompetitive understanding of and appeal to their own Christian faith. What follows illustrates how this appeal to Christian faith might work by expanding on the core of Christian faith that was just outlined.

---

can schematize the corporate life of Christians over two millennia in many different ways to make a point; the intent is never reductionist in the sense of being exclusionary.

6. It should be clear that "validity" refers to the substance of a particular religious faith as distinct from all its various practices. All religions have their fundamentalisms and extremist abuses.

First, the God revealed by Jesus is transcendent and cannot be circumscribed by any finite manifestation or revelation. The transcendent creator of the universe and our earth within it is infinite, unimaginable, and incomprehensible reality; in short, God is absolute mystery. No matter how close and accessible God becomes in and through Jesus of Nazareth, God cannot be reduced to the size of any created reality, not even the humanity of Jesus, because God transcends and yet is immanent to and encompasses the entire universe in creative presence.

Second, Jesus taught that God is present to all reality and to all people in a personal and loving way. This means that all people have the potential to be in contact with this God. Because God completely embraces all that exists, the whole of creation can be an occasion for God's breaking into human consciousness. If God, as God is known to Christians, does not effectively love all persons, is not truly and effectively present to them, and does not in some way offer salvation and fullness of being to them, the revelation of the character of God that Jesus provides is not true and the salvation that Christians experience is called into question. God cannot be reduced to any single experience, revelation, or understanding. God's loving presence to the whole of reality makes it plausible if not necessary that God will be revealed in many different revelations according to historical situations. One of the differences of our time relative to the past is that our new global and galactic perspective shows better how a tribal God, a God who chooses one group over others, more readily appears as an idol for self-worship. To be God, God must transcend all of God's self-disclosures and at the same time and in some measure be reflected in them.

Third, Christianity teaches that, if people live according to various versions of the golden rule, which appear analogously in many if not most religions, they live in an essentially authentic relationship with God.[7] This implies two things. The first is that all who live by the golden rule, that is, they love and respect their fellow human beings as they themselves want to be treated, are following the rule of God as preached by Jesus. They are living by standards that are comparable to those preached by Jesus, not because of Jesus or Christianity but on the basis of their own faith. The second is that from a Christian perspective, this establishes an authentic response to what Christians call the God who graciously and gratuitously embraces all reality.

---

7. Jesus linked together the commandments of love of God and love of neighbor. Matthew develops the principle that the character of persons may be discerned better by actions than by words (Matt 7:15-21). The writer of 1 John develops at length the reciprocity between the love of God and the love of neighbor. See chapter 8, n. 12.

Because God is infinite transcendent mystery that exceeds anything that Christians can affirm of God, Christians can assume that the language of the other faiths describing the ultimate reality they experience in their lives will be a genuine revelation from which Christians themselves can learn. There must be more revelation of an infinite all-encompassing, present, and loving God than can be contained in only one faith tradition.[8]

Many Christians will consider these reflections both as commonsensical and as different from the logic of the Christian faith they were taught. But the challenge that this recapitulation poses to a reductionist reading of it is whether anything has been subtracted from Christian teaching other than various competitive assumptions. There is no reason within a noncompetitive framework for the assumption that, because Jesus is a real incarnation of no less than God (Nicaea), other religions may not have encountered an analogous incarnation of God's presence.

This view appeals to a spiritual encounter of God mediated by Jesus that, precisely in revealing God, shows a God who dwells incarnate at the center of all reality. This is what Dietrich Bonhoeffer sensed spiritually before he could work it out theologically: Christ is not an object of religion but the Lord of the world. "The ground for this lies in the revelation of God in Christ. Christ is the centre of life. . . ."[9] This view found its way into the documents of Roman Catholicism's most recent council, Vatican II. Grace and salvation are available to all people in ways that remain mysterious. The Council affirms no theoretical explanation other than the working of God, who is immanent Spirit.[10] The expectation of God's presence to other religions increases the plausibility of God's incarnation in Jesus. Subtract the competitive assumptions underlying standard Christian beliefs, and Jesus will appear more clearly as a revelation of God's presence to all people. The more God's presence to all people is recognized, the more Christian imagination will be released to find God at work in other religions.

These reflections point to a simple and powerful change of perspective. From our historical perspective religious pluralism appears to be inevitable. One cannot realistically conceive of one human race with

---

8. From the perspective of historically conscious theology, Edward Schillebeeckx writes that God's infinite transcendence overflows the limitations of every historical mediation (Schillebeeckx, *Church*, 166). From the perspective of Christian spirituality, this conviction flows from an encounter with Jesus that recognizes that he mediates a God who is both absolutely transcendent and lovingly present to all human beings. This spiritual conviction motivates this claim.

9. Dietrich Bonhoeffer, *Letters and Papers from Prison* (New York: Macmillan, 1962), 191.

10. Vatican II, *Gaudium et spes*, 22.

one uniform religion. Christianity and other religions as well have resisted this proposition. But this appeal to a noncompetitive view of Christian faith and other faith traditions opens up an entirely new world where religious pluralism is not a negative but the positive natural condition of humanity that is an essential part of human history from its beginning within the evolutionary process.

* * *

This chapter may be fittingly concluded with a proposal that appeals to common sense within a Christian milieu and may have wider application. The intensity of faith sometimes makes it difficult for truly religious people to think outside their narrow sphere of reference. And when this gets challenged, as it is being challenged today, the result can be confusing and even disorienting. In such situations the kind of reasoning that has been offered here may be helpful. But people also need a new kind of experience. This new appreciation of things can sometimes be found by trying on a proposal like a new jacket, wearing it for a while, and allowing it to become one's own. The proposition is this: Jesus revealed a God of infinite proportions and infinite love. This love from God embraces all that comes from God's creative hands. Thus, God is present and personally at work in each individual person and through them in all religions. Wherever and whenever people respond unselfishly and lovingly to others, they have been touched by this love of God, and their religious responses are authentic. Everything else is secondary to the interchange of love and mutual respect. This commonsensical reflection overcomes competitive religion and provides groundwork for interfaith harmony. If the Christian churches tried on and wore this proposition for some time, it would impel concrete behaviors that would build bridges between faiths, promote harmonious relationships with them, and stimulate cooperative action on pressing social issues.

CHAPTER THIRTEEN

Ecclesial Spirituality and Living with Other Religions

In a work published a number of years ago, I characterized ecclesial existence as a spirituality common to the whole church across the denominations.[1] This effort responded to a stalled ecumenical movement by minimizing the divisions among the churches in relation to a core of spiritual existence that all churches share. It softened the historical fragmentation of the church, which seems to be out of control, by recognizing that what appears as divisions may be no more than local adaptations in a wider Christian world. The focus was on the vast area of Christian faith that all Christians and churches actually embrace in common if not together. The best way to describe our corporate ecclesial existence is in terms of a spirituality that holds the whole church together rather than by theological analysis of traditional doctrines or organizational structures. As I have noted many times in this book, by spirituality I mean the way persons or groups direct their lives in the face of some transcendent principle. An ecclesial spirituality refers to the way of life of the members of the church. On the basis of principles and practices learned from Jesus of Nazareth, Christians organize their lives and act responsibly before God.

But there is more. The cosmopolitanism that has accompanied globalization recognizes interdependencies across local boundaries and opens up indigenous identities.[2] Many people now acknowledge that religious pluralism describes the natural condition of historical human existence. From a Christian perspective, just as we have gotten used to a plurality of churches, we are now beginning to reckon with the plurality of religions and their influences on one another. Although religious pluralism represents the status quo, getting used to it does not correspond with the Christianity in which most Christians were brought up. This sets up a tension within Christian consciousness

1. Roger Haight, "The Promise of Constructive Comparative Ecclesiology: Partial Communion," *Ecclesiology* 4 (2008): 1-23. See also chapters 5 and 11 above.

2. Ulrich Beck, *The Cosmopolitan Vision* (Cambridge: Polity Press, 2006).

between a conviction about the truth of the revelation in Jesus Christ and the existence of other religions that Christians have come to respect and accept as they interact with and get to know their constituents. It also raises a serious question about the appropriateness of missionary activity that aims at sharing Christian revelation with others.

These issues are usually discussed in the domain of Christology. But the alignment between the church and Jesus Christ means that the issue is also ecclesiological. In many ways ecclesial spirituality identifies the place where these questions are most sharply felt. And one question among the many has become particularly acute: should the Christian church pursue its mission of communicating Christianity in fields where other religions hold sway? Can one really hold together a deep appropriation of the differences among cultures, the inner freedom of religious belonging, and a conviction that other religions contain revealed truth, and at the same time continue to cling to a Christian mission when in many situations that mission essentially causes conflict?

This chapter describes characteristics of a common ecclesial spirituality that appreciates Christian life in a situation of religious pluralism and yet defends the universal relevance of Jesus of Nazareth and the mission to represent him to all others. On the one hand, I want to respect religious pluralism; on the other hand, I will explain how Jesus and thus the church can be understood not as divisive factors among the religions but precisely as agents of reconciliation. In other words, I find principles in an ecclesial spirituality that both rejoices in religious pluralism and understands how the church has a universal mission not to undermine other religions but to support them. The key to this paradoxical position lies in an ecclesial spirituality that appropriates Jesus not as a particular figure that divides but as one who respects other religions and draws all religions into mutual and friendly exchange. This essay does not provide a formula for mission activity in concrete situations; historical contexts are always unique and always determine the required practical approach. The goal here is rather to explain how such a reconciling mission is possible.

Such a large proposal cannot be definitively defended in a short space. This relatively short chapter bears more resemblance to an extended outline than to a comprehensive statement. The way Christians actually appropriate religious pluralism involves a complex mixture of many factors and is itself plural. From that perspective the goal is to promote ongoing discussion. The use of a series of theses to structure the argument will help to guide the line of thought through a maze of issues.

Truth and Error

Thesis 1. *All religions contain some truth and some error; insofar as a religion is true, it is universally relevant and should be shared.*

This first thesis introduces some of the terms of the discussion and facets of the problem under consideration. The very notion of religious pluralism provides a good place to begin. Pluralism does not refer to sheer plurality, but plurality within a context of unity. Plurality that knows no interaction presents no problem. Also, the plurality of religions is a fact, and this essay engages the plurality of religions as a matter of principle. It does so from a Christian standpoint. The conviction that there should be a pluralism of religions, that religious pluralism is a good, is presupposed here and not defended.[3] But the idea of missionary expansion remains challenging and needs reflection.

One should also be clear about the meaning of truth and especially religious truth. The term "true" means that an idea of something or a proposition about a certain object corresponds in some measure with the reality to which it points, the way things are. Truth is subjective, a state of mind; only secondarily does it mean the way things are. Truth then lies in the relationship between symbols, ideas, and linguistic proposals and the reality they indicate. When people speak of religious truth they frequently imply something normative, as in the expression "the truth." Plainly some things are true but so socially or culturally dependent that they do not travel or are simply not that important. It is true but not universally normative that motorists drive on the right side of the road. It follows that the idea of the normative suggests that some proposals also bear a universal relevance and a weighty importance.

Most Christians affirm the first part of the thesis about the mixture of truth and error in all religions. Its significance lies in the universal relevance of something that is important and true about ultimate reality and about human existence. If something is true in that depth, it bears the character of being normative. Even though words such as "normative" and "infallible" do not really add anything substantial to a proposal that is true, meaningful, and important, the normative quality means that religious truth bears a universal relevance and an inner impetus for people to share it with all human beings. For example, from the beginning the earliest followers of Jesus recognized that Jesus's being raised into God's life was not only about Jesus. It had significance for themselves and for all human beings. This event was

3. Chapter 11 of this work gives reasons why religious pluralism can be considered something positive and good in principle.

important and universally relevant. Humanity itself was implicated. This was not a social, cultural, or religious eccentricity, but a revelation about the destiny of the human as such.

This explains why almost all the Gospel stories of an appearance of Jesus after his death carry a mission motif. Many express the idea of mission in terms of bearing witness. In others it is explicit. In John's Gospel Jesus appears to the disciples and says to them, "'As the Father has sent me, even so I send you'" (John 20:21). The association of Jesus's appearances and his explicit sending corresponds with the implications of coming to awareness that Jesus is alive; the depth and resonance of the Easter experience include a desire to share it. The revelation that the one in whom the rule of God had been encountered was then vindicated by God was not a private experience. It had to be communicated. An analogous impulse should be present in all religions insofar as they represent something that is true, important, and experienced as universally relevant.

If the impulse toward mission accompanies truth itself, and each religion has some purchase on ultimate reality, then each religion should respect the other's mission to communicate. God's status of being transcendent and immanent to all disallows characterizing a whole religion as either true or false; all religions reflect God's immanent presence in some measure, and all do so with inevitable particularity, limitation, and error. A sense of inadequacy before absolute mystery forbids most comprehensive judgments that are exclusive. Recognition that the sources of revelation are culturally conditioned and limited, and that present-day interpretations will always be affected by social location and perspective, should counsel modesty. People today have a definite sense that no single religion can exhaust the absolute mystery of God. These reflections add up to a judgment that each religion, in principle, should be able to learn more about ultimate reality in its own idiom from those bearing witness in another idiom.

Humans as One Family

Thesis 2. *Human beings are one family, so that foundational religious worldviews should uphold a common humanity and not be divisive.*

Classical philosophies and theologies took the unity of the human race for granted; today it can be argued empirically. The account of "creation" from a scientific perspective frequently stimulates a deeper sense of religious wonder and awe than does the mythic story of Adam and Eve. It displaces that story with a vivid sense of human unity, smallness, and contingency accompanied by infinitely complex dependencies. If religious spirituality begins with questioning and wonder, science has provided new religious stimulation. The unimaginable size of the universe, which has evolved through the interaction of stable laws and randomness over an immense period of time, transfixes human attention. Evolutionary biology and paleontology are close to completing the genealogy of our species, *homo sapiens*. With the emergence of the human species, evolution ushered in a new dimension of existence. The common sphere of human intelligence provides a theater in which spectacular dramas unfold. In human consciousness the objective order is framed by self-consciousness and becomes the subject matter of human knowledge. Within human consciousness the whole of matter, the universe of fire, ice, stone, and chemical and biological processes, becomes transformed into a new world charged with meaning and a new kind of intentional and deliberate creativity.

As the story of the biological evolution of the human species becomes widely accepted, it will be obvious that fundamental religious worldviews have to conform to it. The more the unity of our humanity becomes established by science, the less able are religious conceptions of origins realistically to single out or privilege any group above any other. Our common humanity, and more and more our corporate responsibility for one another on our planet, must be accounted for in viable religious worldviews. They cannot be divisive in principle and remain credible. They have to support the unity of the human family and our common responsibility for our natural ecosystem. Religions must build bridges between races, continents, nations, and cultures rather than encourage division. Religions represent ultimacy; that ultimacy has to be understood in a way that is universally relevant and binds peoples together across other spontaneously adopted divisions.

A new appreciation for the particularity of distinct cultures and the autonomy of the religions embedded in these cultures has a bearing on religious truth and its dissemination. There should be no missionary activity that is not invited.[4] This axiom flows from a conviction about the freedom of religious affiliation. It has particular relevance for religious cultures that do not have the resources to enter into dialogue with Christianity or another world religion on an equal footing. They are thus threatened even by the prospect of what may appear as

---

4. The newly globalized world and the sensitivity of particular national and cultural communities, especially in the sphere of religion, have changed the climate for missionary activity. The Dalai Lama formulates this principle with Buddhist simplicity: "Generally speaking, the Buddhist attitude about the issue of spreading its message is this: unless someone approaches a teacher and requests specific teachings, it is not right for a teacher to impose his or her views and doctrines onto another person." See Dalai Lama, *The Good Heart: A Buddhist Perspective on the Teachings of Jesus* (Boston: Wisdom Publications, 1996), 98.

dialogue in an egalitarian context. For example, international urban centers may be far more relaxed about religious pluralism than are rural settings. The history of Christian association with colonialism should make all people engaged in missionary activity hypersensitive to issues of religious freedom. If a religion's missionary activity is causing human divisions, something wrong is going on that bears investigation.

Grounds for a Spiritual Embrace of Other Religions

Thesis 3. *Christianity has grounds for an embracing interreligious spirituality in the conception of a personal creator God.*

With this thesis we move to some constructive premises for a universally relevant Christian mission. Since these are Christian principles, they do not reflect the convictions of all religions, but other religions may find functional analogies within their own belief systems.[5]

In the Abrahamic religions the doctrine of creation represents a common framework of understanding. Early in Christian history this doctrine was made more specific by the notion of creation out of nothing.[6] This belief has an entirely different source than the scientific story. A religious approach to creation does not proceed "outside-in" but "inside-out." The mind does not construct beginnings from observation, and creation in a religious sense does not primarily refer to an event in the beginning. Rather, humans can intuit their being created within the experience or recognition of their own absolutely dependent existence and extrapolate that condition to all finite reality. Not having within one's self power and control over one's own being translates into an experience of being buoyed up by transcendent forces.[7]

---

5. The term "functional analogies" is an adaptation of the phrase "functional equivalents" used by Perry Schmidt-Leukel in an essay comparing Buddhism and Christianity. See Perry Schmidt-Leukel, "Buddha and Christ as Mediators of the Transcendent: A Christian Perspective," in *Buddhism and Christianity in Dialogue: The Gerald Weisfeld Lectures 2004*, ed. Perry Schmidt-Leukel (Norfolk: SCM Press, 2005), 170.

6. Clement of Alexandria and Tertullian make this doctrine explicit over against both classical thought and biblical images of God ordering preexistent chaos. See Jaroslav Pelikan, *The Christian Tradition: A History of the Development of Doctrine,* Vol. 1, *The Emergence of the Catholic Tradition (100–600)* (Chicago: University of Chicago Press, 1971), 35-36.

7. This is a pretheological insight; the experience may occur spontaneously in different ways; it is potentially available to any human being. But from a Christian theological perspective one would explain this experience with a theology of grace. No one better than Karl Rahner has shown how experiences, which appear to be "natural," are grounded in the universal presence and operation of saving grace. The term "grace" may be used as synonymous with the Holy Spirit.

The idea of creation out of nothing should not be understood as though God and the created world coexist as over against each other within a continuum. The creator creating is the "within" of all beings; all things exist within the power of creative energy. God is not an entity, a being, or an identifiable object. God is not a big person in the sky, but is personal nonetheless. How could ultimate reality be less than what evolution itself has produced? This conception of God as infinite and personal creative energy complements the scientific story with an implosion of the creator's concern for all of reality, even for its infinitesimal parts. When the creator is conceived as creating out of nothing, nothing stands between the creator creating and the created creature.[8] This conception places the personal creator God inside all creatures as the ground or sustaining power of their being. And the idea that God's power is itself personal love wraps all beings in a mantle of infinite dignity and worth, of ontological value, despite the random contingency of their empirical coming to be and dying off. Everything exists within the love of the creator.[9] This is the deepest ground of Christian spirituality, and understanding the role of Jesus Christ takes its place within the framework of the God who is creator.

A personal creator God must love that which God creates. It seems reasonable to think that God loves all humans equally and impartially, at least as a premise for their existence. This idea can be found in the Hebrew scriptures, and it becomes explicit early in the Jesus movement. Luke takes two chapters to tell the story of Cornelius, in which Peter concludes that "God shows no partiality, but in every nation anyone who fears him and does what is right is acceptable to him" (Acts

---

8. "Finitude or contingency mean that man and the world hang by themselves in a vacuum, above absolute nothingness. There is nothing that can be brought between the world and God to interpret the relationship between them. This is what people mean when in symbolic language they talk about 'creation from nothing.'" See Edward Schillebeeckx, "Kingdom of God: Creation and Salvation," *Interim Report on the Books* Jesus *and* Christ (New York: Crossroad, 1981), 114.

9. Science tends to understand reality itself as energy. The idea of physical energy provides a language by which mathematical formulas can describe its structures. The Hebrew and Christian scriptures use an analogous metaphor, "Spirit," which refers to the energy of life and existence. But its meaning is very different from scientific energy and has to be understood in a religious way. Spirit in a religious sense is the immanent presence of the creating and enlivening power of God. Primary and secondary causality mean that "God is continuously involved in the dynamic unfolding of creation as its animating source and ground. Creation has no independent existence. It is given *ex nihilo* by the creator God who positively wills its very existence. The openness and autonomy of creation in its dynamic becoming is not contrastive with divine efficacy but is the very gift of that efficacy. *Creatio ex nihilo* explicitly affirms the contingency and open-ended 'play' of creation." See Brian D. Robinette, "*Creatio ex Nihilo,* Resurrection, and Divine Gratuity," *Theological Studies* 72 (2011): 541.

10:34-35; Rom 2:11). This teaching correlates in Luke's theology with a conception of God as Spirit as a presence in the world, acting within history as an immanent energy within creatures. This conception of the working of God's all-encompassing love is not a demoting leveler but a power that raises all to a transcendent level of dignity. Thus, the God who loves those of other religions with the same love by which God loves Christians implicitly asks for or demands a spirituality that embraces all people as they are, within and with their religions. This axiom for spirituality is closely aligned with the second thesis regarding the nondivisive but reconciling impetus of religion.

To sum up this thesis: no closer union between humans and God can be conceived than God creating us out of nothing but God's love. This conception makes God the within of all things and enfolds the whole existence of all people with God's love. But is there a way of interpreting Jesus Christ in such a way that the church's representation of him does not appear divisive?

A Nondivisive Christian Mission Spirituality

Thesis 4. *A distinction between Jesus of Nazareth and later Christian interpretations of him can support a nondivisive Christian mission spirituality.*

With this thesis we move from an all-encompassing spiritual conception of reality to the particular mediator of Christian faith, Jesus of Nazareth who is the Christ. The particularity of any religion, the historical symbols that mediate it and lie at its source, presents the sharpest points of differentiation in interreligious exchange and thus the contentious edge in missionary witness. We begin with the premise that these differences are not bad; they are not something to be overcome. But when they lead to conflict and even open hostility, they undermine the unity of human community and cause undue suffering. The particularity of Christianity comes to a focus in Jesus of Nazareth, and the question of the relation of Jesus Christ to other religious mediators has been discussed in Christology with intensity for decades. But a fresh approach may be found through ecclesiology and especially ecclesial spirituality. At the end of the day, Christians have experienced this problem within the church through which they feel rooted in reality.

Three distinctions that are commonly recognized can define an approach to an understanding of Jesus Christ that will help open up a Christian mission that need not be divisive in principle. Each of these distinctions needs further development than can be provided here. But they are also directly intuitive and straightforward.

First, one can distinguish between Jesus of Nazareth and later theological interpretations of him. Jesus of Nazareth is a public figure presented in the Gospels. Everyone can approach him through the Gospel stories. He was a prophetic figure in his time, but in itself his teaching does not appear divisive today.

This distinction becomes more complex when one scratches the surface. No historical datum and certainly no person in history can be appreciated without interpretation. Therefore one cannot completely distinguish Jesus from the New Testament interpretations of him. Also he is presented in the Gospels within a context and from a distinctive perspective. Thus, one should not understand this distinction in a manner that presumes a separation of Jesus from all interpretation or that Jesus appeared in history in the exact manner in which the Gospels present him. The stories presenting Jesus already are colored portraits of him, and they are received by anyone considering him within an interpretive framework. But the quest for the historical Jesus has shown that one can go some distance in distinguishing the person and ministry of Jesus from later interpretations of him in the New Testament and certainly from later doctrines about him.[10]

The second distinction is analogous to the first but takes it further. It lies in the difference but not separation between a spirituality of following Jesus and formulas of belief about Jesus. There are several ways to illustrate this distinction. One would be to read the New Testament as it developed historically, considering the texts chronologically as they were written, and to read other witnesses through the second and third centuries. This exercise shows how a consistent spiritual attachment to Jesus and following of him gradually generated, through historical circumstance, conversation, and debate, successive interpretations of him in response to new questions. Another way is to consider the plurality of christologies within the whole church at any given time among all who claim a basic and in many respects common Jesus-centered spirituality. In brief, faith as an existential response and way of life is distinct from a particular belief and the many beliefs that may be derived from the same faith.

The structural soundness of this distinction is bolstered by the fact that it appears in other religions as well. For example, the Buddhist Rita Gross distinguishes between "verbal doctrines [that] are ultimately in the realm of *upaya*, skillful means or method, not the

10. The historical interpretations of Jesus range from the popular to the scholarly exegetical, for example, from Albert Nolan, *Jesus before Christianity* (Maryknoll, NY: Orbis Books, 1976), to John P. Meier, *A Marginal Jew: Rethinking the Historical Jesus*, 4 vols. (New York: Doubleday, 1991–2009).

realm of *prajna,* intuitive clear seeing or 'truth.'"[11] Truth is one, true for all: "*prajna* is unitive and the same for all people in all cases. But truth is not a matter of doctrines and doctrines are neither true nor false; they are more or less useful in the circumstances at hand."[12] The distinction says that transcendent truth is apprehended by existential "knowing" or faith, while doctrines, which may appear to be forms of knowledge, are actually objectified expressions of the act of relating to transcendence. What Gross insists on is the coequal status of different faiths and the location of beliefs as practical and variable forms of their expression.[13]

A third distinction, influenced by the doctrine of creation, sees a difference between christocentrism and theocentrism in the structure of Christian faith. Christocentrism makes Jesus of Nazareth the object of Christian faith; theocentrism makes the creator God the object of Christian faith and considers Jesus of Nazareth as the revealer of God and the mediator of faith. This distinction is a real one because the large frameworks within which a given person's faith in Jesus unfolds will be different in each case. But the difference should not be exaggerated. For example, from a Christian perspective, a theocentric position does not undermine the doctrinal conviction of the divinity of Jesus Christ. To hold that a given particular historical symbol, a specific person, thing, or event, is mediator of ultimate reality immediately assigns some ultimate status to that mediator, because the mediator always makes present that which is mediated. That spiritual experience remains. Theocentrism therefore does not undercut the Christian belief in the divinity of Jesus, but it does challenge an anthropomorphic conception of the various formulas of belief in the divinity of Jesus.

These distinctions need more discussion than can be given them at this point. But when the church represents Jesus in the terms of the Gospels, people of other religions may be attracted to him and find what Jesus is referring to in their own religions under another name. Or they may notice analogies between Jesus and the central symbol of their own faith. For example, many find analogies between Jesus and Gautama and the spiritualities they represent. Finding this common ground in historical beginnings and originating spiritualities, as dis-

11. Rita M. Gross, "Meditating on Jesus," in *Buddhists Talk about Jesus, Christians Talk about the Buddha,* ed. Rita M. Gross and Terry C. Muck (New York: Continuum, 2000), 38.

12. Ibid.

13. Ibid., 38-39. When truth is located in the realm of doctrine, *upaya,* or verbal expressions, this "fuels the hope for and often the claim of, final truth in verbal form" and "an adherence to that creed as more important than an understanding of it" (39).

tinct from over-beliefs developed later, provides a place where people of different religions can meet.[14] These distinctions provide a point of entry into a common place for conversation about differences of belief.

Dialogue and Religious Reconciliation

Thesis 5. *Missionary dialogue with other religious communities can represent Jesus as a proponent of religious reconciliation.*[15]

It is not enough to say that Jesus and the church are not intrinsically or essentially divisive. The situation today demands an effort to understand whether the church preaching Jesus Christ can be an agent of reconciliation among the religions. Is this possible?

Missiologists today speak of a goal of mission as reconciliation in personal, social, political, cultural, and ecumenical conflicts. They rarely speak of interreligious conflicts under the heading of reconciliation.[16] Conflicts among religions seem to fall under the category of interreligious dialogue so that interreligious alienation and hostility are not the prominent object of reconciliation. But missionary activity today bears a great potential for creating religious conflict. Can the church be satisfied with the hope that, if it remains a passive presence in another religious culture, it will not become divisive? Or does the church have a positive mission of religious reconciliation? Or should missionary activity be halted because it is an agent of religious conflict?[17] On what basis can the church bear public witness to

---

14. The term "over-beliefs" is drawn from William James, *The Varieties of Religious Experience* (London: Collins, 1971), 488-90. It refers to beliefs that have their roots in spiritual experience; these beliefs grow out of spiritual experience and refer back to it.

15. The missiological literature on the mission of reconciliation is extensive. Here is a sampling of works that have been consulted: Matthew D. Lundberg, "Repentance as a Paradigm for Christian Mission," *Journal of Ecumenical Studies* 45 (2010): 202; Robert Kaggwa, "Is Reconciliation the New Model for Mission? Reflections on the Rwandan Genocide and Conflicts in the Great Lakes Region of Africa," *Studies in World Christianity*, 9, no. 2 (2003): 244-64; Joerg Rieger, "Theology and Mission between Neocolonialism and Postcolonialism," *Mission Studies* 21 (2004): 201-27; World Council of Churches, "The Nature and Mission of the Church: A Stage on the Way to a Common Statement," Faith and Order Paper 198 (Geneva: World Council of Churches, 2005); World Council of Churches, *Mission as Ministry of Reconciliation,"* Preparatory Paper 10 (Geneva: WCC, 2005). Behind much of this writing is the groundbreaking book of Robert J. Schreiter, *Reconciliation: Mission & Ministry in a Changing Social Order* (Maryknoll, NY: Orbis Books, 1992).

16. Stephen B. Bevans and Roger P. Schroeder, *Constants in Context: A Theology of Mission for Today* (Maryknoll, NY: Orbis Books, 2004), 389-94.

17. If the church is to be an agent of reconciliation, it must show signs of being reconciled within itself. When divisions within the church are not reconciled, it cannot credibly play this role. The World Council of Churches makes this point: "This

its faith without proposing itself as a replacement to the culture and faith of its interlocutors? To put it forcefully, can a faith focused on such a particular revealer as Jesus of Nazareth who is the Christ provide anything else than an option that threatens every other religion as an alternative? A few years ago, representatives of other religions told how they shuddered whenever they heard the phrase "Christian mission," because it always amounted to an attack on their own religion. The reaction was analogous to the way many Christians hear the word *jihad* as meaning aggressive violence.

What follows is an attempt to answer this complex question with a response that brings forward some of the principles just laid out.

Turning first to premises, Christian mission presupposes that God's presence and love are entailed in God's creative power that sustains human history from within. God is present in all religions. At some fundamental level this Christian belief, which has analogies in other religions that encompass the whole of human history, should soften the usual reasons for competitiveness among religions. It removes the question of salvation in any ultimate sense from being at stake in Christian mission. God's presence as Spirit and grace undergirds reality itself. The former urgency for mission is removed and replaced by a new urgency for peace in a world churning with conflict. There will be no peace among the nations without peace among the religions. But whether or not religion is mixed up with a particular alienation and violence, religion should be a force of reconciliation.

Mission, as it is envisioned here, will not have doctrines about Jesus Christ as its leading edge. Christian witness and preaching should first of all point to Jesus's preaching of God's values and what a spirituality of following Jesus entails. The Gospel portrayal of the ministry of Jesus of Nazareth shows that he represents transcendent reality that is completely given to the flourishing of human existence. Jesus represents a creator God who is the God of all. Jesus thus supports all that is humanly positive in other religions; he does not compete with but endorses everything that augments salutary human development. Christians should present Jesus in such a way that he underlines everything and does not undermine anything in other religions that promotes human life. Jesus only challenges those practices that attack or neglect human existence in crisis. His prophetic ministry negates only the negation of human life. Discernment of the difference may not be as simple as that, not even within Christianity itself. But this

---

repentance within the church of Christ is itself part of the ministry and witness of reconciliation in the world" (World Council of Churches, "Mission as Ministry," #24). At the same time missionary activity should not be postponed until this intra-Christian reconciliation has been accomplished.

formula defines a mindset and direction of Christian interchange with other religions that provide a way of entering into a reconciling conversation without supremacist language and interpretation.

This strategy does not envisage Christians surrendering their beliefs in Jesus Christ. The distinction of spirituality from beliefs does not imply abandoning them. This point can be clarified by an abstract characterization of stages that put a finer point on the goal of mission, whether it be the mission of Christianity or another religion's reaching out to share its convictions with others.

A first stage consists in bearing witness to Jesus of Nazareth and the kind of spirituality that he preached and engendered in his followers as portrayed in the Gospels. Everyone in their own languages can perceive and appreciate at a basic level what Jesus offers.[18] Analogously, Buddhist literature or teachers bear witness to the teaching of the Buddha and the spirituality it engenders. The Christian may read the life of Buddha, learn of his four noble truths and the eightfold path toward enlightenment. He or she may read the *Dhammapada* and be drawn into the many practices of meditation that promote the mindfulness and compassion that help define Buddhist spirituality.[19]

A second stage consists of a more deliberate interpretation of the spirituality of the other religion and its sources. If one is drawn into the message and person of Jesus, it will not be too long before a person or group begins to appropriate Jesus into their own world spirituality and its beliefs. Thus, for example, Buddhists may interpret Jesus as an enlightened one because of the power of his teaching, the witness of his life, and the authority he enjoys among so many. A Buddhist may "recognize Christ as a remarkable *rupakaya* manifestation of Buddhahood itself, a powerful means through which followers of Christ have indeed communed with and learned to embody liberating qualities of *dharmakaya*" despite differences in understanding.[20] And a Christian might interpret the Buddha as a person who was enlightened and empowered by the Holy Spirit like a prophet in ancient Judaism or as the Gospels of Mark, Matthew, and Luke depict Jesus of Nazareth.[21]

A third stage of mission in both directions consists in dialogue about

18. Missiologists will recognize the analogy at this point with the strategy for mission described by Vincent J. Donovan in *Christianity Rediscovered* (Maryknoll, NY: Orbis Books, 1992).

19. *The Dhammapada*, trans. Gil Fronsdal (Boston: Shambhala, 2006).

20. John Makransky, "Buddha and Christ as Mediators of the Transcendent: A Buddhist Perspective," in *Buddhism and Christianity in Dialogue*, 199.

21. Perry Schmidt-Leukel finds a functional equivalency between Jesus being an incarnation of divinity and the earthly Buddha being an incarnation of transcendent *Dharma*. See his "Buddha and Christ as Mediators of the Transcendent: A Christian Perspective," 151-75.

beliefs. Here theologians and spiritual leaders discuss and compare beliefs to find underlying differences and value them, to notice functional analogies, and to appropriate places where the beliefs entailed in the spiritualities converge. But notice how this dialogue transpires as a third stage of an earlier process or set of premises. In this view of things, the first two stages have prepared a situation in which theological reflection consists in a joint exercise and bears a character of searching into transcendence. The mutual respect and trust that are established in the first stages open up a conversation that is not competitive. This human exchange recognizes deep differences in supposition, logic, and conclusion, and yet remains a shared quest entered from a place where people enjoy a common human existence in the face of transcendent mystery.

In sum, the new situation of pluralism calls the Christian church, as well as other religions, to a mission of reconciliation among the religions. Prior to entering into dialogue about doctrines and beliefs, this situation needs a comparative spirituality based on a fundamental appreciation of other spiritual practices, if not an actual sharing of them. A Christian spirituality that bears witness to the theocentric ministry of Jesus of Nazareth can be appreciated noncompetitively by people of other religions, just as the spiritual practices of other religions can be appropriated by Christianity. This level of spiritual interaction opens up the possibility of the Christian church mediating religious reconciliation.

The Common Bond of Compassion

Thesis 6. *All religions should feel united by compassion for people who suffer.*

This thesis should reflect a common sentiment in all religions. It states in interpersonal terms the consequences of the actual solidarity of the human race. Especially the poor of our common world require the love of their fellow human beings. A natural tendency to feel compassion for human beings who are suffering unites all people, whether or not it is actually elicited or acted upon. This common impulse transcends the religions because it is rooted in a shared humanity. From a Christian perspective, it reflects the will of the creator of a single species, marked by solidarity, all loved by the same God, and invited to be grateful and to show gratitude in practice. The concern for those marginalized from access to the ordinary means for flourishing in society, or for survival, provides a common ethical bond among all people and an imperative for cooperation through concerted action to resist and redress situations of social suffering. Most of the world's major religions share these values and provide a rationale for them.

There should be open interfaith conversation on public social issues, and this can happen prior to theological dialogue. It is true that the social conditions for amicable religious pluralism cannot be presupposed: all people do not enjoy religious liberty and its counterpart, the separation of formal religion and government. Moreover, religious pluralism inevitably tends to carry with it a certain privatization of each one's personal religious views as a mechanism for getting along socially. But religious convictions still have a strong bearing on society; they influence people's political views, public commitments, and actual behaviors. Religious beliefs and practices may in fact be one of the more important factors that determine individuals' public commitments. Despite their particular ideological and pragmatic political alliances, for religious reasons people should be able to unite around a desire to reach out to the poor and to join in efforts to integrate the marginalized into society. Such committed participation forges deep spiritual bonds that can actually accomplish religious reconciliation in particular instances.[22]

* * *

The more we become interdependent and develop a world consciousness, the more we realize that the whole species is absorbed with conflict and needs reconciliation. Can religions help in mediating a spirit that will draw people together rather than help to divide them? What is needed to even begin to think that religion can play such a role? This essay has addressed that question from the perspective of Christianity. It argues on the basis of Christian spirituality, which has its roots in living according to the pattern of Jesus of Nazareth. Allowing spirituality in that concentrated formula to be the leading face of Christian mission can enable the church to represent Jesus Christ as an agent of reconciliation among the religions. The spirituality of Jesus offers no competition to other religions. The appropriation of Jesus's teaching, especially concerning the rule of a loving creator God, supports other religions insofar as they promote human flourishing and concern for the weakest among us.

---

22. No one has done more to bring together the themes of liberation and interfaith dialogue than Paul Knitter. He brings these concerns together around the theme of Christian mission most pointedly in *Jesus and the Other Names: Christian Mission and Global Responsibility* (Maryknoll, NY: Orbis Books, 1996). These themes interact still more pointedly in his intimate dialogue with Buddhism in *Without Buddha I Could Not Be a Christian* (Oxford: One World, 2009), 167-212.

Several decades ago, Wilfred Cantwell Smith proposed an order of progression for interreligious dialogue. It moves from a consciousness of "us and them," to a consciousness of "I and thou" that engenders personal and sympathetic mutual understanding. But the goal of such interchange is to reach a higher "we consciousness," in which people work together across religious differences in a common effort to understand ourselves religiously.[23] A return to Jesus and to the primary religious language of the Gospels may allow the phrase "Christian mission" to be heard by other religions in an unthreatening way and allow the church to become a reconciling force in our present historical situation.

23. See Wilfred Cantwell Smith, *The Faith of Other Men* (New York: Harper Torchbooks, 1972), 129.

CHAPTER FOURTEEN

Trinity as the Central Christian Doctrine

Theologians and church leaders continually speak of the doctrine of trinity as the foundation of Christian faith and life. At the same time, few people have any idea of what the doctrine means after having said that there is one God who consists of three persons. Those theologians who have figured out how three can be one and one three seem to know too much; and those who dismiss the doctrine as impenetrable seem to be missing something.

This attempt to make sense of the doctrine rests on a foundation of two suppositions. The first says that the term "trinity" is not a name of God but refers to a teaching or doctrine about God. Although God is absolute incomprehensible mystery, what we say about God in our doctrines should be comprehensible on the basis of the reasons why we say what we say. In an earlier chapter, it was insisted that God remain absolute mystery. But we still speak about God, and, when we do, coherent reasons should support our speech. The second supposition underlines the monotheistic character of Christian faith. Christians do not believe in three gods, so that any language that suggests that trinity refers to three distinct gods misrepresents Christian faith. The doctrine of trinity does not engage numbers and has nothing to do with how one can be three or three one. Insofar as theologians have become preoccupied with this, they have corrupted the doctrine.

This attempt to retrieve the meaningfulness of this doctrine proceeds in four steps. The first briefly summarizes the story of how the doctrine developed. The second part provides the key to this interpretation. It shows how trinity is a narrative doctrine, because it implicitly summarizes the Christian story. The third part indicates how that story has broken down today so that we need a new version of the story the doctrine tells. The fourth part schematically outlines a new version of the Christian story. The fundamental idea that supports this chapter lies in "narrative," how the doctrine encapsulates the story of Christian experience.

The Genesis and Development of the Doctrine

The doctrine of trinity is a product of the historical development of doctrine. The salient point arising from this history is the fact that the doctrine was not given all at once, that it does not appear as such in scripture, but took over three hundred years to develop. This simple factual point bears importance because it shows that during the first four centuries the church did not have this doctrine in the form that became standardized in the fourth century. This indicates that, just as its fourth-century form was a product of development, the doctrine in its present form is open to new theological interpretation. This limited goal allows a schematic description of this development, which is presented at greater length in all histories of doctrine. What follows qualifies less as a history of the development and more as an analytical commentary on stages of that development.[1]

To begin, the belief in God creator of heaven and earth was in place when Jesus appeared. The creator God, whom Jesus called Father but described with female imagery as well, was the creator God of Israel. But during his ministry and after his death the followers of Jesus experienced in him God's salvation. In other words, God appeared to be immanent and at work in the person of Jesus for human liberation in the different ways in which this was expressed.

How did the growing Jesus movement and incipient Christian community express God's saving presence and action in Jesus? It is tempting to ask how they "explained" God's working within Jesus. But the religious metaphors and ideas they employed are not really "explanations" but ways of communicating the impact that Jesus had on them. Their principal way of expressing God's power in Jesus used "Spirit" language, where Spirit referred to the dynamic life-giving and power-enhancing impulse of God within the worldly sphere. Spirit language reflected the encounter with the effects of God's immanent presence and power. The Gospels of Mark, Matthew, and Luke are suffused with descriptions of Jesus empowered by God's Spirit. John's Gospel, by contrast, is better known for introducing the metaphor of God's Word to express the working of God within him. The "Word" of God contains deep and far-reaching resonance, both in the Hebrew scriptures and in Greek philosophy. In Israel, God's Word commanded: God spoke and it was done. In Greek culture, "Word" translated as "Logos" reflected intelligence and the order of reality. As the Jesus

1. I outline this story in several places in order to ensure a historically conscious appreciation of this doctrine that has been appropriated as a kind of Christian baseline definition of God. See *Jesus Symbol of God*, 471-80; and *Spirituality Seeking Theology*, 171-79.

movement spread out into Greek culture, Word language began to eclipse Spirit language in trying to understand how God was present and active in Jesus.

An important phase in this development occurred when people gradually began to regard the idea of the "Word" or "Logos" of God as an objective form of being distinct from Father God. God's "Wisdom" had been personified in the Old Testament. Personification is a figure of speech in which something that is not a person is portrayed as one. For example, in Proverbs "wisdom" says that she was at God's side when God marked out the foundations of the earth (Prov 8:29-30). Wisdom is a quality of mind, intelligence, and character. In a beautiful literary image, this quality was depicted as God's helper in plotting out the ways of nature. In the New Testament period or before it, God's "Word" began to be personified, first as a figure of speech, but then as a reality distinct from God. In other words, "Word" was no longer appreciated as a figure of speech. Rather than being considered simply an aspect or quality of God, the Word of God came to be understood as an individuality distinct from God the Father. "In the beginning was the Word, and the Word was with God" (John 1:1). This set up a situation in which God the Father and the Word of God were two, and the more the Word of God appeared to be divine, the more it looked like there were two gods. By the early part of the second century some Jews were accusing some Christians of worshiping two gods.

It was not until the year 325 that at the Council of Nicaea this problem seemed to reach a resolution in the affirmation that the Word of God, which was incarnate in the human being Jesus, was fully divine, of the same nature as the creating Father God, and yet distinct from God the Father by a distinction within the single Godhead itself. This decision implicitly carried the seeds of the doctrine of trinity within itself. For what could be said of the Word of God could also be said of the Spirit of God. By the year 381 the decision of the Council of Constantinople was ratified in the West and the whole church had a doctrine of the trinity, about 350 years after the death of Jesus. This long development transpired in the context of the way the world was understood at that time. The conclusion of this analysis can be stated in a straightforward way: the doctrine of trinity as we have it was developed by theological debate carried on in the historically conditioned imaginative framework and languages of a confluence of ancient cultures.

God still remains absolute mystery. But the story of how the doctrine developed is fairly clear. And once the language was in place, it began to function as though it represented objective knowledge of the inner life of God.

The Story the Doctrine Narrates

We now turn to what can be called the narrative character of the doctrine of trinity. The question is this: can the doctrine of trinity be understood as a synopsis of a story? This would be the story of human salvation as the Christian community has encountered it. This analysis is intended to pull the imagination away from the idea that the doctrine of trinity revolves around numbers or anything that can be counted. The importance of this doctrine does not lie in a structural analysis of God's being, of God being three and one at the same time. The analysis proposes to show that the doctrine is important because it tells the story of the Christian encounter with God.

The Narrative Structure of the Doctrine Called Trinity

The doctrine of trinity tells a story of how the Christian community has encountered God. As it stands, this doctrine was not revealed in its propositional form. The formula of the doctrine grew up out of the experience of a religious community that began with Judaism, became committed to Jesus as a revelation of God, faced the problem of the status of Jesus in relation to God, and came to a complex understanding of the one God in the fourth century. In a way, the doctrine is the product of a large committee of diverse people who kept the discussion alive over the course of three and a half centuries.

Its developed form is not found in scripture; it developed in the course of time, experience, and debate. In its finished formulation the doctrine, as distinct from its referent, God, is a human construction.

As such, the doctrine tells the story of how the community experiences God: first as creator; second as being present, active, and thus revealed in the ministry and person of Jesus of Nazareth; and third as God's presence and power within the community. These experiences stretched out over a long period of time. That long history of a relationship with God provides the grounds for recognizing that the doctrine represents a narrative. It tells the story of how the Christian community, reaching back into its Jewish prehistory, gradually experienced new facets of the reality of God in its corporate life.

The Plot in the Narrative of Trinity

The principle that the doctrine summarizes a narrative can be drawn out further by indicating the plot of the story. It is contained in the early creeds. The story tells of God creating the world and all the living things in it. It then tells of a fall or a lapse of human beings into sin. One can depict the Old Testament as Hebrew scriptures that tell the story of God interacting with the Jewish people, chastening them when they are unfaithful, blessing them in their repentance. In the light of the story of Jesus, the narrative then picks up efforts of the early Jesus movement to explain who Jesus was. The New Testament fixed on his role of redeemer along with other metaphors. The many images and symbols of how Jesus is savior become crystallized in the idea of his being redeemer, precisely in relation to human sin. All of this can be found in the development of Christology during the first hundred years after the appearance of Jesus.

The next phase of the story revolves around God as God is encountered and referred to as the transcendent power of movement and life, as divine Spirit immanent in the world. God as Spirit is the predominant language during the first century for expressing the conviction that God was present and active in the ministry and person of Jesus. Especially the works of Luke, his Gospel and his Acts of the Apostles, when they are considered together as companion volumes, portray in historical terms the Spirit empowering Jesus's ministry. After Jesus's death and resurrection the story continues as the Spirit is "sent" by Jesus to animate his group of followers. The Spirit of God, once it too was hypostasized and conceived as a distinct element of the Godhead, became associated especially with the life of the church in history. God who was present to Jesus as divine Word incarnate is also present and at work in the church as divine Spirit. God as Spirit will lead the church to include more and more of humanity until it leads all human beings back to God in the end time. The plot of the sacred story of Christianity that is enshrined in the narrative doctrine of trinity can be summarized in the language of creation, fall, Christ as redeemer, and the Spirit guiding the church through history to the end time.

The Relation of the Story of the Trinity to the Story of Jesus

What is the relationship of the story that is contained in the trinitarian doctrine about God and the story of Jesus that is contained in the New Testament, in the four Gospels and, among these, principally Mark, Matthew, and Luke? The short answer to this question is that the large sacred story of the structure of history gradually grew out of the story of Jesus by means of human reflection and inference. But there is no intrinsic connection in the sense that the large story was necessarily deduced from the story of Jesus, or entailed in the story of Jesus, or required by it. This is a crucial point because this answer to the question of the relation of the two stories allows the further developments that are proposed in the next two parts of this chapter.

How is this the case? The development of the doctrine of trinity took about 300 to 350 years. This is a long and complicated history of the development of a doctrine. It transpired partly within the context of Jewish culture represented by the Hebrew scriptures and the origins of Christianity in Jesus and his ministry, and partly in the Greek culture that suffused the intellectual world of the Roman Empire. The gradual merging of these two cultures within Christian identity and thinking was a *historical* development, and this means precisely a particular development conditioned by context and negotiated by imagination and freedom.

In the light of this history, one can say that Christian self-understanding is made up of two stories, the little story of Jesus, which has four versions in the four Gospels, and the large story, the sacred story of all of history, which developed out of the story of Jesus and which is expressed in the creeds and is summed up in the doctrine of the trinity. The story of Jesus is at the core of the Christian experience; the metanarrative, the grand sacred story of creation, fall, redemption, church, and end time, was derivative and grew up around the Jesus story. But gradually the large story swallowed the small story in the sense that Jesus of Nazareth became interpreted by the grand narrative and the trinity. This reversed and supplanted the correct relationship between these two stories. The grand narrative has to be interpreted by Jesus, who is its source, and not the other way around.

The Failure of This Doctrine Today

One of the main reasons for the failure of the doctrine of trinity today is that few people understand it. Of course, no one understands God. But we should be able to understand our doctrines about God. Even though their content is revealed by God through our religious experience, their construction in language is a human achievement. Their logic should resonate with human experience. Part of the inaccessibility of the doctrine of trinity to religious experience lies in the way it is presented as a resolution of the problem of how one can be three, or three one. Once one recognizes that the content of the doctrine is the story of how the Christian community encounters God and the story of God interacting with human beings, this aspect of the problem should be overcome. But there is another problem as well.

Questioning the Traditional Story

The traditional story is under attack. Just about every aspect of the traditional sacred story that is represented in the doctrine of the trinity has become suspect. All of the elements of the grand narrative are questioned: creation (by the theory of a Big Bang), fall (by evolution), redemption (by demythologization), the origin of the church (by the long story of its development), the character of the church (by religious pluralism), and knowledge of the end time (by a radical sense of randomness and lack of purpose in the universe).

The story of Adam and Eve is recognized as myth, but this way of looking at it still scandalizes the popular imagination. The new scientific story of the universe and the evolution of life on our planet has far more immediate religious power than an ancient creation myth, and it has replaced the Bible story in the secular imagination. Evolution virtually eliminates the idea of a historical human fall affecting all humanity. There are many understandings of Jesus Christ in the New Testament, and "redeemer" is one of many and hardly the most important. Once a fall has been excluded, "redeemer" language loses its premise and supposition. The origins of the church are hotly debated today, but there is a consensus that Jesus did not intend to found a new religion. Many who experience the Spirit of God within the church also postulate that it is the same Spirit that is at work in other religions. And, finally, what do we really know about the end time? Our faith in the future turns into hope, something much deeper than knowledge.

A New Version of the Trinitarian Story

The doctrine of trinity should still tell the larger story that is implied by the appearance of Jesus within the religious tradition of Judaism, but the contents of that story have to be reworked. The story that was designed in the patristic period reflects the ancient Jewish, Greek, and Egyptian conceptions of the universe in which it was conceived. This story has less of a foothold in the twenty-first century; it has no standing within the context of our scientific view of the universe; it has no immediate appeal to the imagination that looks for religious motivation for engaging and participating in our societies today. The large story represented by trinity has to be rewritten.

Retelling the Trinitarian Narrative

One way of reclaiming the doctrine of trinity is to insist on its narrative structure. Then retelling the story of how God has been encountered by Christians would flesh out what the doctrine of trinity contains and preserves. Some of the guidelines for retelling this story are the criteria for a coherent Christian spirituality: the story must preserve the basic faith of the community in how God was active in Jesus for human salvation. The story will testify to the experience of God present and active in the community of the church. It must make sense in the context of how we understand the world in the twenty-first century as distinct from the context of fourth-century Mediterranean culture. In other words, the task here is not to destroy the doctrine of trinity but to bring it back to life by reimagining the Christian story that the doctrine implicitly contains in terms that are meaningful today. What are some of the elements of this story of God that make sense to the Christian community in our world?

Monotheism: One God, Not Three Gods

The story tells of how the one God has been revealed to the Christian community. This first point provides a kind of criterion that the story must meet. The terms Father, Son, and Spirit cannot be woven together in such a way that they appear as three distinct gods; it must be completely clear that the Christian story is monotheistic. We pray to one God, not to any one of three gods, and not to an aspect or a part of God.

Creation

The concept and doctrine closest to the subject matter of this story is creation. God creating, especially creating out of nothing, is the doctrine that most penetratingly designates what makes God God. During the last several decades faith in God, creator of heaven and earth, has entered into a new environment. The religious doctrine of God creating must enter into a dialogue with the scientific story of the emergence of the universe, our planet within that universe, and the gradual evolution of life that up to this point has generated the human species. For many Christians today the anthropomorphic story of Adam and Eve in Genesis and the scientific story of the explosive appearance of the universe are considered competing stories. They are not the same story, surely, but neither are they in competition with each other. The religious idea of being created cannot be validated or invalidated by science. In the story contained in the doctrine of trinity the affirmation of creation relies not on science but on the religious experience of being dependent in one's being upon a power that is not a part of this world but the creating ground of being itself. The two stories are not antagonistic to each other. In fact the scientific story of the emergence of our universe is awe inspiring, and it can easily function as a sacrament for a different religious experience of being within the grasp of an infinite power of being.

God as Spirit as the Energy of the Universe

In the Hebrew scriptures, in the New Testament, and in theology today the Spirit of God refers to God's presence and power as that is encountered within the world, either in persons, or events, or a community, or within the self. God's Spirit refers to the power of God less in abstract terms and more as it displays itself in its effects. These effects range from the prophets and kings who did great things as God's instruments to the many ordinary people who experience divine help or inspiration as they meet a particular crisis or go about daily life. The Bible is filled with testimony to God's Spirit at work in the world and in human lives, and that experience continues today. God is not just the distant creator that leaves the universe on its own, but an ever-present sustaining power of being. This conception of how God relates to the world fits well with the dynamic character of reality to which the scientific story points. God as Spirit can be considered the creative and sustaining energy of God in the evolution of reality. This refers precisely to God's "primary" creating causality and should not be imagined in terms of particular acts within the finite system of this-worldly or "secondary" causality.

Jesus Reveals God as Personal and Loving

Up to this point the story of God and God's creating has not predicated any content about the character of the creator God. Without developing a theory of religious knowledge, it may be presupposed that the only way human beings can learn about God or affirm qualities of God has to involve drawing what can be said of God from knowledge of this world. This does not describe a limitation of God but a structure of human knowing. The content of all human knowledge, including revealed knowledge, has human experience and language at its base, so that all religious knowledge of God is drawn from some this-worldly experience and predicated in a transcendent or infinite way of ultimate reality. On this supposition, the content of a Christian's faith in God is ultimately drawn from and based on the ministry and destiny of Jesus of Nazareth. This does not restrict all that Christians affirm of God to a provenance from Jesus of Nazareth. But it places Jesus's communication of God in a privileged position as the normative framework for a Christian appreciation of God.

The specifically Christian story of God has been channeled to us through Jesus of Nazareth. Jesus tells of God being not only creator, but of being a personal and loving caretaker of all that has been created. Jesus assumes a central place in the Christian story of God as God's revealer and representative. Jesus was so animated by God as Spirit that he can be understood as communicating the Word or self-revelation of God to those who encounter him and his teaching. In other words, trinity summarizes a story of a community's encounter with God in such a way that God as creator and immanent power of being uses Jesus to communicate with humanity. God as Spirit and

Jesus are intimately and intricately woven together. The Christian community had various terms to express God working through Jesus. Besides "Spirit" and "Word," for example, Jesus manifested God's "Wisdom" and "Glory." These symbols express how God has been encountered by this community in the person and teaching of Jesus.

The Spirit at Work in History

God as Spirit is at work throughout creation; Spirit also represents the power of God in history. The story transcends the past tense; it did not just happen in the past but is the story by which the community understands reality now. What Jesus, inspired by the Spirit, said of God is true, so that the Spirit or immanent presence and power of the creator God continues to be concerned about and engaged with the world. God embraces all reality and thus is present to all human beings who make up a self-conscious and relatively free species in their production of history.

A Meaningful End of History

God promises a meaningful end of history and hence *shalom*, justice within a context of peace and fulfillment. The creator God who is also immanent and revealed in the ministry and teaching of Jesus and experienced within the community promises that human life is meaningful. In Jesus, this God says that, in spite of the long history of innocent suffering, justice will prevail in the end. Jesus reveals that the author of the universe and of human life within it is also their finisher and that God will accomplish a meaningful end to this story. In sum, trinity is a narrative doctrine that synopsizes a version of the grand narrative that constitutes the Christian view of reality.

What Is Trinity

It may seem that this discussion has wandered far from the doctrine of three persons in one God. It has indeed, but not in a way that the reasons for affirming the teaching of trinity have been lost. Although the formulation of the doctrine in terms of "nature" and "person" made sense in the fourth century, it seems distant from the current conception of the universe. It seems to occlude the relevance of the doctrine of God for life today by refracting the light of a single personal God into three agencies within the Godhead. Is there a better way of understanding this doctrine in our time?

We began by recalling the fact that this doctrine developed over a course of 350 years and does not appear in scripture in its developed form. The doctrine is the product of a complex development in a specific culture. Without that sense of how doctrines developed, people will not be able critically to question their conceptuality and probe their meaningfulness in a new and different context.

On the premise that one can interpret its meaning in a new language, one way of understanding this doctrine, not the only way to be sure, but a plausible approach nonetheless, will see various aspects of the religious experience behind the many terms that went into the foundation of the doctrine: God as creator; God as Father in Jesus's representation; God's Spirit as a divine force immanent in the world; God's Word that self-communicates and effects what it says; and the early Christian community's experience that God's Spirit was at work in Jesus and in the movement carrying his message forward to communicate it to the world. God as creator, God as Spirit, and Jesus of Nazareth regarded as God's chosen one, together provided the elements that came together over time to form the Christian movement and church. Trinity is a doctrine that synopsizes this historical story, and this appears plainly in the early creeds. As an implicit narrative this doctrine can cohere neatly with a contemporary view of reality. The old story has to be retold in terms that make sense to people for whom the new story of the universe and the evolution of human life on our planet defines our self-understanding. The ongoing creation of God, the immanence and empowerment of God's Spirit in this cosmic process, and the revelation of this creator God in Jesus's ministry can make sense in this new culture. And just as the Spirit of God authorized Jesus as God's revelation, so too can God as Spirit communicate God's presence and power to other religious revealers and mediators.

This interpretation of the trinity as a narrative doctrine, as containing the story of the immanent action of the transcendent creator God within the world, makes sense because it makes sense of human existence. It is not an analytical conceptual doctrine presenting God as a puzzle, but a story that one can identify with. Allowing this story to be one's own, to give meaning and direction to human life, injects hope into the human enterprise. It gives human life a whence and a whither. The content of this doctrinal narrative has its deep origins in the Jewish story of God and its immediate origins in the ministry and person of Jesus of Nazareth. Although its content is quite different from one in three and three in one, it expresses the fundamental belief of Christians in God as God is revealed in Jesus Christ.

Index